Kitchen Secrets

The Meaning of Cooking in Everyday Life

Frances Short

BERG

Oxford • New York

First published in 2006 by
Berg
Editorial offices:
1st Floor, Angel Court, 81 St Clements Street, Oxford, OX4 1AW, UK
175 Fifth Avenue, New York, NY 10010, USA

Berg is the imprint of Oxford International Publishers Ltd.

Library of Congress Cataloguing-in-Publication Data
Short, Frances.
    Kitchen secrets : the meaning of cooking in everyday life /
Frances Short.
       p. cm.
    Includes bibliographical references and index.
    ISBN-13: 978-1-84520-276-7 (pbk.)
    ISBN-10: 1-84520-276-7 (pbk.)
    ISBN-13: 978-1-84520-274-3 (hardback)
    ISBN-10: 1-84520-274-0 (hardback)
    1. Cookery. 2. Cookery—Social aspects. 3. Food habits—
Social aspects. 4. Cooks. I. Title: Meaning of cooking in
everyday life. II. Title.

    TX651.S465 2006
    641.5—dc22   2005035550

British Library Cataloguing-in-Publication Data
A catalogue record for this book is available from the British Library.

ISBN-13 978 184520 274 3 (Cloth)
ISBN-10 1 84520 274 0 (Cloth)

ISBN-13 978 184520 276 7 (Paper)
ISBN-10 1 84520 276 7 (Paper)

Typeset by Avocet Typeset, Chilton, Aylesbury, Bucks
Printed in the United Kingdom by Biddles Ltd, King's Lynn

www.bergpublishers.com

For my father,
who couldn't be here.

Contents

Foreword

My job at St Thomas's was to fry eggs. I fried eggs – egg after egg – from seven thirty in the morning until well after eleven. Rather like those baristas who churn out expertly identical cappuccino after cappuccino or bartenders who with each pint of Guinness they pull aim to draw a flawless shamrock in the head, the trick is to clear your mind, start afresh each time and aim for perfection. Each one can have a consummately golden base, crinkly, crispy bits around the edges and a just-cooked yolk, sheer white over its dome. There may be some who insist on you cooking their eggs they way that they like them – flipped over, hard yolks, almost burnt – but never enough to put you off your stride.

I haven't worked only in hospital kitchens. I've cooked in a marquee, a theatre cafe, a students' union, a hot dog stall, an all-night coffee shop and a vegetarian restaurant in the crypt of one of Christopher Wren's churches. I've worked in the chilly, isolated corner of the butchery and pantry section, under the heat of the grill and in the calm (though not in the face of four hundred forgotten eclairs to be ready in fifteen minutes), more feminine space of 'pastry'. I've waited on, catered from home, taught, worked in recipe development and had my own cookery column. I'm the family cook too – family producing, I have found, perhaps the most exacting of 'customers'. After all, if a two-year-old doesn't like what you've offered, they spit it straight back at you. Five-year-olds and 38-year-olds don't always show a great deal of compassion for the cook either.

Food has always fascinated me, though my fascination doesn't really lie in dis-covering a wonderful restaurant or artisan producer or the best ever recipe for Puy lentils, red curry or lemon tart. I'm not sure I'm a gourmet at all. I'm interested in people and food … why we sometimes seem to be scared of it, why we are so enthralled by professional cooks and the kitchens they work in, why some foods demand an acquired taste. A few years ago I turned from cooking food, at least in a professional capacity, to thinking and writing about it. Early in my new career I went round to a friend's house one evening for an impromptu party. We'd all been asked to bring something to drink and eat and, it being Pancake Day (any excuse for a get-together), pancakes were of course on the menu. There were a dozen or so guests and all apart from myself had brought pancakes in some sort of conven-ient, pre-prepared form. A few had brought them ready-made (Ma Raeburn's and Aunt Bessie's varieties being firm favourites). Others had brought packets of pancake mix. One guest had picked up something new from the supermarket – a plastic bottle of, rather orange I thought, pancake powder that came with instructions to add cold water, shake well and pour straight into the frying pan. Symptomatic, I said, relating this story to Michael Heasman, for whom I was then doing some work, of how cooks no longer cook, of how cooking is no longer about real food. It was a conversation that led to further discussions with his colleagues in food policy, Tim Lang and Martin Caraher, and ultimately to a doctoral study in 'the meaning of cooking in contemporary society'.

I began the research hoping to find out why people can't cook (what other reason could there be for making pancakes from the unnaturally high-in-colour contents of a plastic bottle?) and came out understanding something of why people often choose not to cook. In doing so I gained a certain appreciation of why some love the products of the modern food industry, a little insight into why the informants who made most use of convenience foods were also the ones most likely to offer me something to eat. For cooking for someone in a world where you can eat without really having to shows a level of intimacy too strong, it seems, for the interviewer/interviewee relationship. I found out why a trainee chef like Jez prefers not to cook for his friends but gives them something frozen, preformed and breadcrumbed: easy-to-prepare food that gives him a sense of autonomy as a young adult but that doesn't make him appear fussy and overly attentive, or leave him with too much washing-up. I discovered too why my experience of cooking at home seems barely different from that of my mother – why, despite the years that separate our experiences, my delight at clean plates, an impromptu compliment or help with laying the table is so very similar. The foods may have changed but many of the satisfactions and dissatisfactions, the tasks and skills of the home cook remain much the same.

This book is based on that research, a theoretical and evidence-based study of practices, thoughts, opinions and approaches that aims to disassemble what we think we all know and develop in its place new ways of understanding cooking.

Who Cares about Cooking?

The Subject of Food

Nell, aged four, has decided she wants to make cakes and is with me in the super-market eyeing up decorations and adornments that she considers of suitable gar-ishness. She looks first at me and then with longing at what seem like endless rows of ready-made frosting, colours, flavours and essences, ready-rolled and ready-to-roll 'designer' cake icing, silver balls, hundreds and thousands, sugar flowers and sugar strands, marzipan teddy bears and chocolate numbers, letters, chips, dots (are dots different from chips?) and curls. Her eyes grow even bigger. She has seen the stacks of multicoloured boxes on the aisle opposite. And, though the packaged mixes for superfudge brownies, wild blueberry muffins, lemon drizzle sponge and organic vanilla cheesecake are beginning to tempt me, of far more interest to her is choosing between the Scooby Doo, Barbie and Tom and Jerry cupcake kits.

Born in London in the summer of 2000, Nell experiences food in an endless variety and finds it as much about fun as it is about sustenance. For food, at least in certain wealthier parts of the world, is becoming not only ever more commodi-tized but also as potentially frivolous as it is functional. And, as it does so, a subject long dismissed by serious scholars as being too everyday and banal,[1] too lacking in scope for intellectual elitism perhaps ('everyone eats, so we all feel we can talk about it'[2]), has become increasingly popular as a subject of study and interest. Food fascinates. Many of us can now eat in restaurants serving cuisines from all over the world. We can have what seems like an endless range of food – fast, gourmet and organic – delivered straight to the front doorstep or we can buy it ready-made from the supermarket to reheat and eat in seconds or store in the freezer. We can watch cookery programmes broadcast at peak viewing times or choose from the twenty or more categories of cookbooks available from online booksellers. At the same time, we have become more and more uneasy about the production and distribution of food, more intrigued by its meaning and worth.[3] Food writing and food thought have exploded. From academic to more popular commentary, they now encompass far more than food science, nutrition and how to grow, cook or heal with food. Philosophers ask if food is art but also pose more serious moral and ethical questions. Should we really eat out, cook for pleasure and seek out a gourmet culture when others in the world routinely starve or spend a lifetime malnourished?[4] Snappy, combative titles like *Fast Food Nation*, *Food Politics* and *Food Wars* reveal intricate studies of global food systems and their political and social relevance for the environment and the health and well-being of humankind.[5] Sociocultural histories of salt, saffron, cod, chicken, coffee, potatoes and other food commodities become increasingly fashionable, even ubiquitous.[6] Analyses of culinary practices, beliefs and traditions and the psychological and social influences on what we choose to eat and why have become ever more prevalent as a more general interest in society, lifestyle, consumerism and taste has grown. Dominant themes of contemporary social studies – globalization, identity, consumerism, commodification and rationalization – can regularly be found in current food writing, research and debate.[7]

The State of Cooking

If the study of food has often been somewhat overlooked in the past, then the study of food and food practices in the home, as those who have begun to think and work in this area often complain, has been largely ignored. A lack of research and real evidence, however, hasn't stopped the state of cooking and eating in the home from being keenly and eagerly debated. Yet, though there may be some who cheer the growing diversity of sophisticated, exotic and convenient ingredients to cook with and the plethora of glossy cookbooks and food manuals now available, there are few who write with eagerness about the freedom from the kitchen granted by the products of modern food technologies. Far more food writers and commentators appear to deplore the rise of convenience eating and the products of a global food industry than applaud it.

Many, for example, agonize over 'the decline of family meals'. Home-cooked meals eaten together are seen as fostering good eating habits, good conversation and an appreciation of good food. They are viewed too as the cornerstone of family ritual and family life, the fabric of society. Their replacement by eating in front of the television and solitary refuelling 'on the run' is frequently and regularly taken as an undisputed step towards poorer diets and eating disorders and weakened family unity and, ultimately, even social order.[8] Research suggests, however, that claims like these may be a little overenthusiastic, even premature. For it is easy to quote from research that shows 'family meals appear to play an important role in promoting positive dietary intake' and disregard conclusions from the same study that 'family meals are clearly not extinct'.[9] And, whilst a study in Japan found that mealtime conversation is important in the socialization of children, it revealed too that children are generally happier and gain more from eating with their mothers than with their fathers. Mothers tend, the research found, to chat to them about school and friends whereas fathers are far more likely to quiz them on current affairs and their aims in life.[10] Meals are not neutral, straightforwardly supportive occasions, it seems. Power relations and gender roles are established, acknowledged and represented at the dining and kitchen table.[11] For every paean to the family meal it is possible, though perhaps requiring a little more dogged sifting of the literature, to find comments on family mealtimes as hierarchical – gender, relative and child divided – and as places where fierce power games are played out. All too often, it has been argued, meals together can become 'teeth clenching tests of nerve' about eating and conversing with due decorum and respect,[12] or eating food you don't particularly like, perhaps, with relatives and in-laws you barely know.[13] Family meals can all too easily turn into a fight over finishing dinner, growing big and strong and leaving the table.[14] Those who are obliged by financial or schedule reasons to eat with their children dream of civilized adult company. Meanwhile, parents who view a meal together as an act of giving, love and communication can be left with little more than a thwarted moment of irritability and tension, says Susie Orbach. For children far prefer to just eat and go.[15] Don't even try it with the under-fours, warns child psychologist Penelope Leach. Toddlers and pleasant meals at the table just don't go together.[16]

By making everyone eat the same kind of food in the same way and at the same time, isn't the family meal, asks Jane Jakeman in an article that challenges 'food snobbery', merely an instrument of family government, a means of instilling discipline and codes of behaviour?[17] There is, after all, evidence that eating disorders like bulimia nervosa can be in part the product of mealtimes where parents dominate conversation and use food to manipulate, as well as evidence that meals together can benefit children's emotional health, sense of attachment and long-term eating habits.[18] It is also difficult to prove that the family meal – in its 'traditional' democratic, communicative and sociable form – has ever really existed, let alone whether it is in decline. As is often pointed out, in many communities around the world and until very recently in the West, few except the wealthiest have had any sort of dining tables, crockery or eating implements.[19] It could be that the family meal is alive and well but has taken on different forms. For families today there may be social significance not just in an occasion where everyone eats the same food at the same time and in the same place, but in an occasion where friends and family gather together to eat, but eat different foods. There may be meaning in a home-cooked meal eaten by family members but at different times, or in a meal eaten together but cooked by others, perhaps even commercially.[20] Yet, despite the lack of any real, extensive evidence of its health and social benefits, and the indications that it has a darker, more negative side, there is still overwhelming allegiance to the ideal of the 'family meal'.[21] (The corollary, point out Alan Warde and Lydia Martens, that more meals with friends, colleagues and even strangers may be beneficial for wider, non-family, social relationships, is rarely considered.[22]) Whilst we may all be familiar with meals that amount to little more than bursts of angry indignant eating or what seem like hours of nervous chewing and stilted conversation, most of us still feel compelled to at least occasionally organize a 'meal together'.[23] As Lotte Holm says, commenting on her study of the family meal in the Nordic countries, people will go to great lengths and endless endeavours to plan, create and conduct such occasions.[24] Indeed, if you are not sure how to have a family meal, then there are numerous websites that can help you decide on where to eat and how to set and decorate the table, that can give you advice on how long the meal should last, what tasks to delegate to which family members and what foods and subjects of conversation are well suited to and enjoyed by every age group.[25]

Other writers and commentators have preferred to focus, not on the decline of the family meal but on 'the impoverished state of domestic cooking'. It's not particularly difficult to find articles and reviews that describe a public 'who are ever more divorced from primary foodstuffs in their raw state and whose idea of cooking is assembling several pre-cooked, components from cartons, packets and tins'.[26] Children, we are told, can use a computer and programme a video before they can boil an egg or bake a potato.[27] Convenience foods and ready meals, microwaves, fast food and takeaways, freezers and processors routinely get the blame. By 2020, comes the warning, kitchens may become a thing of the past.[28] The death of home cooking has been foretold.[29]

Academically, this demise has been spoken of more in terms of a loss of cooking skills, of a deskilling through a move towards ever more routinized and depersonalized 'cooking' reliant on processed, prepared food.[30] Industrially, commercially made food, says George Ritzer, using food preparation and cooking to help explain his treatise on the rationalization of contemporary society, is marketed as realistic and efficient, as giving people greater convenience and greater control over their lives. Ultimately, though, he argues, pre-prepared, convenience food is irrational in that it requires few and relatively easy skills to 'finish off'. Those who no longer require cooking skills to eat or provide food for others, he argues, will obviously no longer acquire cooking skills in the course of doing so. Their lack of skills will compel them to continue using prepared foods and leave them without any skills or know-how to pass on to the next generation. They and their children, in turn, are denied a choice to cook in the name of the choice not to cook.[31]

Concern about the plight of domestic cooking, and the impact any deskilling might have on eating habits, diet, health and well-being, is the focus of a number of debates in a variety of academic disciplines. Many working in food policy, health promotion and education, for example, have increasingly taken the position that cooking skills and knowledge can improve diet. A deficit of skills, therefore (and it is now often taken as implicitly understood that deskilled cooks and cooking are a feature of contemporary society[32]), is seen as hindering people's ability to prepare and cook fresh, raw food and understand what goes into the ready-prepared food they eat instead. Advice to, say, grill and steam food can only be followed if you know how to grill and steam.[33] Home-made soup, for example, can be cheaper than shop-bought soup and can very probably be made with less salt and preservatives. But it may well be a waste of time trying to impress that upon a public who have no knowledge of how to make soup. Furthermore, if you cannot cook, you surrender, as Australian food writer Cherry Ripe puts it, your food choices and nutrition and those of your family to people whose interest is purely financial.[34] 'Cooking skills prepare people to make choices in a fast changing food world,' say food policy specialists Martin Caraher and Tim Lang, arguing that without skills 'choice and control are diminished and a dependency culture emerges'.[35] Some campaigners in the UK have suggested that the deskilling of home cooking is a purposeful process on the part of the food industry: a means of increasing profit that is aided and abetted, they claim, by government policy on the teaching (or lack of teaching) of cookery in schools.[36] Indeed, there has been uproar in many quarters that changes to the national curriculum in recent years have not only meant that cooking is now optional for many age groups but also that it is taught as part of design and technology rather than home economics: an approach that is commonly regarded, despite a few who maintain that it is wholly appropriate and empowering for life in a modern, industrialized society,[37] as inferior and commerce-led, based more around designing food packaging than practical home cooking skills. How will the next generation learn to cook, ask campaigners, if their parents have been deskilled and school cookery classes have all but vanished?[38]

Social scientists and scholars of culture, history and modernity have other concerns. Their interests also lie in examining if or how modern food systems alleviate a family's or household's reliance on an individual cook – or, more pertinently perhaps, as research shows that it is still largely women who do the majority of the everyday food preparation and provision, how they free women from the kitchen.[39] More usually, however, cooking in the home is discussed in a similar way to eating practices and the family meal, in terms of how the use of industrially prepared, commodified food products and the decline of traditional abilities threaten family relationships and cultural identities. Rather than being discussed for its potential to emancipate, the 'homogenous, instant and convenient' food of commerce and industry is far more likely to be described as irrevocably damaging to local cuisines, traditional craft skills, family practices and family life.[40] Ready meals, fast food and microwaves are seen to threaten the social order. The words of historian Felipe Fernandez-Armesto sum up the views of many:

Cooking was a precious invention because of the way it forged community. Contemporary eating habits threaten to unpick this achievement. Food on the fly feeds the values of hustle, nourishes the anomie of the post industrial society ... The loneliness of the fast-food eater is uncivilising. Food is being desocialized. In the microwave household, home-cooking looks doomed. Family life must fragment if people stop having shared meals.[41]

For the Slow Food movement, the decline of cooking and the loss of regional, artisan produce are synonymous not only with a loss of tradition and family life but also with the abandonment of ecological care and civic pride. They have more prosaic gastronomic concerns, of course. Slow Food USA, for example, has charged itself not only 'to improve the relationship of human beings with their environment and each other' but also with promoting an appreciation and enjoyment of wholesome food and a revival of home cooking and the kitchen.[42] Its concerns mirror those of many food writers, who worry that, as cooking and eating together become less a part of daily life, there will be more and more of us who will be able neither to participate in nor to appreciate the aesthetics of real food and good cooking.[43]

Ambiguities, Complexities and a Lack of Evidence

As with the family meal, these are powerful claims in the face of limited evidence. For studies of home cooking practices and the relationship between culinary ability, food choices and eating practices remain noticeable by their absence. Two UK government-led public health surveys in the mid-1990s, however, did include sections that focused on measuring cooking ability and food knowledge against income, gender, age and so on. Both asked similar questions about sources of cooking knowledge, confidence in being able to cook from basic ingredients, frequency of cooking and the number of main meals bought ready prepared. They asked, too, about confidence in using techniques such as boiling, frying, microwaving and stewing and about preparing a range of generic foods, including white fish, rice, pulses and root vegetables.[44] Both studies reached the conclusion that positive attitudes and confidence play a key role in what we cook and how often we choose to do so – a conclusion supported by other studies carried out with community groups and in schools to look at the relationship between cooking skills and food choices. Mothers who improve their skills become increasingly confident, find greater enjoyment in cooking and use a wider variety of foods. Children become more interested and choose more widely as their experience of food and cooking grows.[45] However, it appears that the relationship between confidence in cooking and actually doing so is not as straightforward as it may at first seem. One of the public health studies found that those who never prepared a meal did not necessarily hold more negative attitudes towards doing so than those who cooked regularly. The other found a similar ambiguity in that its respondents might describe themselves as being generally confident about cooking whilst also admitting they lacked the confidence to use particular techniques or cook specific foods – a contradiction also seen in a Portuguese study, in which, despite the fact that they cooked far more frequently, girls were found to be no more confident about doing so than boys.[46] Further incongruities can be seen in market research. Surveys have found, for example, that 81 per cent of seven- to fifteen-year-olds might think cooking is fun and 63 per cent think it not too complicated but only 29 per cent can cook a full meal,[47] or that 91 per cent of home cooks say they enjoy cooking, yet only 61 per cent say that they rarely use convenience foods.[48]

Despite the fact that these two public health studies were conceived in the light of the concerns about the deskilling of home cooking, with no knowledge of the level of cooking skills in the past against which to measure their findings, neither found that they could really comment on whether or not cooking is in decline or skills disappearing. They are problematic, too, like most current debate about home cooking, in the way that they treat concepts and terms like cook, cooking skills and ready prepared. Debates about the family meal have progressed, at least to an extent, because alongside debate over their possible decline there has been a corresponding discourse about what constitutes a family meal. Definitions have been disseminated and disputed.[49] In what different ways can the term family be interpreted? What do we mean by a 'meal'? What conditions surround a family meal? Can it be five minutes' eating together at breakfast or a shared tub of fried chicken? This kind of conceptual and terminological enquiry hasn't been done in relation to cooking. Terms and phrases like 'basic ingredients',' 'dish', 'homemade' and 'cooking from scratch' are regularly used without any explanation or clear definition. 'Ready meal', 'ready prepared', 'processed' and 'convenience' are expressions which typically appear without reference to any clear-cut level of 'prior to household' preparation. Used interchangeably, they are a means of describing foods as being somehow opposite to some, similarly vague, concept of fresh, raw ingredients. Who qualifies as being 'a cook'? It is simply 'someone who prepares food for eating', as dictionaries suggest, or can it be a more loaded concept, associated with certain abilities and responsibilities? And what does 'cooking' mean – making a sandwich for a packed lunch or reheating a pizza to serve with salad and Caesar dressing straight from the bottle? Or can making food only qualify as being 'cooking' if it includes the use of 'fresh, raw foods' prepared 'from scratch'?[50]

Even more relevantly, perhaps, for all that has been spoken of the deskilling of home cooking, phrases like 'cooking ability', 'culinary knowledge', 'traditional cooking skills' and 'assembly skills' remain largely unexplained and without interpretation. What is a cooking skill? It is usually understood as being straightforward – a practical technique such as barbecuing, frying, cooking rice, peeling vegetables, making stew, curry or apple pie.[51] But this simplicity can lead to confusion.

It can be puzzling when, for example, a survey lists microwaving – reheating, defrosting, cooking? – alongside grilling, frying and boiling rather than something seemingly more comparable such as 'using an oven',[52] or when researchers deem grilling a cooking skill but not making toast, list boiling potatoes as a skill but not mashing potatoes, or highlight in a recipe for pizza base only 'rubbing in' and 'kneading' as skills, ignoring such abilities as rolling, mixing or checking for the right consistency.[53] Is it at all appropriate to measure people's cooking ability, and in turn make grand judgements on the state of cooking in contemporary, Western societies, by their confidence to poach, roast or stir-fry?[54] Can a survey of people's ability to make white sauce, cook a Sunday roast or bake a cake really provide any insight into the role of cooking in everyday life?[55]

Skills experts and industrial sociologists warn that, to be insightful, an appraisal of a practical task must be informed by a thoughtful, detailed analysis of the skills in question.[56] A purely mechanical interpretation is of little use. No activity, job or task is purely practical, they say. All rely on skills of judgement and understanding: 'a cook opens the oven door, examines her cake (perceptual skills), and then closes the oven door for further baking or removes the cake from the oven'. It is not our manual ability but our cognitive, perceptual skills that inform us whether the cake is cooked and determine the mechanical action that follows.[57]

Detailed analyses of cooking skills and knowledge, however, are all but absent from current work and thought on contemporary cooking despite its decline and deskilling being regularly declared by any number of food writers, government bodies, social think tanks and serious scholars.[58] There is certainly little mention of Harry Braverman's 1970s deskilling theory. Braverman maintained that, in modern societies with industrialized systems of production, the worker is no longer involved in a complete task from its conception through its entire execution to completion. He performs only the mechanical aspects. Whilst the skilled artisan had autonomy over his work, a craft identity and a sense of self-worth, the deskilled worker in a rationalized system is alienated both from his own work and that of his co-workers and as a consequence becomes dissatisfied and unhappy: a process, Braverman argued, that is self-perpetuating in that deskilled workers require ever more simplified work and the ever more simplified work they then do deskills them still further.[59]

It is not difficult to see how this idea, this approach to skill and ability, has been so easily and eagerly applied to contemporary home cooking, characterized as it is, or as regularly claimed, by industrially prepared foods, cooking by assembly and technologies such as the microwave.[60] Debates, however, include no extended descriptions or analyses of the processes that are seen as being at work. There are very few explanations, and very little detail, about how people learn to cook, never mind how this might be affected by using convenience foods. Nor are there any descriptions of how cooking with pre-prepared foods requires fewer or different skills than cooking with fresh, raw foods. The mechanisms of the suggested deskilling of domestic cooking, and any dissemination of the argument against relevant theories such as Braverman's, remain largely unexplored and undeveloped. And in turn, of course, debates about the relevance of people's cooking skills and home cooking practices to their ability to control their diet, appreciate good food, sustain stable family relationships and to the wider social order are difficult to extend.

A further awkwardness for any argument that home cooking is in decline is the rise of gourmet food culture and cooking as a recreational, leisure activity. Market surveys reveal that many of us enjoy cooking, entertaining guests with special meals and trying out new recipes.[61] Microwaves, meal replacements and junk food exist in a world where glossy cookbooks, celebrity cooks and innovative and refined cuisine also prevail.[62] My local and quite small bookshop has over three hundred cookery books on its shelves and a quick search of Amazon.com produces forty-four categories of cooks' tools and gadgets, including eleven pages of cookie cutters, 504 (count them) different kinds of spatula and 106 types of ice-cream maker. Furthermore, research shows that people still expect the kitchen to be the most expensively fitted room in the house and for it to cost a substantial amount more than their annual holiday. And when they buy a new kitchen they spend a considerable amount of time investigating ideas, drawing up plans and choosing designs and colours. Most are keen for it to have a table to eat at.[63]

Does this 'epitomise an apparent move of cooking from a chore or production skill to a section of the leisure industry', as Martin Caraher and Tim Lang suggest?[64] And, if it does, does that make this a counter-argument to claims that cooking is being routinized, degraded and deskilled?

Are we food-bereft, convenience junkies, passive consumers and assemblers of ready-made foods, alienated from traditional cooking skills and in thrall to food producers and retailers? Or budding gourmets and knowledgeable foodies, eagerly devouring specialist TV programmes and cookery books, seeking out local produce and exotic ingredients as we try out new recipes and cuisines? Paradoxes abound. Supermarkets and shops may be stuffed full of endless new varieties of ready-prepared, packaged, tinned and frozen foods but its also easier to find and cook better-quality food than ever before. For all that there are 'diminishing contrasts' there is also 'increasing variety'. Foods eaten across seasons and in different social groups, regions and nations are becoming ever more similar, professional and domestic cookery less differentiated. At the same time, the variety of foods and different styles of cooking available to us steadily increase.[65] Instant, reduced-fat, toffee-flavoured cappuccino sachets, sliced, longer-life white bread, pre-trimmed purple-sprouting broccoli florets and lasagne – ready-made with carbohydrate-reduced pasta – exist alongside fair-trade Colombian Supremo, artisan-baked, sourdough rye bread and boxed deliveries of muddy, freshly picked, locally grown vegetables.[66] Anyway, how can cooking be in decline when more and more men, we are told, are taking it up? If teenagers graze throughout the day on foods they can prepare themselves, even if they only prepare frozen pizza and the occasional sandwich, aren't they still likely to be more knowledgeable about food and cooking than their predecessors, who had to rely on the skills of whoever in the household was 'cook'?

Towards a Theory of Home Cooking

Those few who have set out to investigate the attitudes and practices of home cooks and the state of contemporary cooking have been forced, however reluctantly, to admit that, without any real, empirically gathered evidence, claims as to its decline and deskilling are hypothetical.[67] 'In the absence of studies of everyday cooking practices,' says David Sutton, writing about his research of food and cooking in the Greek islands, 'we remain in the realm of speculation.'[68] Like others involved in this area of academic enquiry, Anne Murcott has repeatedly stressed that a systematic, theoretically based framework for thinking about domestic cooking is essential if debates are to progress and useful policy is to be developed.[69]

In the study upon which this book is based, I set out to establish that framework, to define cooking ability and explore the meaning of home cooking. I wanted to understand people's cooking practices and skills, their approaches, beliefs, values and opinions and how these relate to their use of convenience and real, raw foods, how often they cook and their sense of themselves as being a cook. I aimed, too, to develop debates about the social significance and place of cooking, as well as arguments about its decline.

With no convention for its study or existing 'set of works' to which to turn, developing a theory of domestic cooking proved neither simple nor straightforward. I had to trawl through literature and research for details that might be informative and search out social and cultural theory that could provide direction and a grounded, philosophical structure. I had to constantly rework and re-evaluate ideas, intuitions and judgements. I read, thought, spoke to experts, scribbled down interesting and invaluable comments. I developed explanations and abandoned explanations. And, whilst writing this book, new ideas, thoughts and evidence have meant that I have had to continue going 'back and forth', thinking, note-taking and reassessing. Though for the sake of readability it is presented in a far more ordered and linear way, the next chapter describes this process.

–2–

Who Knows about Cooking?

Finding Out about Cooks and Cooking: Reviewing the Literature

Whether the focus is on a single food or commodity, the techniques of cooking and kitchen management or the cuisine of an age, restaurant or region, cookbooks and food philosophies, histories, memoirs and musings have been around for centuries.[1] Finding out about home cooking and people who cook might seem then to be relatively unproblematic – there is plenty of accessible, readable literature to which to turn. Yet cookbooks and memoirs are primarily books for cooks, rather than about cooks.[2] A creative and resourceful researcher such as Janet Theophano might make use of memos written in old cookbooks or the clippings and diary pages kept within them. (She explores the daily domestic lives of previous generations of women through the stories of family occasions, advice on making do and coping with sickness and thoughts on managing servants and local and world events that they noted in their cookbooks.[3]) But we have no assurance that the printed text of these books really does represent people's actual cooking practices and abilities.[4] As Laura Shapiro says about studying food in history: 'popular cookbooks tell us a great deal about the culinary climate of a given period, about the expectations and aspirations that hovered over the stove and the dinner table … What they can't convey is a sense of day-to-day cookery as it was genuinely experienced in the kitchens of real life.'[5] In the same way, contemporary cookery books don't necessarily reflect contemporary cooking practices.

Theoretical Approaches to the Study of Food and Cooking

To get some kind of background and structure for my study I turned to sociological and social anthropological studies of food. A study like Luce Giard's, which focuses on home cooking as a means of examining how people claim some sense of autonomy and individuality in an increasingly consumerist society, is rare, though.[6] More usually, academic studies have looked at food preferences and choices rather than practices. Their approach is generally analytic, however, supported by social theory and based on research of people's actual behaviours and attitudes. With their varied and contrasting perspectives rooted in conventions of social and cultural study, they helped me develop alternative, more systematic ways of thinking about cooks and home cooking and provided me with indications of where to look to find detail and more specific insight.

A number of overviews of the sociology of food describe and classify these different theoretical perspectives.[7] There are slight variations within each, but most usually they are organized into three different types of approach – the symbolic, the developmental and those that are gender- and family-based. Before I move on to examine the details about food practices – specifically cooking – in the wider literature, these are the three classifications that I have used in the paragraphs that follow to explore the broader social theories.

Research in the last twenty-five years or so has made domestic food ways and food arrangements more visible. Family and household studies have revealed that the hierarchical organization of the family or household can be seen as manifest in the different members' entitlements to food and in the subjugation of the tastes and preferences of some to those of others.[8] In terms of cooking, various studies have set out to show that 'the actual labour of food preparation is embedded in domestic power relationships'[9] and have found that, though men do cook, doing the cooking is generally women's work. It is women who are responsible for feeding the family, it is they who are the guardians of food-related health and well-being. Yet, despite consistent findings that women take on the bulk of the everyday food work, the research shows too that women do not generally have autonomy over what is prepared or how it is cooked. They plan and provide meals around their partner's and children's food preferences, tastes and requirements, diaries, schedules and more emotional food demands. Finding 'feeding the family' both oppressive and rewarding work, women are drawn into 'social relations that construct and maintain their subordinate position in household life', argues Marjorie DeVault.[10] Even in the most egalitarian of households, cooking and feeding are perceived as 'women's work' – an association that is so strong it is seen as a 'natural expression of gender', as 'womanly' rather than 'manly'.[11] Most of the 'housewives' who took part in Anne Oakley's study of domestic work thought cooking to be potentially the most enjoyable of the many household tasks that have to be done. However, cooking can easily, they explained, become the most dissatisfying and tiresome when busy days, others' demands and culinary 'standards' mean that inventiveness and expertise are thought below par and the food served not as good as it should be. 'I'm trying to be better at it than I need to be,' says one of Oakley's informants. 'I feel I've got to cook something interesting, and the effort that goes into that every night is a bit much really.'[12]

Symbolists and structuralists look, not so much at individuals, families and households, but at the rules that govern people's food practices, rules that cross cultures and social boundaries. For Mary Douglas our food choices, in particular the frequency and regularity with which we eat different foods, help us structure our lives and differentiate between the times of the day and from one day, or time of the year, to another. The food we eat and how and when we eat it tell us whether we are marking an anniversary, celebrating a time of the year, perhaps, or simply refuelling for the day ahead. Wherever you are in the world, elaborate meal structures, special foods and different types of eating and serving implements (say, more than one course and/or cutlery and crockery in some parts) mark an occasion that only certain, clearly defined people are allowed to take part in. Less formal eating events, Douglas explains, warrant fewer rules and discriminate less. You may well offer the window cleaner or plumber a cup of tea, she points out, but you would be far less likely to ask him or her to share your lunch or stay for dinner if they finish late.[13]

Symbolists have also explored society and culture through taste. They see people's choice or taste, in home decoration, clothes, cars and so on as well as food, as a learned process, a means of showing status, group membership and individual aspiration. Those who take a symbolic approach have argued that food tastes and preferences are, rather than purely physiological and linked to aromas and the flavours perceived by the tongue, also cultural. Preferred tastes are acquired, albeit subconsciously, and become physiologically preferred tastes at some point, showing an attachment or affiliation to a certain social group. A taste for dark chocolate and bitter coffee might show sophistication or aspiration to another class. A liking or not for the taste of alcohol might show religious or ethnic allegiance or entry into the 'greater sophistication' of adulthood.[14] Pierre Bourdieu believes taste preferences, including those of food, are an expression of individual identity and status. He argues that the higher social classes use 'good taste' to differentiate themselves from the lower classes. But as their tastes are soon adopted by those 'beneath them' trying to emulate 'their betters', to hold on to their higher status they have to keep acquiring new tastes and discarding old ones. Hence that which makes for 'good taste' is forever changing.[15] Sooner or later, oak-aged Chardonnay, crème brûlée and squid ink risotto go the way of Black Forest gateau, coq au vin, kiwi fruit for garnish and Liebfraumilch.

Amy Bentley's work on food riots examines both the symbolic nature of food and its connection with the social, economic and political phenomena of an age, the spark for food riots and protests coming, she says, not merely from being deprived of sufficient food, but from being deprived of certain, more meaningful foods (be that meaning derived from religious significance, tradition or social distinction). The lunch counter sit-ins of the post-Second World War civil rights era in America for example, she believes, were not just the result of a lack of food. They were a demand from African-Americans to be able to order and consume 'a Coke', now for many a disfavoured reminder of an increasingly powerful food industry perhaps, but nevertheless one greatly valued by the protesters of the time as a symbol of Americanness and democracy.[16]

Other scholars, though not eschewing symbolic meanings completely, are interested in how the food ways of a given society or culture develop and alter over time, and how these changes relate to the broader social, political, economic and cultural changes that are also occurring. For, in a given place and at a given time, what food is chosen and when and how it is eaten are seen by many as reflecting the unique cultural arrangements and social policies of that place and time.[17] Jack Goody, for example, has looked at the reasons why some societies, like France or China, develop both low and high cuisines, concluding that elaborate high cuisines, markers of taste and distinction, develop in more hierarchical societies where there are elite institutions and professional male cooking.[18] Drawing on this theme, Stephen Mennell has made a study of the social, economic and cultural history of England and France and the very different ways their respective food practices and cuisines have developed. He asks a similar question to Goody's: why did an haute cuisine develop in France but not in England? The explanation he arrives at is that the intricate haute cuisine of France arose from the elite, male-dominated, Paris-based courts and the aristocracy. The less elaborate and less technically complex cuisine of England, on the other hand, developed in the female-oriented kitchens of the gentry's rural country houses, where good-quality food was more readily accessible.[19]

Alan Warde has also looked at food practices and choices, including, at least to an extent, food preparation and cooking, in his study of how class, gender, lifestyle, generation and so on influence taste and consumption in contemporary Britain. It is not surprising, he concludes, that people are wary of the food they eat and sometimes unsure about cooking it. For they have to constantly make sense of and deal with four overarching antinomies that are continually and fiercely played out in representations of food and cooking: the opposing tenets of care and convenience, economy and extravagance, novelty and tradition, and health and indulgence.[20]

It is not difficult to appreciate Warde's argument. We're all aware of the endless magazines that give recipes for inexpensive food to impress, tempting the reader to make gourmet dinners for six and other such marvels 'for less than a fiver'. Food companies, on the other hand, never fail to tell us that buying their frozen pizzas shows our families we care more than buying those of their rivals – though we're not convinced we shouldn't make them something proper instead. Should I whip up something new and exotic for dinner, be a bit creative, or should I go for something more comforting with home cooking appeal? Surely I'm not being a health-obsessed fanatic if I say no to a slice of double chocolate fudge cake and grande caramel latte?

Food, Identity and Difference

Both academically and popularly, the last few years have seen interest in the symbolic aspects of food, particularly food as a marker of identity and difference, escalate: so much so that Anna Willets has described the oft-used phrase 'you are what you eat' as being 'hackneyed'.[21] Colloquially at least, our food choices are now entirely accepted as being an integral expression of who we are, what we believe in and what we value. Public opinion research in the United States, for example, shows that vegetarians are thought to eat broccoli, quiche, brown rice and avocado sandwiches and are assumed to be anti-war and pro-drugs and to drive imported cars. Gourmets, in contrast, are expected to favour caviar, oysters and French-roast coffee and are regarded as liberal, drug-taking sophisticates. Fast-food eaters, on the other hand, are generally considered to be religious, conservative and liable to wear polyester.[22]

Food preferences are seen to mark out gender. A sixteen-ounce T-bone steak is man's food. Prettily wrapped gourmet chocolates that promise romantic fulfilment must be for women because men eat machismo-affirming, king-size, chunky chocolate bars in dark brown wrappers.[23] Food highlights age or generation. Smiley potato faces, baked beans and apple slices can only mean a meal for a child, right? Food also marks out otherness. They eat horse meat, we don't. They eat pork, we don't. They eat pumpkin pie, we eat mince pies. They eat fast food, we eat organic. As Alison James says when she asks 'How British is British food?', 'what I eat may reveal that I am English or Cornish, a Hindu or a Jew, a child or an adult or an international traveller or trendsetter. It may also, more prosaically, indicate my social class or status.'[24] Learning about what is 'other' is how we learn and affirm our own identity.

Academically, food and how 'who we are' – our distinctiveness in terms of socio-economic group, religion, gender, lifestyle, age, cultural group and so on – is constructed, interpreted and reproduced through our food preferences are much debated. Introducing *Food, Drink and Identity* its editor, Peter Scholliers, talks about becoming a vegetarian in 1968, when he was fifteen.[25] His long hair, dark clothes and left wing sympathies, he says, gave him a position, a particular status both in his own eyes and in those of others. Through his vegetarianism he was situated in relation to that which was 'other' to him. Some may argue, he points out, that identity such as this, acquired from adopting a vegetarian ethos or from affiliation to a football team or political party, is less fixed and less true that that which comes from family, religion, nation and ethnicity, others that it is impossible to make such distinctions. But, whatever stance is taken, Scholliers explains, it is generally agreed that 'identity contributes to how individuals and groups perceive and construct society, how they give meaning and how they (re)act, think, vote, socialise, buy, rejoice, perceive, work, eat, judge or relax'.[26]

Cuisine

Scholliers goes on to make the point that identity and sentiments of belonging do not only come from our food choices and preferences. They come too from how we organize, serve, prepare and cook food. Cuisine – distinctive ingredients and flavours, dishes and their trimmings and accompaniments, styles and methods of preparation and presentation – is vitally important to our understanding of who we are.[27] Most Westerners expect food to be served on plates and eaten with a knife, fork and spoon. They take it for granted that certain flavours 'go together', that sweet follows savoury and that three main meals are eaten daily despite the fact that these patterns and ways of combining, cooking, serving and eating food are culturally specific and far from universally 'normal'. Cooks in schools, offices and hospitals are all well acquainted with the problem of interpreting – preparing, pre-senting and serving – a particular dish or recipe in the same way as clients who come from very different cultural settings and social backgrounds. It may well have been chosen to appeal to the group in question but food will remain uneaten, as research of residential homes in Stockholm found, if it doesn't smell, taste and appear exactly as expected.[28]

Cuisine or culinary culture and its relationship with identity, especially national identity, is most often viewed simply, colloquially. In the popular imagination there is such a thing as Italian cooking or Thai food. Lasagne comes from Italy, goulash from Hungary.[29] Dictionary definitions tell us that cuisine is 'a characteristic manner or style of preparing food: *Spanish cuisine*'. For sociologists, social anthropologists and other social scientists, however, it is not that simple.

'What makes a cuisine is not a set of recipes aggregated in a book, or a series of particular foods associated with a particular setting, but something more,' says Sidney Mintz. 'A cuisine requires a population that eats that cuisine with sufficient frequency to consider themselves experts on it. They all believe, and care that they believe, that they know what it consists of, how it is made, and how it should taste.' For Mintz, a cuisine can only truly exist if people regularly produce not only the food and cooking of that cuisine, but also opinions about it. Therefore national cuisine, like Russian cooking or Greek food, cannot really exist. It is an artifice, he argues, based tenuously around the foods of a particular area and/or a political system. (Haute cuisine, on the other hand, is, Mintz suggests, something very different. Symbolic of a socially stratified, hierarchical society with an elite to cook for, as Goody has said, it may contain out-of-season foods and the 'best' of products grown elsewhere; it may even be defined by its complexity or difficulty to prepare.[30]) Not that presenting or describing restaurants, cookbooks or television food programmes along nation-based lines is necessarily meaningless or pointless, say Ian Cook and his co-writers of a number of articles that examine culinary authenticity. Whether in a guide or in common consciousness, identifying an establishment as a Spanish bar or Vietnamese cafe, a dish or recipe as Turkish, Moroccan or German creates a story about the food, distinguishes its differences and how it is 'other' to the food of the mainstream culture. It provides a structure for individuals to negotiate those differences and their choices about what to eat, how to eat and perhaps where to eat. Like Mintz, however, they argue that these are identifiers that rarely have anything more than a tenuous link to a 'true' cuisine with its prescribed dishes, techniques and foods and its shared beliefs about standards to be met, what is 'good' and what is not.[31]

'As American as apple pie' is a peculiar analogy of national identity for the English, Dutch, Irish and probably others who associate apple pie as definitive of their culinary culture too. 'I only like real Norwegian food,' protests an eight-year-old from Norway, 'the best of all is spaghetti and pizza.'[32] Yo Sushi is a chain of American-style, British-owned 'Japanese restaurants' that has branches in Greece and Dubai.[33] Cuisines are notoriously difficult to pin down. They continually change, blend and interbreed.[34] Culinary tradition is a hugely indeterminate concept and examples of its ambiguity and awkwardness are far from difficult to find. The potato, for example, is 'traditional' to many European 'cuisines'. Yet the potato only arrived in Europe in the seventeenth century and it didn't 'catch on' until much later.[35] Chillies are indigenous to South America but are synonymous to many of us with, amongst other places, the hot, spicy cooking of India – India being a country where chicken tikka masala, a favourite 'Indian dish' in Britain, doesn't even exist, it being a recently 'invented' combination of the kind of creamy, tomato sauce which the British apparently love and a Punjabi way of cooking chicken in a tandoor oven.[36] Beef sukiyaki too became popular in the 1980s and was regularly presented on restaurant menus in the UK as a sophisticated and authentic Japanese dish, says Katarzyna Cwiertka in her paper on the making of culinary traditions. Yet sukiyaki – meat or fish cooked in a single pot with miso and sweet soy sauce – is only known as such in certain parts of Japan. Moreover, as eating beef was only allowed in Japan from the end of the nineteenth century, sukiyaki would more 'traditionally' be made with game.[37]

It is as it changes and as it transforms that cuisine can reveal, it is argued, the shifting values, beliefs and identities of a society or culture. Drawing on the cookery writing and recipes of the time, Michael Wildt describes how the cooking of immediate post-war Germany was not only thrifty and reliant on substitute foods but also specifically German, regional and local. It reflected both the material and cultural poverty of the time and a society, he says, that was trying to reaffirm its nationhood and assure itself of who it was. From the mid-1950s, however, 'international' food arrived. Secure enough now to look further afield and associate with the rest of the world, West German cookbooks and magazines eagerly proffered recipes for things like Irish stew, Viennese rice, Portuguese meatballs and mutton chops à l'italienne. Yet recipes from outside Europe, says Wildt, noting one for banana salad described as 'African' rather than coming from a specific country, were rare: a reflection perhaps, he suggests, of a desire to participate, to be seen as European again. With time and greater financial, emotional and political security, food and recipes in post-war Germany increasingly became less about assuaging hunger and cooking efficiently and economically and more about satisfying an appetite for difference and variety, for the fancy and the pretty and for celebratory, party food alongside more mundane daily meals. The instruction was increasingly about how to 'dress dishes nicely'. There were time and money enough now to garnish with aspic and flotillas of cucumber boats, to fastidiously carve radishes and to decorate with chopped, boiled egg even the potato salad of every day.[38]

National cuisine, then, can be interpreted as mirroring broader social, cultural, economic and political changes. It can also be consciously manufactured, argue the authors of a paper that looks at how the food served at ministerial meals during Sweden's European Union chairmanship in 2001 was designed, to present a very particular national image. Sausages, slow cooking methods and fermented, soused and preserved foods were thought too robust and 'homey' to serve. They were also deemed too difficult to make look sophisticated or to adapt to the traditions of internationalized cuisine with its tendency to favour quickly cooked fillets of meat or fish and side vegetables, separately prepared and plated for each individual guest. Moreover, products new to but grown in Sweden, such as shitake mushrooms, were considered un-Swedish and inappropriate. 'The food presented was [that which] confirmed old beliefs that certain areas have certain foods, and the nation was presented as homogenous, with no "new" food influences from immigrants, or food contacts with the world outside.'[39] This use of food as a political tool can also be seen at an earlier meeting of European Union ministers in Newcastle, England. As a 'showcase for the country's food', says Henrietta Green, who helped draw up menus, she was instructed that 'all the dishes had to sing out "British"'. The produce used had to be of the very best quality, seasonal and representative of the region – in other words, all of the things that we in Britain are constantly being told our food very definitely isn't any more. The final menu included salmon from the River Tweed, local leeks and potatoes, oysters farmed in Lindisfarne, venison from Northumberland and petits fours of miniature 'traditional puddings' like apple crumble, marmalade tart and lemon meringue pie:[40] not a chocolate brownie, panettone or New York toffee cheesecake – surely seen far more frequently on restaurant menus and in supermarkets and contemporary cookbooks – in sight.

In her book, *Something from the Oven, Reinventing Dinner in 1950s America*, Laura Shapiro considers the fluidity and artificiality of culinary traditions, food ways and cuisine.[41] In post-war America, says Shapiro, 'hoping to rid themselves of freeze-dried army leftovers and profit from new technologies', the food industry attempted to convince women that cooking was difficult. They tried to persuade housewives that they couldn't do without the tins and packets and the frozen, dehydrated and canned products that they now could, and for profit reasons wanted to, supply. Those that used them, they claimed, could then give themselves over to the more glamorous, sophisticated and satisfying side of cooking – the garnishing and glazing, the prettifying and decorating. Inundating them with recipes and information, food manufacturers set out to invent a new cuisine based around their bottled, canned and freeze-dried pre-prepared products. They even attempted, Shapiro explains, to introduce new meal types and times, for recipe suggestions like 'tomatoes sprinkled with cheese, banana and mayonnaise and browned in the oven' and 'muffins covered with canned apple slices, red jelly and then broiled or grilled' were impossible to classify as belonging to either breakfast, dinner or lunch.

Cooking for Leisure

The symbolism of food preferences and practices, of their connections with self, cultural, religious, class, gender and national identity, has become an ever more popular area for study in recent years because food has increasingly, at least in Western societies, become something that can be purchased and used for pleasure. Dining out, cooking for recreation, wine and chocolate tasting and watching food-focused travel programmes and cookery game shows on television are the practices and pastimes of wealthy, food-rich societies. Food and cooking can now be a form of leisure, as much about relaxation, enjoyment, cultural acquisition and performance as they are about any biological imperative to eat.[42] And, with the explosion from the 1980s onwards of cookery books, food magazines and television cookery, serious and academic interest in food and cooking in the media and as a leisure activity has grown too.

Martin Caraher and Tim Lang have looked at the influence of celebrity chefs and television cookery on people's cooking practices and abilities. Interestingly, despite the fact that their report makes little reference to media theory and the study takes more a functional than a symbolic approach, their conclusions that these programmes and the people who appear on them have little direct impact on people's actual cooking practices and skills but may expose them to broader cultural food and cooking beliefs reflect the views of media theorists.[43] John Corner, for example, whilst making the point that empirical research into the effects of the media on attitudes and behaviour of any sort is difficult to find, explains that there is general agreement among those working in this area that any influence there is is largely indirect. Amongst experts the media is widely acknowledged, not as imposing false consciousness and directly changing public attitudes, but as 'producing unconscious categories through which life is experienced and understood'.

Television, for example, has become the measure of quality in everyday practices, a definer of reality. It provides larger-than-life standards by which the more mundane actuality of the real world can be measured and perhaps judged as disappointing and dissatisfying.[44] For, unlike the situated cultures of 'traditional' societies, the mediated cultures of 'modern' societies are not founded on the values, beliefs and tastes of groups who are bound to a specific time and place and the people around them. Ready access and exposure to and daily use of media technologies mean that they come into contact with the thoughts, experiences and behaviours of those who they will never meet and who live in places and times they will never visit.

The food cultures of post-industrial, technology-oriented, Western societies are therefore mediated food cultures. We experience and understand our food, cooking and eating practices not only through those around us but also through the media – from cookery columns and real-life stories in men's and women's weeklies, from food and lifestyle articles in Sunday newspapers and from the manner in which food and cooking are treated in television soaps, historical drama and crime shows, as well as in specialized cookery programmes. Yet, as Sandie Randall, who has written extensively on how food and cooking are represented on television, has pointed out, how we make sense of media messages about food and apply them in our everyday lives hasn't really become a subject of scholarly interest,[45] a neglect, Randall thinks, which suggests food and cookery in the media are mostly approached as being straightforward, as being (in the manner of Caraher and Lang's study) about information and instruction. This is a surprising neglect too, she suggests, when one considers the somewhat cult, sub-obsessive status of cooking today, with its foodie web pages, recipe software, famous and celebrity cooks, specialist cooking holidays and the new-found convention for the food memoir and food-oriented biography – surprising too, perhaps, when one considers the frequency with which commentators and campaigners tell us reproachfully how these days a deskilled and incapable public 'loves to watch' but doesn't actually 'do' any cooking.[46]

Drawing on the work of symbolists and semiotic theory, Randall looks at how food, cooks and cooking are represented on television, and at how these representations, the words, gestures, images and perspectives used, are then interpreted by viewers and reproduced as food beliefs, food culture and ideology. A critical analysis of a single episode of Rick Stein's *Taste of the Sea* is the focus of one of her articles.[47] In it, Randall reveals how the messages conveyed in a seemingly uncomplicated programme looking at the lives of Cornish fishermen, the histories of their trade and the landscape in which they work, whilst providing a selection of fish and seafood recipes, are in fact far from simple. *Taste of the Sea* has been designed, Randall argues, to create a sense of intimacy and co-presence with the viewer. The life-size, head and shoulders presentation of Stein, the simulated eye contact of everyday conversation, the use of slang and occasional swearing, glimpses of Stein's home life and his staff at work are all devices by which the audience is drawn into a complicity with the presenter. Stein is presented as thoughtful, intelligent and philosophical. A staff party shows a certain paternalism. We learn that he is an Oxford graduate, she explains, his voice-over peppered with literary and musical quotations. In sum, the different images establish Stein as an expert and an authority. In a similar way, Randall goes on to explain, *Taste of the Sea* is made up of a succession of short segments, different stories of different lengths that are independent of each other but that together reinforce a set of 'dominant themes' and 'cultural norms'. Various concepts – community, family life, the shipping forecast, Cornish regionalism and traditions – are layered up in order to portray Britishness, at least Britishness of a particular kind. For this is a romanticized world that idealizes country living, British 'seaside holidays' and working-class jobs. It is a process of mediation that, Randall believes, transforms food production and preparation from an everyday craft and necessity into a pursuit of leisure and art, that shifts cooking into the realm of the auteur.[48]

Research like Randall's, as she herself points out, is scarce, though. Like so many other aspects of contemporary food and cooking, debate about the influence and role of the written media on daily home cooking practices is difficult to develop, she says, because there is little real evidence. Yet, as in the case of the decline of the family meal or the impoverished state of home cooking, that hasn't stopped it being the subject of enthusiastic debate. One issue often discussed is the effect of the sheer quantity of readily accessible advice – food columns and articles can now be found in all types of journals and newspapers – on people's food and cooking approaches and practices. Does it give us a chance to access areas of knowledge and expertise that we might not previously have had? Or does it leave us overwhelmed, searching bewildered for a 'way in'? For, on the one hand, the readily available and huge quantity of guidance, information and instruction, presented variously as travelogue, anthropological insight, memoir, cultural analysis and historical research, as well as practical cooking advice, can be seen as democratizing. Transcending class and cultural boundaries, it gives everyone the chance to be aware of, and to gain cultural status through being aware of, new foods and new styles of cooking. On the other hand, it can be argued that this vast, ever increasing quantity and variety of information about cuisines, foods, recipes and techniques goad the individual to acquire ever greater food knowledge. Rather than feeling enlightened and culturally informed, however, we bow under the pressure and resort to ready-prepared foods,[49] the deluge of cookery books, recipe leaflets and restaurant guides and their disorientating entreaties – to care for families but be quick and convenient, to remember tradition but stimulate with something new and interesting, to indulge yet always consider health and to 'have a treat' whilst watching the purse strings – hastening our 'descent'.[50] Equally anxiety-inducing, it is argued, are the glossy, stylized pictures that frequently accompany recipes and that tell us just how good our food could or should look. They may, of course, be inspiring, just as the increasing precision and quantification (preparation and cooking times, nutritional content and so on) found in recipes may remove uncertainty and increase confidence.[51] Yet this positive view is more often than not overshadowed by a more negative approach that believes didactic, contemporary-style recipes do away with the need to develop skills of timing, judgement and planning. Indeed, recipes themselves are a subject of great contention, for, whilst they can be seen as making elaborate food preparation easier and allowing the replication and experimentation that facilitates and encourages complex and haute cuisine, they can also be viewed as inflexible constructs of ingredients and methods that halt creativity and spontaneity.[52]

Finding Out More about Cooking: the Study and its Aims

With a range of informing, guiding philosophies and theoretical comment on the social study of food in place and (as described in the last chapter) the gaps in knowledge and understanding of cooking in everyday life established, the next step was to develop research that could provide evidence that would move current debates forward, beyond conjecture.

My overall purpose with the research that informs this book was to take a sceptic's approach and disassemble current, accepted but often unevidenced views, building an alternative, evidence-based way of thinking about domestic cooks and cooking in their place. I wanted to look at cooking from the perspective of people who cook, to describe and explain their real life experiences of cooking. By examining their thoughts, reasonings, joys, satisfactions and dissatisfactions, difficulties and abilities, I aimed to develop this new area of study and interest. The specific objectives of the research were to:

- Find out what expressions like 'good cooking', 'cooking ability' and 'basic cooking skills' really mean to the people who use them.
- Examine how people approach cooking, what they think and feel about it.
- Explore the connections and discrepancies between what people can cook and what and how they do cook.
- Explore the connections and discrepancies between what people think about cooking – how confident they are, whether they enjoy it and so on – and what and how they cook.
- Develop a theoretical framework that allows domestic cooking to be treated as a serious subject of social enquiry.
- Examine the appropriateness of claims that contemporary home cooking is being deskilled and devalued.

The aim of the study was not to provide numerical data that would allow comparisons between social characteristics like age, class, education, income and gender: research that could show for example, the percentage of women who enjoy cooking, the contrasting percentages of the middle classes and the working classes who regularly use ready meals or the number of university-educated respondents who say Jamie Oliver is their favourite television chef. I wanted to focus on individuals and their day-to-day experiences rather than on broad social groups, numbers and causal patterns of behaviour. I wanted to understand what concepts such as 'learning to cook', 'ready meals', 'enjoying cooking' and 'using pre-prepared foods instead of cooking' mean to those who cook. To do so, to provide insight into people's real cooking lives, I took a qualitative, interpretative approach to my study.[53]

The research took place in two stages. Early findings had shown me that a two-part design would be a useful and appropriate way of exploring a subject where the existing research is limited, for it would allow the study to be developed horizontally in the first place (a wide number of issues explored broadly and generally so that key themes can emerge) and then vertically (a focused, detailed examination of those key themes).[54] Both stages were designed around fairly loose, semi-structured interviews, using topic headings and prompts rather than inflexible, precise questions. Those who took part in the first, more exploratory stage also gave me a guided tour of their kitchen. They kept cooking diaries as well, listing for each meal or snack, over and beyond a cup of tea and a biscuit, say, what they ate, how they prepared it, who prepared it, where the food was served, who ate it and who wrote the notes. I did not use observation, a method of collecting data that might at first seem particularly relevant to the study of something as practical as cooking, for a variety of reasons. First, I did not aim to appraise or measure people's cooking skills. Secondly, the literature review had shown me that many practical tasks involve perceptual and conceptual abilities that are tacit and mostly unobservable. And, thirdly, I felt it very likely that becoming 'part of the furniture', a neutral observer in someone's private kitchen, would be a lengthy and potentially unworthwhile process.

In both stages I selected people to take part opportunistically. Friends, family, colleagues and sometimes people who had already contributed to the study suggested individuals who they thought might make appropriate informants – people they worked with, lived with and knew socially. I also advertised in colleges and the workplaces of friends and associates. If the 'qualities' of the people who were suggested or who came forward were useful to the study at that point, then I gave them some information and asked if they would like to take part.

Couples aged between thirty and fifty from different social, financial and occupational backgrounds informed the first stage of fieldwork. All those who took part had lived in England for twelve years or more and as couples they had all lived together for over five years. Each couple had different living arrangements, differing through the presence of children or a lodger, the occasional extended visits of older children, and so on. All claimed to 'keep regular hours' in that, however they were employed, they tended to work somewhere between seven in the morning and ten o'clock at night. The informants had very varied occupations. One man described himself as unemployed whereas his wife worked as a marketing manager. Another male informant was in 'occasional employment', he said, whilst his partner described her job as secretarial. One couple who took part consisted of a self-employed painter and decorator and a part-time school meals' supervisor. Two lawyers made up a further couple. One woman had 'an administrative occupation' whereas her husband was employed on a part-time basis in delivery work. Two female informants described themselves as full-time housewives, one being married to a writer whereas the other said that her partner worked as a freelance subeditor.

I chose to study couples in the first stage because I aimed to investigate a wide range of issues. The shared experiences and views of couples, I felt, could provide depth via different viewpoints of the same cooking experiences whilst limiting the diversity of data and so keeping it to a manageable level. Topics I discussed with them included 'childhood experiences of cooking and eating', 'current cooking practices', 'the role of ready meals' and 'typically British food'.

After I had analysed data from seven couples, it became apparent that a number of recurrent themes – cooking with fresh, raw ingredients has to be 'worth it', for example, good cooks have some degree of natural talent, pre-prepared foods are accepted and normal – were evident. I then designed the second stage of fieldwork to substantiate, refine and explain these themes. Those opinions, beliefs, values and practices that I thought might be general or universal were 'tested out' as being such on sixteen (seven men and nine women) very different people. Though two had been born elsewhere, as with the informants who took part in the first stage, all those who contributed to the study had lived in England for more than twelve years. Two were in their late teens, four were in their twenties, five in their thirties, two in their forties, two in their fifties and one in her sixties. Two informants lived alone. One lived with her nine-year-old son. One of the younger informants lived for part of the week with her parents, another spent most of her weekends at her boyfriend's parents' house. Another described herself as 'flat-sharing' with a friend, yet another as living alone when at college and living with his parents during holidays. The remaining nine informants all lived with partners; two of these nine had teenage children living with them, four had one or two children under ten and three had no children. The sixteen informants had very different occupations. Two women described themselves as housewives, one claiming income support and the other her pension. Three informants had clerical or secretarial positions. Nanny, freelance writer, bookkeeper, hospitality student, doctor, musician, youth worker, receptionist, restaurant manager and accountant were other occupations. Two informants described themselves as 'working in education', one with adults for a local authority and another in the theatre. The sixteen informants had very different experiences of cooking. Two had professional cooking experience: one was an ex-chef and restaurant manager and the other a hospitality student taking cooking classes at college. One young woman lived with her parents but also worked as a nanny and had to cook for the children in her care whilst another went home regularly to help cook for her ailing mother. Two informants were single men who lived alone, though one often had his teenage children to stay. One woman was nearing her seventieth birthday and had been cooking and providing food for others since her early twenties. Another had to cook for herself and her nine-year-old son on a very limited budget. Yet another had two part-time jobs and cooked for her husband and her two teenage children. Two of the informants had very young children – under the age of five – to cook for. One of the younger informants lived in a shared house. She cooked for herself but shared a kitchen. Two of the male informants had very little experience because they lived with partners who 'did all the cooking', they said. Another lived with a partner but, as he 'worked nights', they both cooked for themselves and ate at different times.

These different cooking lives enabled me to determine not only which themes 'held true' across informants whatever their experience, food responsibilities, age and so on but also where there were variations in approach and practice. Further, studying a group with very varied experiences of cooking and responsibilities for providing food for others meant that I could find and describe a wide range of different cooking skills and abilities. Topics I discussed with the informants, as a means of exploring the key themes that emerged in the first stage, included 'the importance of learning to cook', 'using recipes', 'making a pizza' and 'watching cookery shows on television'. (The thesis that reported on the study and papers published since provide further details on the approach, design and process of the study.[55])

I have described the informants as two groups, rather than individually, so that data, the words of the informants, are not traceable back to a particular person. Comments and accounts from those who took part in the study are only used in this book, as they were in the original thesis, to represent typical answers and emerging patterns and help explain or give evidence of themes, values, concepts, skills and so on. They are not used to attribute a particular occurrence, belief or perspective to a specific characteristic, say, income level, gender, cooking experience or class status, because that might encourage a feeling of false representativeness or stereotyping. For example, unless otherwise stated, a quote about using pre-prepared foods from a bookkeeper in his forties with two teenage children would only be used to help explain an approach towards using pre-prepared foods found generally amongst the informants. It would not be included to illustrate how middle-class men, people living with teenagers, bookkeepers or people in their forties feel about using pre-prepared foods.

This book is based on the findings of my study, on the papers, books and expert views that informed it, and on the articles, debates and conversations that have resulted from it. But essentially, and most importantly, it relies on and is inspired by the cooking lives of the thirty people who took part, their accounts of their cooking experiences and their thoughts, views and opinions. To help protect their anonymity, the names by which I call them are not their real names.

–3–

What do Cooks Think of Cooking?

What does it Mean 'to Cook'?

To cook something is to apply heat to it, John, a one-time student of mine, declared, insisting that preparing a salad was obviously not 'cooking', nor was making sandwiches or whisking up a smoothie or milkshake. Food writers often take a similarly inflexible approach. For many there is only one true meaning of cook and that is to prepare food from scratch. Cherry Ripe, for example, is adamant that cooking means taking fresh, raw ingredients and turning them into a meal. It is very definitely not 'following the numbered pictograms on the back of a packet, and microwaving for x minutes'.[1] Others speak almost disdainfully of how today's '"cook" can use pre-packaged mixes to make an array of "homemade" foods – cakes, pies, pancakes and waffles'[2] and of survey respondents who nominate making baked beans on toast, cakes from packet mixes and chips as their cookery skills – evidence, surely, of the degradation of home cooking.[3] Dictionary definitions tend to take a similar line to John and are generally of the 'to prepare food for eating by applying heat' type,[4] though some versions are a little more adventurous, offering things like 'to practise cookery' as well.[5] Anne Murcott, however, writing about the study of food in sociology, identifies a very different meaning. 'Cook' can also be used, she explains, to refer to – in the same way as washing up, shopping and doing the laundry are tasks – the household task of cooking.[6] But what of the home cooks themselves? What do people who cook mean when they use the word 'cook'?

'If I'm cooking for myself I'll just cook pasta and have it with pesto,' said Claire in response to my asking her 'how much cooking' she does. 'I very rarely *cook* for myself. I never really experiment *cooking*-wise.' In this one statement Claire uses 'cook' in three different ways. She uses it to mean preparing something to eat and to refer to applying heat to pasta, presumably by boiling in water. When she emphasizes cook, however (where I have used italics), Claire appears to be alluding to something more complex, more abstract: an aspect of cooking that is more highly valued and that is somehow 'proper'. For Claire, boiling some pasta and reheating a ready-made sauce to go with it are not 'proper cooking'.

People who cook, my research revealed, associate 'proper cooking' or 'real cooking' with those meals and snacks that are highly valued, like weekend food or a meal for guests. 'Proper cooking' also involves more effort and a greater use of foods that the cook considers more unusual and more special. 'We cook things that are sort of easy and straightforward during the week but at the weekend we try and *cook*,' explained Jules. 'We don't necessarily eat with the kids at the weekend and we try and cook slightly more interesting things. We might spend a bit longer over it and try out new recipes.'

People who cook also use 'cook' in the way that Anne Murcott has highlighted, to mean 'doing the cooking', the task of making and providing food. Kate's response to my question 'how much cooking do you do?' was to describe a day's worth of activities, including things such as making coffee and pouring drinks:

> Per day, I start off in the morning when Peter and I have breakfast before I go to lunch. On a workday the children will have their breakfast at nursery, so typically a workday would involve a bowl of cereal for both of us, a coffee for Peter and water for me. If he's starving, Josh can grab himself a yogurt out of the fridge. When I get home about five o'clock the children have already eaten their meal so then it's really just organizing food. (Kate)

They use cook too, as can be seen in Wayne's comment that he likes his vegetables 'cooked but not cooked to death', to refer to the straightforward application of heat. They do not, however, use 'cook' in the way that many food writers and experts do, to mean the preparation of food 'from scratch', from fresh, raw ingredients only, even when they are talking about 'proper cooking'. Mark is proud of his 'quite mean Carbonara', it's the only thing he has ever 'really *cooked*', he explained. But he makes it, it transpired, with a packet of dried Carbonara sauce mix. Nor are those who describe tasks like making sandwiches, grilling burgers, using cake and batter mixes or reheating frozen pizzas as 'cooking' necessarily the least able cooks. Indeed, those who are most likely to interpret and use 'cook' in this way are generally those, usually women, heavily involved in food preparation and cooking for family and friends on a daily and often all-day (at least that's how they say it feels) basis. They are interpreting the word 'cook' in a similar way to that identified by Anne Murcott, understanding it as meaning a household activity other than, say, doing the washing, tidying up or cleaning.

If 'to cook' has no precise or definite meaning, then neither do phrases that refer to levels of pre-preparation, such as ready-made, convenience or from scratch. Food writers and scholars often associate ready-prepared and pre-prepared, for example, solely in connection with chilled or frozen meals and foods requiring only reheating.[7] Yet the people who cook that I spoke to used terms like these indiscriminately. Ready-prepared can be used to describe a chilled vegetarian lasagne or frozen chocolate cheesecake but, as with phrases like 'convenience food' and 'bought', it can also be used to refer to such foods as skinned chicken breasts, dried pasta and frozen vegetarian sausages.

Recently, however, researchers have begun to query the meaning of 'cook' (and other related phrases) and become aware of its complexity or 'plasticity'.[8] They are increasingly appreciative of how survey results may be interpreted incorrectly or unsatisfactorily as a consequence, even if some cannot get away from the slight horror of 'cook' not necessarily meaning the preparation of food from scratch. 'Despite most pupils stating that they were not taught enough about cooking at school a "whopping" 9 out of 10 said they could cook good meals themselves!' a report of a study of the cooking practices and approaches of schoolchildren exclaims in mock confusion. 'However,' the report adds, 'it was evident from the focus group discussions that "cooking" often meant heating and eating convenience and ready made dishes.'[9]

The ingenuity with which people use 'cook' and the varied, sometimes highly abstracted, meanings they bestow upon it proved to be a first sign for my study that home cooking might not be the simple, practical and rational activity it is often constructed as being. In fact, I would now argue that the complexity of the meaning of the verb cook reflects the complexity of the domestic practice of cooking and the approaches of those who do it – a complexity I examine in this book. In this third chapter I look at the beliefs, values and interpretations that surround cooking in the home, approaches that were shared by the cooks I studied, whatever their age, generation, gender, income, food responsibilities or cooking experience.[10]

Prepared Food is Just Food

A child has to learn at what times of day particular foods are eaten in the society or culture in which they are growing up. He or she has also to learn how they are eaten (fork and spoon, knife and fork, fingers or chopsticks, say), how they are usually combined (a two-year-old may well have a tantrum if they are told they can't eat their toast with custard or dip carrot sticks in chocolate spread) and how they are usually prepared, cooked and served (on individual plates, 'family style' in a shared bowl or wrapped in banana leaf). First though, they have to learn what food is, what people, and more specifically 'what people like them', eat. For food is not just what an individual *can* eat and will provide nutrients and energy. Food is cultural and it is socially constructed. Fido is perfectly edible but in most of the world he is not considered to be food. Arugula, escarole and radicchio are salad to some and weeds to others.[11] The child brought up in the UK or USA who eats caterpillars and grass from the garden or the cat's food from its bowl is eating something that will nourish them but is not eating what is generally deemed acceptable as food. The same child will probably learn that horse meat and insects are not considered food by 'people like me' and that bread, rather than, say, rice or cassava, is the staple that comes with many meals.[12]

In *Can She Bake a Cherry Pie* Mary Drake McFeely describes how, astounded though she is now, as a young, newly married woman she used to make baked beans 'from scratch'. Nostalgic about a rural past that she had never known, she felt driven to do so as a way of experiencing and reflecting on, she suggests, the lives of her female predecessors'.[13] Her recollection of making baked beans struck a chord with me for I can clearly remember my glee at finding a recipe for Boston baked beans when as a student I first began cooking for myself. Driven by curiosity (how could you *make* baked beans?) I was ultimately disappointed by the treacly, mustardy, spicy, sweet yet savoury concoction that bore no resemblance to the gluey, orange yet, for me, 'proper' version. Drake McFeely herself writes of her own similar surprise at discovering that Campbell's Black Bean Soup could be made from scratch with dried black beans.

Years later I would discover that baked beans are one of a number of pre-prepared foods that domestic cooks wouldn't ever expect to make, even if they may do so, as I did, on the odd occasion, as a matter of course. In their food diaries many of the informants who took part in my research explained in great detail how they made such things as 'vegetable kebabs' and 'shepherd's pie' but gave no information about other foods listed, such as 'oven chips', 'veggie burgers' and 'chicken Kiev'. One cook meticulously described the making of a 'whiskey and chocolate cheesecake' for a dinner with friends but gave absolutely no information about the 'chocolate mousse' that she put in her daughter's lunchbox. The explanation for the lack of information came with her bewilderment (when I interviewed her) that anyone would expect her to make chocolate mousse for a child's packed lunch. She took it as read that I would understand (as indeed I did) that she was referring to a little pot of chilled ready-prepared dessert.

For contemporary home cooks it seems that there are any number of pre-prepared foods that are 'just food', which have their own identity. They do not expect to ever make, on a regular basis at least, such things as bread, ice cream, breakfast cereals, fruit yogurt, burgers, peanut butter, butter, jam, salad dressings or sliced cooked meats such as ham and pastrami. The use of pre-prepared versions seems to be considered normal and entirely acceptable. There's another reminder here, too, of the difficulty of defining phrases such as ready-prepared, fresh, raw and pre-prepared. It is, after all, relatively easy to understand why a chilled tray of Chicken Pasta Bake might be described as pre-prepared and a whole, uncooked chicken as raw even if it is ready-plucked, trussed and freed of its insides. Foods like dried pasta, easy-cook rice, sausages and rolled oats are far more problematic to describe or classify. That definition of this kind relies more on the prevailing food value system than any analysis of their 'pre-preparation' is an argument that I shall return to later. But wouldn't it be right to suggest that many of us would be more likely to label the tin of Thai curry cook-in-sauce available in Sainsburys or Walmart a 'convenience food' than the jar of Thai green curry paste found on the shelves of an oriental supermarket?

This acceptability of pre-prepared foods proved to be a real opening into understanding how contemporary domestic cooks view, value and understand the practice of home cooking. Unlike many food experts and scholars, cooks themselves, I found, do not necessarily start from the position that cooking with convenience or pre-prepared foods is less acceptable than cooking with fresh, raw foods. They are just 'part of cooking'. Many of the cooks that I spoke with, like Eamon, even talk of preferring the taste of prepared versions of foods that, if they so wished, they could cook themselves: 'I do like being able to produce a reasonable, edible and attractive meal and I don't necessarily do it from scratch either. If it involves knowing where to buy the best tart that's going to be really nice, that's exactly what I'll do.' Some even aim to cook food 'as good', they said, as that which they can buy ready-made and part-prepared. Even capable cooks and those who do express doubt about pre-prepared foods being as 'good' as raw foods are ultimately perfectly happy to cook with them on at least some occasions. As Jules said, 'it's sad that there is such a big trend towards using pre-prepared foods but I think its fine and we do use them sometimes'.

When to Use a Ready Meal, When to Make an Effort

Christmas dinner is a special and rare occasion governed by precise and strict rules about food choices and the preparation methods used. It comprises a number of highly valued foods, mostly eaten infrequently throughout the rest of the year, served in a rigidly sequenced order. Anyone who has ever served roast beef instead of turkey or cheesecake instead of Christmas pudding or abandoned the sprouts or cranberry sauce will know that twinge of guilt and/or disappointment coupled with a fleeting glee that they have broken the rules. Breakfast, in contrast, is usually eaten on a daily basis, comprises foods that are not particularly highly valued and has far more informal rules about how they should be prepared.

Mary Douglas researched and analysed the food practices and choices of both her own household and, with colleagues, those of a number of working-class families in London. She found that there are many rules determining how often different foods are prepared and consumed, the types of food chosen for a particular meal or snack and the preparation and cooking techniques that are then applied. The rules governing each separate meal reveal its relative importance and the social relationships involved. In the Douglas household, for example, workmen and visiting strangers would perhaps be offered a drink but meals were shared only with family, close friends and special guests.[14] It is these kinds of food rules, points out David Sutton in his study of food practices and habits on the Greek island of Kalymnos, that mean someone, say, 'a migrant returning to his village after a long absence', can '[on] coming upon a large meal in progress recognize and categorize the type of feast being enacted'.[15]

Drawing from Douglas's work on the rules of meals, Anne Murcott's study of young Welsh mothers included an examination of the food preparation and cooking methods they used. In particular, she looked at the rules behind the food choices, serving methods and preparation techniques of the highly valued 'proper meal' or 'cooked dinner'. To qualify as such, she found, the meal had to be hot and it had to include roast or grilled meat and at least two kinds of vegetables, one of which had to be green and boiled.[16] More recently, Anne Murcott has reviewed her earlier studies and suggested that it may be time for a rethink. She speculates that perhaps, within contemporary societies where both industrialized and craft modes of food production (home cooking and pre-prepared, convenience foods) exist, the rules underlying food choice and preparation practices may well be changing.[17]

Yet, rather than developing these analyses of the rules and structures that underpin domestic food choices and practices, the main focus of academic interest and debate in the last few years has been on their breakdown.[18] Alongside fears about the possible risks of industrialized and globalized food production and anxieties about food additives and adherence to nutritional guidelines, there has been growing concern about the breakdown of 'traditional' domestic food practices. The decline of domestic cooking and the meal is a topic that dominates food talk as the twenty-first century progresses.[19] These anxieties represent, says sociologist Claude Fischler, a move from gastronomy towards 'gastro-anomie', or food disorder. 'We feel fear, unease and are raising very broad questions about modern food practices,' he says. 'Never have we been so free to decide what to eat and at the same time we often feel that we are digging our graves with our own teeth.'[20]

However, it seems, as Murcott suspects, that cooks do follow some sort of guidelines. Liz, for example, has some very definite ideas about what kinds of foods and dishes are appropriate for different – and in her case highly differentiated – meal occasions: 'Once every three or four weeks [I cook chicken and vegetable kebabs]. I would imagine I wouldn't generally do it just for me and my husband. I would do if people are over. It's not something for a dinner party 'mind, it's something for tea.' The foundations of these guidelines lie in the value that cooks place on different cooking occasions. As my research findings revealed quite clearly, some cooking occasions (meals or snacks) are valued more highly than others. Most usually, weekday cooking occasions are thought less important than weekend cooking occasions and evening cooking occasions are thought more important than daytime occasions. Cooking for adults constitutes a more important occasion than cooking for children and cooking for guests is valued more highly than cooking for the family.

It was generally agreed that a Saturday dinner for guests, for example, is more highly valued in terms of the cooking done and the food choices made than a Saturday dinner 'just for us'. However, although all the cooks who took part in my study differentiated between the cooking practices they associated with each, how they differentiated and the degree to which they differentiated varied enormously among individuals. Some described making a special shopping trip or providing more courses, others may use 'different and interesting foods' or new recipes, they said. Some, but certainly not all, associate a greater use of fresh, raw foods with cooking for guests. And, although there are cooks who will cook 'all day' for a special meal or important occasion, most think one or two hours is appropriate. Roughly half an hour generally seems to suffice for 'just me' or 'just us' at home, with a video or dvd perhaps.

Breakfast is a less important cooking occasion than dinner and as such cooks appear to differentiate less between a weekday breakfast and a weekend breakfast than they do between their evening meal equivalents. In general, it is only a breakfast on holiday or when guests are staying that adds much importance to the meal as a cooking occasion. It is only then that 'fresh croissants', 'sausage and eggs', a 'full breakfast' or a 'quick trip to the shops' are more likely than the toast, cereals or bread provided by the weekly or fortnightly shop. Breakfasts, though, even special ones, rarely warrant the trying out of a new recipe or a look through cookery books for fresh inspiration.

These guidelines may appear relatively simple, but they take on a greater subtlety and sophistication when the 'effort and reward relationship' (noted briefly by Roy Wood in *The Sociology of the Meal* and by Luce Giard in her study of French women 'doing cooking') is also taken into consideration.[21]

Preparing large quantities of food is an effort, though so too is preparing small quantities. Washing up, asking for advice and finding and using recipes are all an effort, as are preparing messy foods and making special shopping trips. Also thought an effort are preparing everyday food and meals 'just for us', making food for special occasions, cooking 'dishes', serving more than one course and cooking with 'fresh' foods rather than 'pre-prepared' foods. In short, in a world where you don't have to cook from 'fresh', 'raw' ingredients, most cooking tasks are regarded as an effort on at least some occasions. Being prepared to make an effort involves being confident that sufficient, compensatory reward for doing so will be received. And reward for cooks takes many different forms. It can come from others' enjoyment of eating the food they have prepared but it comes also from satisfaction with the standard or appearance of the food in question or from others' appreciation of their ability, either as a cook or as a host. It can also be found, as Jaclyn's words show, in the cook's enjoyment of the cooking process itself:

When I have the time I love it. I actually really enjoy doing all the preparation and spending the time because its quite a relaxing thing to do then. But if I come home, and I'm not usually home till half past seven or eight, then the last thing I want to do is start cooking. I don't find it relaxing then. (Jaclyn)

Reward can also come from slightly more obscure sources like the attaining of personal aims such as, in the case of quite a few of the people who took part in my study, getting the children to eat 'something healthy' or 'something green'.

The greater the importance of a cooking occasion, the greater it is felt the effort applied should be. Cooking for guests, generally considered the most important type of cooking occasion of all, is usually understood as requiring the greatest effort and potentially offering the greatest reward. In particular, cooking for guests may require the effort of cooking from scratch, or at least the use of a greater quantity of 'fresh', 'raw' ingredients than is normal for the cook in question. Cooking a weekday breakfast, on the other hand, is generally thought 'not worth the effort', providing, as it does, insufficient compensation for a few minutes longer in bed.

Conversely, as Mick describes below, putting greater effort into a cooking occasion can elevate it in terms of importance and simultaneously increase the associated reward:

When you've got guests coming round you want to make the meal a bit of an event … You want a meal that will have a number of courses so that it goes on a while and you want to cook something a bit special that you have put some work into. You feel good about it and they respect the fact that you've gone to some effort. (Mick)

If someone cooks and they don't feel that they receive enough of a reward for the effort they have put in then they may feel disappointed, unsatisfied and even frustrated. Kate explains how she once went to the trouble of making an extra large quantity of beef casserole to portion and give to her father to keep in his freezer. Tripling the quantities and searching in vain for the right size pan, she found she 'didn't quite get the proportions right'. The resulting casserole didn't taste as flavoursome as normal and Kate felt disappointed: 'it can be so annoying when you spend time on something'. Showing similar disappointment, Genevieve, one of the women who took part in Luce Giard's study of cooks in France, recalls her past efforts cooking for her son:

When he was little, I made a effort, you know, to vary his meals, to never give him the same thing twice. I made imaginative efforts. I gave him some green beans with half a potato and half a carrot, and I mixed it up with some chicken. I made him his meals, but I would get so upset – he didn't want anything! I made so much effort without results that I let go of everything, well, I abandoned many things. (Genevieve)

Her son's refusal to eat the food she 'cooks' is for Genevieve a sign of his abandonment of her, says Giard, his rejection of her offer of love.[22]

The existence of these discerning guidelines and this organized approach to tasks of food provision and the use of fresh, raw and pre-prepared foods supports Alan Beardsworth and Theresa Keil's claim about the reconstruction of food choice. Though they are talking of food practices in general rather than specifically of cooking, they suggest that people, rather than being anxious about the multiplicity of food choices, flavour principles and fashions of cuisine made available in Western food systems, find it 'quite normal and essentially unproblematic'. And they do so because there *is* 'a relatively stable overall framework within which the choices, whims, fashions and fads of a pluralistic approach to eating can be played out'.[23] There are guidelines. The first decision for the cook is not 'what food do I cook?' but 'what is the occasion?' or perhaps 'who will be present?' or 'what type of meal is befitting?'[24]

Learning to Cook

Culinary memoirs proliferate, *French Lessons: Adventures with Knife, Fork and Corkscrew, Comfort Me with Apples, Recipes and Remembrances from an Eastern Mediterranean Kitchen, Waiting: The True Confessions of a Waitress* and *Kitchen Confidential* being just a very few of those that have been published in the last few years.[25] Often rather nostalgic, they most usually recall cultures or eras where cooking is 'real' and cooks, whether domestic or professional, are talented and skilled at what they do (and those who are not, tend to be amusingly not so). My own childhood cooking memories of packaged, dehydrated Vesta chow mein and Bird's trifle would probably not pass muster for such a memoir. I can remember eating my mother's coffee and walnut cakes, shepherd's pies and apple and blackberry crumbles and I can remember it being my job from the age of about eleven to make pudding for Sunday dinner. But neither held, nor hold, my imagination in quite the same way. I loved tearing opening the boxes and gathering up all the little packets that fell out, noodles that went soft in water and noodles that curled, crisped and bubbled in the frying pan; a foil-lined packet that you emptied out into a little heap of lumpy, dried powder, but add water, simmer, stir and watch as it swells and turns into chow mein! And then there was the tiny little silver sachet of soy sauce to pour over as you ate. I remember the trifle sponges wrapped in plastic, the jelly crystals, the squishy pouch of sherry syrup, the pink, brown or yellow custard powder (strawberry, chocolate and regular) and the Dream Topping.

'Pre-prepared', 'convenience' foods often get a bad press, yet this has not always been so: 'Labour for hours making a strawberry shortcake and what do you have at the end? Dessert. But with Bisquick and frozen berries, it was a "dessert masterpiece", according to a 1954 advertisement.'[26] In the post-war years,

explains food historian Laura Shapiro, packaged and convenience foods were synonymous with style, the glamorous alternative to daily drudgery in the kitchen.
(Some would argue that they were merely sold as such – the food industry needed
a mass market for the processed food that had been developed in order to feed the
armed forces.[27]) My mother, though both amused and slightly bemused about it
now, can remember serving fish fingers to dinner guests. Processed foods were the
means for the time-pressured housewife to 'properly' care for her family whilst
offering sophisticated, foolproof results: 'processed food from scratch', as Erika
Endrijonas has neatly labelled it.[28]

Today, the role of pre-prepared, convenience foods in the deskilling of home
cooking is usually taken as implicit. It is generally accepted that they require few
skills, other than that of assembly, to prepare. Yet I believe I acquired a whole range
of skills from my early experiences with Vesta and Bird's. I learned to stir and
whisk, simmer and fry, rid custard of lumps, add rice to 'stretch out' the chow mein
and judge when the jelly layer of the trifle was sufficiently set for it to be safe to
pour over the custard layer without the whole thing imploding. Those intriguing
and 'easy-to-use' little packets not only inspired me to cook, they encouraged my
mother to let me cook, reducing as they did some of the more tiresome aspects of
cooking, like the weighing out of ingredients and the washing-up.

Despite concern about the state of contemporary domestic cooking, there is
very little research about 'learning to cook' and the focus of the work there is, most
of which has taken the form of public health surveys, has generally been not on
how people learn to cook but on the sources from which they learn. Learning to
cook has generally been treated as a straightforward, purposive process. Surveys
ask questions such as 'when you first started learning to cook, which of any of
these did you learn from?' and 'who taught you to cook?' Sources for respondents
to select from including 'mother', 'father', 'grandmother', 'school cookery
lessons', 'booklets from food producers', 'television' and 'books and magazines'.[29] 'Few parents teach their kids to cook,' says food campaigner Prue Leith,
introducing one such survey, her choice of words providing an image of cookery
lessons in the kitchen rather like a dance class in the school gym or a music lesson
at the piano.[30]

The cooks I studied, however, spoke of a far more informal process. On the
whole – things tend to be a little different on important cooking occasions – experiencing new foods, techniques and combinations of ingredients, whether via
friends, the television or the written media, and putting new abilities and ideas into
practice are an unpredictable process. Claire, for example, described how she had
recently picked up a leaflet in the supermarket but that it was still 'in a drawer at
home'. It 'looked really nice', she told me, though she couldn't remember if it was
a starter, a main course or a pudding. Martin talks enthusiastically of a recipe for
a 'fantastic' red cabbage stew made with 'loads of cheese and butter beans and

stuff' that he has made ten or fifteen times. He had seen it on the back of a *Hello* magazine that he had flicked through at his sister's house one afternoon.

It's not only that the use of sources of instruction is haphazard but that the application of any information or instruction gleaned is equally so. 'Things I make are sometimes inspired by seeing something on telly,' said Mick. 'But then it becomes a case of thinking maybe I could try that with that. I don't really do it, but I might throw together similar flavours.' Likewise, Corrine might see something she likes in a cookery book, but then think 'that would be better if I did that with it'. She can't help but add her own ideas, she explained. And, for Amrit, the process of learning to cook has been far from straightforward. He had made many 'mistakes' along the way:

> [I've learnt to cook] watching other people, from programmes on tv ... through trial and error. When I first started to cook, I would chop up all my vegetables, the onion and the garlic, chop it all up and put it into the pan. And then it would be 'that's cooked but that's not', 'the onion is raw but the garlic is burnt so there's got to be some sort of system here'. So I eventually learned to cook things in some sort of order, put different vegetables in at different times so it's not a case of 'the mushrooms are shrivelled to bits and the carrots are raw'. (Amrit)

Very few people appear to read specialist food magazines, television cookery programmes predominantly offer passive viewing and easy-going entertainment, and recipe leaflets thrown into shopping trolleys at the supermarket invariably end up in the bin. The acquiring of cooking abilities is an arbitrary process; people pick up cookery tips, ideas and inspiration 'by chance' as they go about their daily food and cooking business. Although they may seek out and/or use a recipe or advice on an important cooking occasion, they do not purposefully set out to learn to cook or become 'a cook'.

Supporting other research that shows the importance of interpersonal learning, my study found that people spoke most favourably of tips, ideas and instruction gained 'one-to-one'.[31] Mick, for example, has regularly made couscous and roast vegetables since he tasted some that a colleague brought into work and explained how it had been made, and Debora is often inspired by the food she eats at a particular friend's house:

> My friend made a gorgeous spicy pasta thing that she just literally made off the top of her head. That was beautiful and I asked her for the recipe. I've tried it myself ... but with a bit of fish and things. I often do that now. She does a lot of Chinese cooking and things and she just tells me the different spices and what to put in. (Debora)

Advice and information from friends and family provide confidence and trust via direct and 'real' experiences of cooking, tasting, eating and advice giving, I found:

which is a shame, because, as the next section will explain, today's home cooks appear to prefer to cook alone.

Cooks Want to Cook Alone

The cooks I spoke to don't really want help with the cooking. Well, they do, but they would prefer someone to take over the cooking of certain meals rather than helping them out with the tasks of a particular cooking occasion. 'We have arguments about how to make a sauce,' said one; 'He doesn't like to cook with anyone else around,' complained someone else; whilst a third confessed, 'I'm a bit difficult to share a kitchen with.' Elspeth and Martin often share the cooking of an evening meal, one taking over from the other as they bath the children and put them to bed. Romantic cooking 'à deux', however, didn't on the whole go down that well. Cooking with someone else is likely to be a recipe for upset, irritation and disagreement, I was told: 'He's always looking over my shoulder and saying "but what about this?" or "can't you cut them a bit smaller?"' explained Claire. 'In the end I usually just think "well, you can do it yourself then".' Eamon dislikes, he said, having to help out those who have come into the kitchen to 'give him a hand': 'If I think I know what I'm doing then I'm much happier doing it myself. If I think the person who I am with doesn't know what they're doing then I find that quite frustrating because its actually quicker to do it yourself in that sort of situation.' When people cook, they prefer to be left on their own in the kitchen. 'There are just times when you want to say "this is my meal",' said Mick, '"I, personally, have gone to this much effort for you".' Kate prefers to 'prepare things in "my way"', especially when her family, particularly her in-laws, are around. This desire or preference to cook alone is particularly true on those occasions when the cook wants or feels obliged to make an effort, get a lot done or relax and enjoy cooking. It also appears to be an especially prevalent approach amongst those who see cooking primarily as a hobby or interest and mothers who find it less stressful and productive to cook when their children are out or have gone to bed. 'If they go to sleep I can get in the kitchen and do things ... if not I get up very early,' said Kirsty.

In current food debates, individualization is a motif more usually connected with eating and consumption than with cooking.[32] Pre-prepared foods, microwaves and takeaways are seen as encouraging family members to graze and snack separately throughout the day, governed only by their own schedules. The individualized nature of home cooking remains largely ignored. Cooking alone, of course, means not only dismissing your partner or in-laws from the kitchen but also your children, the impact of which may be of great significance and consequence when considered in the light of findings that show the increasing leisure focus of home cooking.[33] For it is on occasions when the cook likes to be left alone, whether because the occasion is an important one or because he or she is a keen and interested cook, that fresh, raw foods are most likely to be used. Conversely, when a cook is cooking for a less important occasion or is a cook who views cooking more 'as a job to be done' than a form of recreation, 'pre-prepared' foods are used in greater quantity and other people are more likely to be included in the process:

> Keeley, who's one, often sits on the work surface whilst I cook and she helps me. She's always really interested in how things are cooking. If they're in the microwave she wants to watch it till it pings and she wants to watch things under the grill. I think they're both a bit young to really learn to cook but if you ask them to go and 'find the pasta' or 'find some eggs' or 'find some crisps' they would both know where they were stored and what you did with them. They're both quite well aware of what food you need to cook and what food you don't need to cook or what I keep in the freezer and why things need to be in the fridge. (Liz)

> She's made little fairy cakes and things. Occasionally I'll try and get her involved if she's keen to help. I mean she can do things like open a tin or I'll let her stir the beans or something but nothing more adventurous than that. (Elspeth)

The accounts of the people I spoke with certainly suggested that any debate about the transference of cooking skills from one generation to another should consider the effects of solitary, recreational cookery with at least as much emphasis as those of the use of pre-prepared and ready-made foods.

The Ubiquitous and Autonomous Recipe

In *The Domestication of the Savage Mind*, a study of oral and written cultures, Jack Goody describes how the recipe 'reigns supreme' in contemporary Western food culture. He points out how a cookery book is almost always a collection of recipes, how a food column in a magazine or journal will invariably include at least one and how recipes are generally regarded as 'the right and proper thing to do'.[34] Similarly, Dena Attar found in a study of school home economics classes that teachers assumed the recipe to be the starting point for the cookery process.[35]

The approach of the home cooks I spoke with does little to belie the observations of Goody and Attar. Individuals varied, a point I'll explore in Chapter 5, but even if they never used recipes their response to my mentioning them was that they are a simple fact of cooking. Many, for example, interchanged between using the terms 'cookery book' and 'recipe book'. Amrit describes 'cooking' as 'dabbling and trying and following recipes' whereas for Tayla 'learning to cook' is synonymous with 'learning her [mother's] recipes'. A mother with two small children says she will think about 'teaching them to cook when they are old enough to read a recipe'. David, on the other hand, refers to the creative abilities he used to make pasta shells, tapenade and 'some sort of garlic sauce I poured over peppers and covered in Parmesan' in terms of 'not following a recipe': 'I didn't actually follow a recipe. Well, it was a vague recipe that I sort of remembered from somewhere. I just sort of did it.'

Goody points out that for thousands of years cooking and cooks have managed without formal, written recipes, as they still do in many societies and cultures around the world. Yet despite the fact that they are a 'cultural construct' the implicit legitimacy of the recipe in contemporary food culture can be found, not just in the words and approaches of people who cook, but also in those of many academics, researchers and writers. It can be seen in *Consuming Passions. Food in the Age of Anxiety*, an academic book that explores food choice and practices at the end of the twentieth century and which deconstructs the family meal, analyses the rise of eating disorders and constructs moral frameworks for ethical eating. Most of the chapters in this book are prefaced or concluded with a recipe.[36] In another example, Antonia Demas, reporting on her study of food and cookery lessons in an elementary school, advocates the use of experiential cookery: the learning of cooking skills through experience, creativity and design rather than through rules and precise instruction. But, in spite of this thoughtful, analytical approach, she goes on to describe how the study inspired the children who took part to 'create recipes', how it gave them sufficient confidence to allow them to 'develop their own recipes'.[37] With so few words to describe a 'combination of foods for eating', it seems the term recipe slips easily into speech.

David Sutton talks of how on the island of Kalymnos in Greece people deny that they ever use recipes. They hold measurement and precision in disdain and believe that, in terms of learning to cook, recipes and written instruction can do no more than provide a memory jog for existing know-how.[38] The people who cook who took part in my research had some very different approaches to using recipes. Elspeth described herself as being 'completely obsessive about following recipes'. 'I get a real sense of satisfaction following them to the letter to see how well it turns out.' Her husband, however, she explained, is 'much more inventive, much more likely to just throw things together'. 'I'll just substitute things and chuck something in if I think it'll work,' he said, 'I'm very liberal with recipes because I'm lazy. She takes absolutely no artistic licence whatsoever,' he went on to explain, 'she'll be looking at a recipe with me and I'll say "we could try that" and she goes "no we can't because that says double cream and we've only got single cream".' Ash often experiences something similar: 'I always believe in doing what the recipe says [the first time you use a recipe] and I get criticized for that. My family makes fun of me. I say "no no … it says cayenne pepper" and my wife says "well we've got something similar" and I say "let's do it the way it says and then if you don't like it, change it after".' In contrast, Liz feels very strongly that she is too impatient to follow recipes. If she did use one, she said, she 'would probably think "oh no I don't have to do it that way I can do it this way" or " no, I don't actually have to have a red pepper it can be a green pepper'". Kirsty's position on using recipes, on the other hand, depends on what kind of food she's making. If she is baking, then, like Ash and Elspeth, she will follow the recipe 'religiously'. If she isn't baking, then her stance on using recipes is more reminiscent of Liz's:

> When I'm baking, yes, I tend to follow them word for word. That's because – and it probably comes from school – I remember someone saying 'you can't mess around with baking'. 'There has to be two eggs and there has to be this amount of sugar and there has to be this amount of butter and that's it … there's no better way of doing it.' And that's been drilled into me somewhere along the line. So with baking I tend to take my baking book into the kitchen and read it as I go along. Anything else I tend to look at the recipes and read them through and go 'da da da … yep, no problem … I can do that' and shut the book and go and do it. But that's just my arrogance probably. (Kirsty)

Whatever their approach, most of the people I spoke with, even if they didn't exactly defer to recipes (as some did), held them in a certain kind of respect. Liz said that if she was to follow a recipe she 'would have the confidence to mess around with it'. And Mary meanwhile, a cook quite happy to add extra flavouring, different spices or substitute certain ingredients, told me, 'I wouldn't fiddle around with basic quantities,' whereas Elspeth explained, 'I'll go to recipes because then if it goes wrong I can say, "well, it's the recipe. I followed the recipe".'

Getting it Right, Getting it Wrong

Success and failure are concepts never far from a discussion of home cooking. 'It didn't work', 'it came out right', 'sometimes it works' and 'it just didn't look right' were typical of expressions scattered through the food talk of the cooks who took part in my study. Of course, sometimes they are not much more than a turn of phrase – as in 'you can't go wrong if you've got enough garlic in it' – but not always. Frequently, food, the product of cooking, is classified as being right or wrong, a success or a failure. Jean, for example, a part-time school 'dinner lady' in her fifties, who has cooked for her family for more than thirty years, said that she'd really like 'to learn to do different dishes, like chicken things and that'. 'I can do them,' she added, 'but they don't look right, they don't come out like other people do them.'

It is on an important cooking occasion that 'you are more worried that it might go wrong', more concerned that 'you've cooked it right'. And it is cooks who are interested in cooking, it seems, those who see it as a specific hobby perhaps, who are more likely to aim to cook successfully. For some people who cook, 'getting it right' is part of the enjoyment of cooking. Texture, taste, appearance and aroma can all be right or wrong, correct or incorrect. Dishes, foods seen as being of a specific cuisine and titled recipes are far more closely associated with this belief than combinations of foods without titles and more tenuously linked with any particular cuisine. Grilled cheese, steak and chips, the barbecue for a great-aunt's birthday party and the cheesy bake thing made from Tuesday's leftover risotto are less likely to be seen as being either a success or a failure than Aubergine Parmigiana, Lamb Pasanda,[39] Jamie Oliver's Baked Beetroot with Balsamic Vinegar, Marjoram and Garlic (note the capitalized title)[40] or, from a River Café cookbook, Bruschetta with mashed broad beans or *Bruschetta con fave crude* (no capitals here, but notice the two titles and the italics).[41]

Using pre-prepared foods can mean less concern for the cook about 'getting it right'. They care less about whether the Scooby Doo cupcakes made from a packet mix have risen perfectly than they do about those made 'from scratch'. They're not bothered about the technical standard achieved when they're preparing beans on toast or making a casserole from a couple of frozen chicken breasts and jar of mushroom pasta sauce. This kind of cooking is in many ways a less emotional experience than cooking 'from scratch' because the result is far less a reflection of ability, expertise or the effort taken. (There is also, of course, less potential for the enjoyment and satisfaction that comes from displaying skills, achieving 'success' or 'making an effort'.) Cooking with fresh, raw ingredients that can also be bought prepared is also problematic as 'standards for home cooking are increasingly being influenced by convenience foods', as the authors of a recent study on the development of a community food skills initiative conclude, their informants stressing that 'sauces should be like the ones that come from the packet' and that 'fish should resemble that from the take-away or the supermarket freezer'.[42] Of those who took part in my study, Ash described how he once tried to make scones but, when he compared the finished result with the ones he can buy in the supermarket, he concluded that he 'got it wrong': 'Making scones would be difficult because you are working with flour and getting the texture and consistency right and because you are going to say "does it look like ...?" something you have eaten before or you've bought somewhere. If it doesn't then you didn't get it right.' Elspeth would rather buy a pizza than make one herself because they 'just don't measure up'. Tayla, a nanny, finds only disappointment and lack of success in the lemon meringue pie that is not brilliantly yellow like the ones 'in the picture' and the irregular, slightly swollen and misshapen gingerbread men she bakes for her charges that look nothing like the ones she buys:

> Things look so lovely in a nice book and everything. And then you do it and you look at it and think 'oh God'. And you try and make it look better but it never looks the same as it does in the book ... Lemon meringue pie [didn't turn out the way I expected]. The lemon underneath the meringue wasn't yellow at all, it was a sort of browny, beigey colour ... and the meringue just shot over the sides. It was awful. And it tasted awful. I don't know how I managed to go wrong with the meringue but I mean it just spilled

over the sides. There are just loads of things that I've done from recipes which are so … well. Like gingerbread men. They're just the classic. I mean they never look the same when you get them out the oven. You cut them out all nicely and they look right before you put them in the oven. But then they look just like Mr Blobbies when you take them out. … We buy Sara Lee [lemon meringue pies] now. I may try it again with one of the mixes because all you have to do is make the pastry and then you just mix the rest of it. I'll probably try that but I wouldn't start it from scratch again. (Tayla)

Proponents of 'experimental cookery' teaching methods[43] make the point that, if twenty people follow the same recipe for a sponge cake, the huge number of variables – variations in ingredients, equipment, individual technique and oven temperature (who has ever had their oven serviced or the temperature gauge calibrated?) – would make it surprising if any two cakes are the same. Which of the cakes is correct? Of the twenty cooks, who has been the most successful? Recipes and the illustrations and photos that often accompany them, say Linda McKie and Roy Wood, then compound this issue of 'successful' cookery by presenting a prescriptive and idealized 'standard' to be met. 'The recipes and illustration say "your dish should look like this",' they explain, and 'a failure to produce a copy of the original – however approximate – is a matter for regret, perhaps even shame'[44] – the result being, of course, a disappointed and deflated cook, their confidence knocked. As cookery writer Nigella Lawson says: 'Believing that there is always some higher authority telling you what is right and what is wrong is not going to help you.'[45]

Yet the people who spoke with me about cooking also talked of how using a recipe can also lessen the need to be successful. That same voice, that higher authority which says how something 'should be' is also the one that can make the cook confident, that can take responsibility for the result away from the cook. One woman I interviewed, calling herself 'Mrs Recipe', says that for fear of failure and disappointment she always uses a recipe when trying something new because then she has 'something to blame if it all goes wrong'. Ash, too, uses them when he cooks, not only because they increase his confidence and 'success rate' but also because they help him understand any reasons for failure: '[I will follow a recipe] exactly as it is. The first time I would always do so because it makes me feel confident. You had the recipe, you used it and you followed the instruction, right? So if you get the consistency wrong, for example, then you can say "why did it go wrong?"'

Contemporary food culture is one in which cooking follows 'manifold fashions', new varieties of pre-prepared convenience foods are 'constantly made available'[46] and the recipe, as was remarked on earlier, 'reigns supreme'.[47] It is also one in which food campaigners inform cooks that 'there is often a prescribed method of cooking many favourite dishes but it is also possible to add a little something of your own',[48] the Chambers definition of a cookery book is a 'book of recipes for cooking dishes'[49] and schoolteachers have been found to present the recipe to children as 'normal and necessary'.[50] Later, I shall examine how this prescriptive conceptualization, coupled with a plethora of advice and information about cooking, negatively affects people's food practices, the frequency and regularity with which they cook and their use of fresh, raw and pre-prepared foods. After all, the now much maligned 'cooked dinner' or 'meat and two veg' found by Anne Murcott to characterize home cooking in the 1980s[51] has no real title, is rarely if ever the subject of a written recipe, illustration or photograph and is not readily available pre-prepared. Out of favour it may be, and unlikely to provide as much of a cooking challenge or sense of achievement as a dish or recipe with its recorded, fixed identity[52] and glossy, glamorous photo, but it is a meal or style of cooking less likely to be judged as being right or wrong, less likely to flatten a cook's confidence. And more practically, as Jack Goody has pointed out, a cook can use up what is available or substitute foods for others more easily 'if one does not think one is preparing Tripe a la mode de Caen, but simply cooking a dish of tripe for supper'.[53]

The Creative Cooking Ideal

A good cook can prepare 'interesting food' and 'original food' and makes 'food that looks good'. As Jaclyn says, 'I suppose [a good cook can make] a variety of food with novel ideas and nice presentation, looking completely stress free as they were doing it. Someone who can make different types of food that I wouldn't try usually.' People who cook view the abilities of those who they feel don't need to follow recipes, the skills of those who can cook 'professionally' and make food like 'everyone on the telly', as the most desirable. Rarely is feeding a family on a budget, cooking healthy food, self-provisioning or being time-efficient mentioned in association with good cooks or good cooking. Even the ability to 'just make something from nothing' is connected with being stylishly creative rather than economical. The values of contemporary cooking lie firmly, it seems, in the field of what Anne Oakley has called the 'creative cookery ideal'.[54] The cook who describes how he 'browns the meat off' when making a casserole and how he 'adds a bouquet garni before he lets it all cook through' was seen by the people I studied as being interested in cooking and as a good cook. He was regarded as having and using greater skills than the cook who 'slings a tray of diced lamb from the supermarket into a casserole dish' and quickly adds some chopped vegetables, dried herbs and the dregs of a bottle of wine. For the people who cook who took part in my study, it is professionalism, knowledge of cuisine and culinary terms, the aesthetic and the pleasing rather than resourcefulness, organization, know-how and self-sufficiency that is of 'cooking value'.

Oakley suggests that a value system, a 'creative cookery ideal' such as this increases the burden of housework and results in dissatisfaction in 'the job done'.

'Standards of achievement exist of which the housewife is permanently aware, but which she cannot often hope to reach due to the other demands on her time.' For 'husbands demand meals at specific times, small children cry when their stomachs are empty, the hour that might be for cooking competes with the hour that ought to be spent washing the floor or changing the beds'.[55] More recently, however, Phil Lyon and his colleagues, in an article that looks at the deskilling of contemporary domestic cooking, have argued that cooking provides a useful and accessible opportunity to demonstrate creativity. For them it is the creative dimension of home cooking, coupled with the declining everyday drudgery of preparing and providing food (brought about by the often unacknowledged benefits of developments in kitchen technologies, they say), that will 'hold future practitioners to the craft'.[56]

Yet the impact of the creative cooking ideal on home cooking might not be as direct or unequivocal (whether negatively or positively) as either Oakley or Lyon et al. suggest. For the findings of my study revealed that home cooks are both burdened and inspired by creativity. On special occasions – for weekend dinners without the children, perhaps, or when entertaining guests – cooks sometimes like to rise to a challenge, to be daringly creative and to enjoy the esteem in which they are held for being so. On occasions that offer less reward – evening meals squeezed between work and social commitments, breakfasts, snacks, packed lunches and family meals with demanding relatives – they often wish to just get on with the job and to be free of the pressure to produce varied and interesting food.

Chefs and Cooks

Some nights I'd like to be able to cook like the people at Ma Cuisine, some nights like Rick Stein. I wish I could do all that. I've never eaten at the Roux brothers' ... but that's the sort of thing.

(Patrick)

Domestic cooks rarely distinguish it seems, between what they do cooking-wise and what the professional cook, cooking for a wage in a place of employment, does. Generally, chefs and cooks are not seen as having different tasks, aims or sets of skills and knowledge. John calls his wife a 'good chef' whilst Aidan says, without a hint of irony, that he never took home economics classes at school because he didn't want to become a chef when he left. Professional cooks are viewed comparatively by home cooks. They're seen as 'being more successful' and as making 'fewer mistakes'. They are 'more artistic' and able to 'produce nicer things'. A trained and professional cook, one of my informants suggested, would be 'ideal for a dinner party'.

The valued qualities of the chef don't appear to be that far removed from the qualities associated with the creative cooking ideal. And just as creative cooking is connected with special meals and guests rather than with efficiency, nutrition and the family, the professional chef is connected, not with those who cook in fast-food restaurants, supermarket coffee shops or the kitchens of hospitals and schools, but with 'five star' restaurants, celebrity chefs and television cooks who publish books. In the food talk of domestic cooks, I found that calling your wife or son-in-law a 'good chef' is unlikely to mean that you associate them with those who deep-fry chips and prepared, ready-seasoned chicken pieces in franchised TexMex restaurants, scooping ice cream from a tub whilst defrosting a slice of pre-portioned chocolate chip cheesecake – or with those who manage to produce two thousand meals for forty pence a head in a university canteen.

The significance of this lack of differentiation between domestic cooks preparing and providing food on a daily basis and professional chefs cooking at the prestigious end of the catering spectrum probably lies less in its existence than in the influence it has on domestic cooking practices and food choices. The lack of a clear acknowledgement of the differing set of abilities and knowledge, different contexts, environments and goals, and hugely varying levels of practical experience may well be of critical importance for the home cook's cooking confidence and/or their desire to 'make an effort'. After all, it is highly likely that a television chef has worked at his or her trade for fifteen years or more and may have cooked for ten hours a day or so throughout those years. Yet home cooks are given the impression in food articles and on television cookery programmes that they can easily prepare in their own kitchens the haute cuisine practised in resource- and equipment-laden professional kitchens by highly trained and experienced professional cooks.[57] They try the complex, complicated recipes of professional chefs and, finding them difficult to follow and the results disappointing, feel they lack skills and any aptitude for cooking. 'The rise of the chef book', Nigella Lawson has commented, results in a situation where people who can cook feel that they can't.[58]

Writers of professional cookery books make the point that the approach taken by the professional cook and the domestic cook towards using recipes and applying and acquiring cooking skills is very different. The professional cook, they argue, works within a craft or cuisine that has established methods, techniques and standards. The recipe is a guide, particularly for those learning their trade. Using a recipe provides experience and understanding of those different craft techniques and methods and of how they combine with different foods. The domestic cook, they go on to say, perceives cooking as a series of discrete and largely unconnected food experiences. Home cooks are very unlikely to learn a formalized craft or cuisine in its entirety, gaining experience of one set of interrelated methods and techniques before moving on to another. Using a recipe is, more often than not, simply a means to an end.[59]

In Chapter 7, I shall argue that a mystique or myth surrounds home cooking, that the high ideals of creativity, glossiness, professionalism and cooking success impose themselves on everyday domestic cooking and feeding, propelling the state of 'being able to cook' (never mind being a 'good cook') way beyond what perhaps it might be. There is, however, a further myth-making ideal to beset the home cook, and that is the endless pursuit of the interesting and the different.

The Quest for 'Different and Interesting' Food

The cooks in my study, I found, enjoy cooking most when they are free to experiment, when they can 'try different things' and 'not just run-of-the-mill stuff':

> I started to experiment with things and use people as guinea pigs. I'd invite somebody round to dinner and cook something unusual rather than something I would cook just for us. (Aidan)

> Soups ... I tend to experiment with them. I don't know why soups particularly. And desserts. I never really experiment with main meals. (Claire)

Domestic cooks like 'interesting recipes', 'recipes that are a bit different'; they like pre-prepared foods because 'you can make something interesting in less than twenty minutes'. Their enjoyment of cooking is greatest when they are 'free to experiment':

> Sometimes I will go out and buy specifically interesting things because I enjoy preparing and cooking interesting dishes. (Amrit)

> A friend did a chicken and pine nuts sort of salad. It was very nice, something different. (Jaclyn)

They can't really explain what they mean by different or interesting food and cooking; however, it's just 'more than the usual peeling carrots and cooking pasta'. Maybe, said Ash, 'it's something which the family hasn't eaten for a while' or something you might get in a restaurant. There is no doubt, however, that this kind of cooking is highly valued. Difference, novelty, variety and interest are concepts intrinsically linked in the minds of home cooks with 'real cooking', professional cooking, creative cookery, good cooks and cooking for special and important occasions.

That the desirability of variety in food choice is an overriding ideological precept in contemporary Western society is widely accepted by academics and scholars. The relentless search for new taste sensations and eating experiences is seen by sociologist Deborah Lupton, for example, as adding both value and a sense of excitement to life.[60] The quest for variety and difference is, argues Stephen

Mennell, the most striking feature of food and cookery writing in women's magazines in recent decades,[61] an argument that is borne out by findings from Alan Warde's study of food columns in women's weeklies from the 1960s and the 1990s. The magazines of the 1990s, Warde explains, 'make a point of emphasising variety as a fundamental virtue of consumer culture'. They feature wildly diverse ingredients and foods from all over the world. A single issue of *Prima*, for example, contains thirty-nine recipes and 176 different ingredients, including garam masala, Chinese five-spice powder, chilli powder and cayenne pepper, hoysin sauce, Worcestershire sauce and soy sauce, almonds in five different states, three types of margarine and seven types of sugar.[62] The observation of the young people who took part in research for *Health Which?* that more hands-on experience of 'a wider range of more experimental and exciting foods' may make cooking in schools more relevant to adult life suggests that this need for variety and difference is culturally deeply ingrained.[63]

That the ever continuing search for new and different foods is not only a manifestation of a food system characterized by anxiety over food choice but also an agent of it is a frequent and popular subject of academic debate.[64] Yet there may be more practical implications. The constant 'trying out' of new recipes and experimentation with techniques, foods and styles of cooking may mean that contemporary cooks fail to acquire those skills of judgement, understanding and timing that come through experience and the repetition of tasks.[65] Grandmother, on the other hand, could effortlessly cook her recipe for apple pie or chicken dumplings whilst surrounded by all her arguing, rowdy offspring and grandchildren because she had done so many times before:

> Grandma would invite the three of us over, pull out the pie tins (which were probably older that our parents), the rolling pin and the five ingredients that had made her apple pie famous all over town. As we combined the three ingredients that made up the crust (one pound of lard – Grandma preferred Crisco – six cups of flour and just enough water to make the whole thing stick together), she would tell us stories of when she was young.[66]

Today's cooks may never expect or be expected to cook the same apple pie every Sunday. Good cooks should try out different recipes – the 'trying out' of new recipes, foods and combinations of ingredients and methods being accepted as a distinct 'part of cooking' by the informants in my study:

> They [good cooks] would ring each other up I presume and exchange cookbooks and try out the recipes and so forth and throw lots and lots of dinner parties. (Dean)

> Just for two people it [cooking] gets a bit 'oh, I can't be bothered' to try out a new recipe or something you haven't done before. (Seth)

After all, with only a very quick Internet search cooks may find recipes for Dutch, American, French, Tuscan and English apple pie, lattice apple tart, apple strudel, brown sugar apple pie, caramel apple flan and sourcream apple pie. They can just as easily find advice on how to make a filo, rough puff, streusal, shortcrust or flaky pastry case – if they don't decide to make it with a cream cheese dough or biscuit crust, that is.

The Natural Cook

TV chef Nick Nairn is presented with a bag containing rabbit, haggis, frozen peas, onion, tomatoes and parsnips. In just a couple of minutes he has come up with a selection of different dishes (albeit with a few additional ingredients) – rabbit casserole, char-grilled rabbit salad, pan-fried haggis with a pea puré and curried tomato soup – which in not many minutes more he has finished, ready for tasting.[67] How does he do it?

'Natural ability,' joked Amrit, 'well, you'd have to completely isolate someone from any cooking environment and then present them with a dish and say "what does that need?" And I doubt very much whether anyone would go "I've never tried this before and I've never heard about it but if you put a bit of basil in there …".' In the prevailing belief system of the cooks who informed the study, Amrit's rational, though slightly ironic, approach is unusual. Home cooks do believe that, yes, cooking skills are acquired by practice and experience, but there is an underlying suspicion, a little nagging doubt, that to be a good cook an element of natural ability is required:

> I used to think that there was a plot out there because everybody knew better than me. But I've learnt over the years that its not so, that in fact a lot of people are trying out as they're going along and they find out as they experiment. Although people do seem to have this natural ability, don't they? (Corrine)

> Why is it that you try to do the same dish and somebody is always good at it and you're not? Because they have a gut feeling of how its going to come out? Cooking is all about having the ingredients in front of you and what comes out at the end. You just don't know until you've done it. So how can somebody consistently get it right and some people can't? I mean they must have some natural flair for it, something innate that comes from within them. (Ash)

Alongside, perhaps contributing to, this belief that good cooking and good cooks (or perhaps just 'able cooks') require a little additional natural talent, domestic cooks find it difficult to describe or explain what cooking skills are or what constitutes cooking ability. 'Oh, I don't know', 'perhaps being a bit more bothered?', 'I'm not sure' and 'using conventional practices?' are typical of their somewhat quizzical responses to the questions I asked about doing so. For some, the term cooking skill means techniques like chopping, mixing, stirring and so on. Geraldine sees the skills of making a strawberry tart as rolling out pastry, slicing strawberries neatly, preparing some sort of cream and glazing. To make scones, however, 'you just mix up the ingredients, dollop it on the foil and cook it'. For others, cooking skill is a more vague concept, something to do with timing and determining whether something is cooked or not. 'There's always something hanging in the balance' when you make bread, says Corrine, because 'the oven and things can affect how they come out'.

Nick Nairn is presented as a natural who with his special talent can magically create a selection of delicious and highly presentable dishes from a collection of 'mismatched' ingredients.[68] Yet he probably has many years of experience. Rather than a natural, he is more probably an experienced, expert practitioner of his craft. The char-grilled rabbit salad and curried tomato soup are probably not dishes or combinations of ingredients that he has made before, plucked from a vast memory of disparate and unconnected recipes. Nor are they a lightning strike of creativity and inspiration. What Nairn does is search through his knowledge of culinary techniques and methods, the skills he has amassed from hours and hours of experience, and apply them to the foods the contestant has supplied. It is his 'repertories of memories and imaginations', as Nathan Schlanger phrases it, which enable him to design and create in this way. He picks out the most appealing, the most likely to please the eye as well as the taste buds, something that will cook on the hob, something for the oven, something else that the contestant can help with without getting in the way.[69] He knows how to make soup and how to curry it, he knows how to make a vegetable puré, how to char-grill and he probably knows numerous ways of making a casserole. It is the timing, judgement and organizational skills he has acquired through the years of practice that make him so astoundingly quick, so competent at juggling five or six pans, so able to finish 'on the bell'. These are the hidden, perceptual and conceptual abilities that, skills experts say, when unrecognized and unappreciated give rise to the belief that a task requires a certain aptitude, a special talent or knack.[70]

Cooking ability is the subject of the next chapter.

—4—

Who can Cook?

The Death Throes of Cooking

'There is a prevailing view that we are in the middle of some kind of food revolution,' says Matthew Fort in a newspaper series looking at contemporary food issues. But the deluge of cookbooks and television food and cookery programmes and the huge diversity of foods available in our supermarkets are, he declares, 'manifestations of the death throes' of domestic cooking rather than any kind of evidence of an uprising.[1] Equally dramatically, restaurateur and food campaigner Prue Leith predicts that, as 'most Mums and Dads cannot cook' and 'what cooking skills there are, are not getting passed down to their children', the twenty-first century will see the demise of home cooking.[2] Elsewhere, food writers bemoan their readers' lack of basic cooking skills, market researchers argue that an ever decreasing number of people have and use cooking skills and public health experts worry that having cooking skills is now thought of as old-fashioned.[3] From community websites and broadsheet journalism to consumer surveys and political and social think tanks[4] and in countries as widespread as Canada, Zimbabwe, Singapore, Turkey and France, home cooking skills are an issue of concern.[5]

Worries about a decline of cooking are not only far-reaching, they are also far from new. Back in 1882 food writer Baron von Rumohr wrote that 'not inheriting a "traditional" cookery based upon the sensible preparation of local products and so resorting to "soul destroying" books, the "respectable virtuous wife" no longer knows how to prepare meals'.[6] In 1932 a public health report in Scotland criticized the 'ignorance and laziness responsible for much bad cooking ... Too many housewives arm themselves with the frying pan, the teapot, and the tin opener,' it complained.[7] Today, convenience foods and new kitchen technologies continue to be blamed for the demise, the ready meal and the microwave being seen as particularly culpable. New methods of food storage and preparation are seen as having deskilled the buying, preparing, cooking and eating of food. If you cannot cook, you buy pre-prepared foods, if you use pre-prepared foods you do not acquire cooking skills. And so on.[8]

Yet, though many have made reference to the deskilling and decline of home cooking, few, as was noted in Chapter 1, add much substance to their claims.

Whilst we may assume, perhaps, that writers and commentators are not including themselves, they fail to tell us who it is that can't cook. Academics offer little detail about what cooking skills are being lost or the process by which they are disappearing.

What is a Cooking Skill?

The recipe given below for a popular dessert in the UK in the 1990s, Free-Form Apple Pie, looks at first glance relatively straightforward:

> Dust a rolling pin with flour and roll 340 g shortcrust pastry into a 35 to 40 cm circle. Don't worry if the edges are uneven. Fold the pastry in half and then half again, lift it onto a baking sheet and then unfold. Pile 6 finely sliced apples tossed with 80 g granulated sugar, 2 tbsp cornflour and 1 tsp ground cinnamon in the middle of the pastry circle leaving a 4–5 cm border all round. Next, fold the 'pastry border' over the apple slices. Brush whatever pastry is exposed with 1 tbsp milk and sprinkle over 1 tbsp granulated sugar. Bake at 190°C for 45 minutes or until the apples are fork-tender.

The first time I taught with this recipe at an evening cake- and bread-making class however, I missed something. Yes, I thought to describe how to roll pastry and how to fold it into quarters so as to be able to transfer it safely to a baking sheet. I remembered to explain why it's important to slice the applies thinly and evenly, and how to sprinkle the sugar 'chef-style' by using the underside of your fingers and throwing it lightly up in the air so that it disperses evenly over the pastry. But I neglected to mention to the class how important it is when you 'fold the pastry border over the apples slices' to cup the pastry in the palm of your hands, lifting and lowering it gently down. Don't pick it up with your fingertips and pull it straight over, I should have told them, or it will immediately and irreparably split in two, which is, of course, exactly what happened, leaving a class of disappointed cooks – a snippet of cooking knowledge the wiser maybe, but with a far from photo-perfect apple pie to take home.

Despite the fact that most of us are, at some level, quite aware that cooking involves a host of these nameless abilities, any amount of inadvertently gathered know-how, debate about the decline and deskilling of cooking more usually treats it as an uncomplicated and largely technical activity. Food preparation is generally regarded as 'a practical and not theoretical pastime, a manual not a mental activity'.[9] Understanding of the concept of cooking skill has tended to remain unsophisticated; in current debate cooking skills are generally interpreted as straightforward and as being self-explanatory. This can clearly be seen in public health and market research surveys, in which respondents are asked about their abilities to make jacket potatoes, for example, joint a chicken, prepare a salad or peel vegetables. They are questioned over whether they can bake, boil or microwave, make a chicken casserole or a Victoria sandwich, and about their confidence in cooking such foods as white fish, fresh green vegetables, pulses and rice.[10] Testament to the death of cooking has been seen in a lack of knowledge about how to cook cuts of meat such as brisket, fore rib, chump and loin. An ability or inability to boil an egg has on more than one occasion been regarded as providing useful evidence of the state of home cooking skills, an indicator of whether the public still know how to cook or not.[11] As the writers of 'Deskilling the domestic kitchen: national tragedy or the making of a modern myth?' point out, most published work on cooking usually 'evades definition entirely', there being an assumption, they suggest, that interpretation and understanding are neither ambiguous nor problematic[12] – an assumption that can be seen, perhaps, in Alan Warde and Kevin Hethrington's description of barbecuing as a 'simple' skill.[13] Practically, yes, barbecuing may involve little more than placing a piece of meat or fish, say, on a grill over hot coals. But anyone who has ever tried to barbecue a steak to meet a friend's request for 'medium rare' or cook fish so that it doesn't disintegrate and fall into the flames or has worried that chicken is sufficiently 'cooked through' to keep guests safe from food poisoning might not agree. Cooking in the open air with basic implements and over an unregulated heat can be anything but simple, especially when there are the exacting standards of a particular cuisine, guests or family to be met.

Making reference to similar techniques of chopping, boiling, frying and stirring, Margaret and Wayne, two people who cook and who took part in the study upon which this book is based, describe two very different cooking experiences. Margaret explains how she makes chicken Zorba by stuffing pitta breads with fried chicken strips marinated in freshly squeezed lime juice and mint picked from her garden; how she serves it with boiled new potatoes and a dressing of yogurt into which she has stirred some chopped tomatoes. Wayne, on the other hand, describes a dinner he recently made for himself from ingredients grabbed from the chilled cabinet of his local supermarket on the way home from work. He fried a few chopped mushrooms, stirred them into a reheated carton of Napolitana tomato sauce, which he then poured over boiled, 'freshly prepared' tagliatelle. Both used the same 'cooking skills' – boiling, chopping, stirring, frying and so on. Yet, whereas Margaret might be spoken of as cooking 'properly', Wayne is more likely to be seen as 'not really cooking', as merely assembling a selection of convenience foods. An approach to cooking skills that focuses on the technical aspects provides very little chance to gain any real insight into, say, the food choices made by Wayne and Margaret or their respective roles as home cooks.

Within the broader field of social science, particularly in the work of those who have studied food habits as a way of exploring social, family and gender relationships, a wider, more comprehensive approach to the concept of cooking ability can be found. It is an approach more in line with Anne Murcott's and Anne Oakley's understanding of cooking as a household task, like tidying up, shopping and washing, than with definitions of it as 'applying heat to food' or 'traditional skills of making meals from scratch'.[14] Luce Giard's eloquent description of French women cooks, for example, reflects the varied skills and seamless artistry she feels they bring to 'doing cooking' – a task, she says, that involves constant calculation of timings and budget and endless adjustment to the environment and ingredients, social demands and people's likes, dislikes and diets. Doing cooking involves 'knowing what to do when milk turns on the stove', 'making the stew go a little farther', 'remembering that Beatrice cannot stand chocolate cake' and 'bearing in mind that the local fishmonger will be closed all week'.[15] Likewise, the researchers who studied the food and cooking lives of people in the Nordic countries speak in their report of how making dinner 'may start in the morning, before leaving home … or with a glance in the refrigerator, the freezer or cupboard'. Making dinner involves any number of questions and considerations long before any actual food preparation begins, they point out; '"What do I have at home that needs to be eaten?" "What do I need to buy?" "What do the children like to have?"'.[16]

Home cooks, the findings from my study revealed, use many different skills and abilities as they go about their daily cooking lives. They are often skills that are difficult to define, owing little to the techniques listed in the surveys, studies and writing described previously. 'You don't stand and watch fish fingers cooking,' Liz was at pains to point out. 'You put them on and then go upstairs and get a load of washing, bring it down and put it in the washing machine, turn the fish fingers over and then take the clean washing upstairs.' John, meanwhile, creates what he calls 'hotchpotch meals' from leftovers in the fridge. He doesn't follow recipes or use precise quantities, he is keen to explain, he just gets an idea of what he wants to cook. And Kirsty, hurrying off to work, 'drives her husband daft': '"What do you want for your tea?", "I haven't finished my breakfast yet", "Yes, but I might have to get something out of the freezer and defrost it!", "Just cook me anything", "How do you want your anything, fried or boiled?"' She has to be an organized cook, she explained, because she has to do a lot in a very little time.

The Realm of Home Cooking Ability

Cooks use a range of techniques. The cooks I spoke with flip pancakes, slice mozzarella and bread, fry eggs and potato waffles, grate cheese, boil pasta and open cans, cartons and packets. They sometimes mix salad dressings and batter, grill fish, chicken nuggets and pork chops, pour milk and juice, roast chicken, ovenchips and pumpkin and reheat pizza, baked beans, coffee and ready meals. They use practical skills that have little to do with any specific techniques – the washing, squashing, scrubbing, trimming, rolling, tugging, tearing, folding, wiping and arranging described by Michael Symons in his history of cooks and cooking.[17] Yet, as they go about the daily business of making and providing food, they also use a range of skills and knowledge that are far less easy to define.

As can be seen in the following paragraphs, the realm and range of domestic cooking skills are vast. They can be practical and technical, but they can also be perceptual, conceptual, logistical and emotional.

Understanding and Judging

The Frenchwomen in Giard's study are able to identify the exact moment when custard begins to 'coat the back of a spoon' and should be taken off the stove to prevent it from separating.[18] And, just as on another occasion their sensory perception might intervene to let them know that the smell coming from the oven means the cooking is 'coming along', Gay knows that 'you've got to get the consistency just right for a scone to be nice and light'. She is using her perceptual abilities, abilities that can only be acquired from practice, from applying mechanical skills, from being aware of the feel and texture of the dough and relating that to the final product, the baked scone. It is skills like this that can perhaps best be acquired from making mistakes – from being able to compare the dryish, more solid scones made when you just knew you hadn't added quite enough milk and the mixture was too stiff but carried on regardless, with those that were light and moist and began with a softer, more pliable dough. Sometimes called tacit skills, because they are difficult to identify, these perceptual abilities concerned with the senses of sight, sound, smell, taste and touch are also called secondary skills, because they are gained via the application of manual or mechanical skills. Tacit, perceptual or secondary, their acquisition comes from experience of the understanding stages of a task, the moments when information is absorbed, processed and then used to inform the action that follows.[19] Perceptual cooking skills include understanding of the taste, colour and texture of foods and how they will react when combined or heated. 'Just by looking at this [recipe for watercress soup], you can see the ratio of how much butter to potatoes you want,' Amrit told me. 'You just need a wodge on your knife. You want the flour to just thicken the soup but not so much that it makes it stodgy and tasting of flour.' Any practitioner of a craft or activity will with regular experience begin to develop what James Scott, explaining the concept of 'practical knowledge', describes as a 'repertoire of moves, visual judgements, a sense of touch, a discriminating gestalt for assessing the work'.[20] Jules, for example, is fairly sure that she can usually pre-empt problems and adjust quantities when following recipes: 'I think I'd just improvise at this point. If I'd followed the recipe and if it just didn't feel right, the pastry is falling apart or the sauce is too stodgy …, then I would think "right, it needs more flour" and bung a bit more in even if it's not what the recipe said.

In his study of food and memory, David Sutton relates how Chinese recipes often call for the cook to add ingredients to the wok at the point when the oil is 'almost' smoking – 'A direction that assumes the cook has enough experience of failure to identify that turning point', a perceptual ability that relies on remembering what happened last time in the same or similar circumstances, with the same or similar ingredients.[21] It is prior experiences and memories of them that mean Claire, without weighing or measuring anything, can add milk and water to flour until she has a batter 'of the right consistency' for what she wants to make.

Timing, Planning and Organizing

In order to examine the cognitive demands of familiar practical activities, David de Leon studied ten people preparing a meal in their own kitchen.[22] He concluded that timing is a crucial aspect of cooking. Yet De Leon found that, even though his participants did generally consult timing equipment at the beginning of a cooking session and calculate an end time, and often glanced at a clock or their watch during its course, by the end its more formal, precise use had usually been abandoned. Rather than relying on precise structured times his participants checked in with their clocks, timers and watches as a way of taking stock and realigning themselves, of reflecting on what part of the activity had just been done and what would be best done next. It was one of a whole range of different strategies his participants used, he found, to manage and time food preparation. Belinda, for example, who made rice and a pork and sausage casserole, realized just after she had begun that most of the necessary preparation for the casserole could be done whilst the rice cooked, so she prepared and started to cook the rice first. Benny, who made a similar meal of chicken and rice, decided that as rice doesn't take long to cook, he would start with the chicken. Neither cook's approach, says de Leon, is simply concerned with making sure that everything is ready at the same time. Both are drawing up very loose, informal plans, organizing their work in a way that will make it less stressful by giving themselves enough time to deal with any difficulties or unforeseen circumstances that might arise: 'By identifying [the] more time-consuming processes of their activities, and engaging in these early on, Belinda and Benny increase the likelihood that improvisation will be a viable strategy.'[23]

Even though Aidan himself describes his skills simply as the ability to get all the different part of the meal ready to serve simultaneously, this same kind of strategy to 'stay in charge', to manage time, is clearly evident in his account of making Sunday dinner:

> Traditional Sunday roast with all the proper trimmings, like the roast potatoes, the gravy and all that, can be quite hectic. You have to be very organized to do it I think, otherwise you just end with everything being cooked at the wrong times. Having done

that several times you kind of get into a routine. I can almost wash up as I go some-times. 'Use this pan ... put some stuff here ... wash the pan' and by the time I've washed it, I can go back and do something else. (Aidan)

There is a further aspect to timing, says de Leon. Meeting the deadlines set up by external factors, such as friends arriving or a particular television show begin-ning, depends upon timing of a more formal kind. It requires planning and sched-uling. For Eamon, organization is always a feature of cooking but it takes subtly different forms, he says. 'There's cooking food right at the last moment, food that you can just plonk down and eat because there are only two of you.' There's also, he explains, 'the "we're going to sit down at eight o'clock and eat" cooking for guests'. Organizational cooking skills take many forms. Kirsty plans the evening meal first thing in the morning before she leaves for work. Many of us are most probably familiar with her experiences of having to remember on a Monday that on the way home from work you must buy bread and sandwich filling of some sort for Thursday and Friday's lunch boxes, because you will be busy on Tuesday and Wednesday. Organization like this is a logistical skill that involves conceptualizing the activities of the day ahead – work, childcare, household stuff, leisure and social commitments – and fitting food preparation and cooking around them (or for some, of course, fitting other activities around cooking). For Debora, the types of meals she makes depend on what else she has to do. A one-pot oven-cooked stew, for example, though cooked 'from scratch', is useful on a busy day because it requires little attention:

If I've got a lot to do then I might think 'right, I'll do a quick and easy meal tonight' so I can get on with everything else. Or I might just make a stew. You can literally throw it all in a dish, put it in the oven and leave it to get on. And then you do whatever you've got to do. (Debora)

To maximize the time she has with her family, Kate's organization starts with a list of all the meal occasions she has to provide for in the week ahead and moves to the supermarket, where she buy the prepared foods and ready meals she allo-cates to the different occasions. Jules and her partner prefer as far as possible to cook their weekday, evening meal with fresh, raw ingredients and to eat it with their two young daughters. As they work and both they and their children have busy social diaries, this gives rise to some sophisticated organizational skills being put into practice. For their evening meal they will often prepare food on one day that is suitable to be adapted with other ingredients (most probably picked up from local shops after collecting the girls from school) and served in a slightly different guise on the next. Though the food must be something that they are both able or wish to cook, Jules explained, it significantly lessens the amount of time they have to spend cooking and gives them more time with their children.

Creating and Designing

Creative ability comes in many forms. 'I may do a sandwich or something,' said Dean, 'I'll look at it and think "yeh, I'll put this in and bung some Hellmans [mayonnaise] on top".' Giard's French cooks can make the most of leftovers in such a way that their families and guests believe they are eating a completely new dish.[24] Likewise, coming home from work without a planned meal is never a problem for David because as he said, he can always 'make *something*':

> I would probably go for pasta. I would make a tomatoey based sauce and add whatever else I'd got to it. I don't tend to have much meat in but I've usually got cheese to shove on top. And I usually have vegetables of some kind. I either chop them up and make a salad or chop them up and make a sauce for pasta. (David)

Creativity and design skills involve conceptualizing or visualizing the intended or desired end product. They require an understanding of such things as the length or difficulty of a task or how to carry out a task with materials or ingredients that have not been used before.[25] Jules spoke of how she occasionally recreates ready meals she sees in supermarkets. 'I'll see what ingredients are in it and think "oh that's a good idea I would never put those things together".' Even though she has never used those particular foods in combination, she has the ability to conceptualize how the end result is reached and the perceptual and mechanical skills necessary to achieve that result.

However, creating food does not appear to always require a clear vision or idea of an intended outcome. Mick's description of making his evening meal from the contents of his food cupboards or from some fresh vegetables and a pre-prepared sauce is not dissimilar to David's. Yet Mick's more casual approach suggests that, unlike David, he doesn't always have a particularly fixed result in mind when he begins. There is an accidental element to the food he 'creates': 'Cooking for me is getting some vegetables and some sauce, some stir-in sauce or something, and doing it like that ... I would take the sauce and mix it with stuff that could cook quite quickly. Maybe I'll just get some Oxo cubes, some vegetables, some rice out. I just make it up as I go along.'

Knowing and Discerning

People who cook may know that a pizza with a mozzarella and tomato topping makes it a Margherita, that it is essential for health reasons to fast-boil red kidney beans and that the basil used in Thai cooking is different from that used in Italian cooking. Some may have knowledge of food hygiene, chemistry, nutrition and the history and geography of food, cooking and cuisine as well as of food fashions.

Different cooks know different things. Cooks in Colorado may know that, at the higher altitudes in which they live and cook, water and fat boil at lower temperatures and baking soda is more efficient. They may know to adjust cooking times for baking, deep-frying and boiling accordingly.[26] But it is doubtful whether many cooks in London, including those I spoke to, are aware of these differences.

This kind of knowledge is academic knowledge. It is knowledge about a task or activity that can be acquired without direct experience of it, that can be taught. It enhances understanding of a task, and in doing so can increase confidence in performing that task. The cook who opens the oven door and has to judge whether the cake is ready or not will probably be more confident about making their judgement if they know *how* a cake rises and cooks – what chemical reactions occur, what role the beaten egg whites, the yeast or the sour cream plays.[27] It is debatable, however, whether understanding of complementary tastes, flavours, textures and combinations of ingredients (or lack of knowledge in the case of Helen, who complained that she 'never knows what goes with what') qualifies as academic knowledge. If it is accepted that there are many foods that 'naturally go together' – thinking maybe of tomato and basil, couscous and chickpeas, roast beef and horseradish or lentils and coriander – then it can perhaps be seen as possible and credible to teach people about 'what goes with what'. Social scientists, however, are more likely to understand preferred flavour combinations, tastes and textures as being absorbed through social and cultural experience and connected with self-identity, lifestyle, status and so on. Why else would people come to acquire a taste for such 'bitter' and 'unpleasant' things as espresso coffee, whisky or gin and excruciatingly hot chilli sauces?[28]

Empathizing, Caring and Coping

Does the task of cooking begin with the opening of packets, the switching on and off of the oven or the writing of a shopping list? Or does cooking start when contemplating the family planner or leafing through a much-loved cookery book in search of inspiration? In their report on cooking and health in the UK, Tim Lang and his colleagues refer to both 'cooking skills' and 'general food skills'. For them, 'cooking skills' include grilling, microwaving, shallow frying and casseroling, activities that have something to do with the adding of energy or the direct preparation of food. 'General food skills' cover everything else.[29] Though slightly crude, perhaps, this is at least an attempt to get to grips with the definition and classification of cooking ability. Part of the difficulty in doing so lies, of course, in the ambiguity of the verb cook, a more expansive interpretation of which allows in turn for a broader understanding of cooking ability, knowledge and skill. Because Luce Giard in her study of women 'doing cooking' uses a wide interpretation of 'cooking' she is able to identify and refer to a whole range of different cooking abilities they use, including many of the kinds of tasks that Lang et al. call 'general food skills'. Similarly Marjore DeVault in looking at 'feeding work', providing food for the household or family, can equate cooking ability not only with those aspects that are practical and logistical, but also with those that are emotional.[30]

People who cook use many different and difficult-to-categorize mental abilities as they go about the business of preparing and providing food for themselves, their families, guests and friends. Compiling menus and organizing food for the week or days ahead may include knowledge of what ingredients are available (either in the shop, the fridge or the limits of the budget), what kinds of occasions will be taking place and others' taste preferences and dietary requirements.[31] Kate's 'logistical nightmare', as she called it, requires that when she does the weekly shop she take into account the largely separate mealtimes of each member of her family. She must remember their divergent tastes and needs, as well as those of the numerous friends and relations who frequently visit. Menu planning for Geraldine can even include consideration of the weather: 'the temperature is about ninety and you ask your husband what he would like and he says meat and potato pie', she laughed. Debora, meanwhile, always tries to take her friends' likes and dislikes into consideration when she cooks for them: 'Normally I do something like a roast dinner, a lasagne, a pasta dish or just something to that person's taste because some of my friends are vegetarians or whatever. I'd judge it on whoever was coming. I know what someone likes and what they may not like so I judge it on the person.'

Many cooks have to be able to prepare food to consistent standards because those for whom they cook prefer foods, tastes, textures and colours to be familiar and dependable. Grilled fish fingers should never be too black, chocolate cake must be chocolatey (but not too chocolatey), fat should be kept to a minimum and fish must never have bones or a head. Tomato lumps are cause for immediate rejection, though puréed tomato is fine. Carbohydrates and proteins should never be mixed on the same plate or in the same dish, and meat, well, it's just unacceptable – unless, of course, it's chicken and it's the weekend and there's nothing else.[32] Nor is it enough just to know and shop for food that satisfies others' preferences and/or requirements: the cook also has to be able to prepare that food to an accepted standard or style. Corrine worried that she resorts too frequently to using tinned and packet ready-made curry sauces. But her husband is 'so fussy', she said. 'If it's not exactly to the right temperature, well, you can imagine.'

For some the emotional work of cooking centres on the stress of dinner parties and cooking for friends. Keen to show she makes an effort, Jaclyn often finds that an experience she hopes will be enjoyable becomes frantic and stressful. 'The "the food isn't ready and your work mates are at the door scenario",' she calls it: 'Once when I was cooking for some people I was running really, really late and it was supposed to be a relaxed and recreational thing. It turned out to be quite a stressful event because things weren't ready and I knew they were going to be arriving soon.'

The emotional work of cooking for Kate comes to the fore when she prepares Sunday dinner for her husband's family (though she feels pretty much the same about cooking for her own). There can, she agrees with the old proverb, be too many cooks in the kitchen, only so many suggestions that a cook can take:

> I don't want ten million people flapping around me and increasingly as you get older and there are children the kitchen can become the hub of everybody's social activity and I very often feel 'get out of the kitchen … I can't concentrate … I need some quiet … If you want the meal burnt then all mill around me and if you don't then go into one of the other rooms and let me get on with it.' (Kate)

Coping with the emotional work of cooking requires skill. Some people, including Eamon, it seems, have the timing and planning skills that allow them to effortlessly prepare a dinner for guests without a drop of sweat breaking on their brow; skills that perhaps Jaclyn has not yet acquired. Kate, though she has difficulty coping with relatives, finds that with experience she has developed the skills that enable her to cook even if her young sons are in the kitchen with her. 'Kids', she said, 'are always trying to pull your legs when you're at the hot cooker. It's dangerous and you have to constantly move them away.' Yet she has learned to be aware, whilst chopping, stirring, frying, loading the dishwasher and answering the phone, of what they are doing and how close they are to the pan of boiling water on the stove or the sausages under the grill. She has learned, she explained, not only to give them tasks, but what tasks they can do safely and what sort of tasks will hold their attention.

Cooks' Skills and Cooking Skills

Cooking skills, then, can be seen as more than a set of manual and technique-based abilities, far more than just the discrete practical skills surrounding the physical preparation of, and application of heat to, food. Interpretation can be dependent on how cooking is defined and on whether the focus of definition is on the capabilities of the cook or the requirements of the cooking task.[33] A task-centred perspective might see making bread as requiring or utilizing a range of techniques, including mixing, kneading, rolling and shaping. A person-centred approach, on the other hand, would take into consideration the perceptual, conceptual, emotional and logistical cooking skills used or required by the cook and the circumstances or context in which making the bread took place. It could then be shown how there are different skills involved in, for example, making bread with the help of a recipe, making bread without a recipe but with constant interruption or making it in a professional kitchen with state-of-the-art equipment but pressured for time.

Understanding or defining cooking skills as a set of techniques is not wrong: it just cannot provide the same depth of insight into people's cooking practices, food choices and their beliefs about cooking that a more cook-centred, contextualized and detailed approach can. As skills experts say, there is no definitive or conclusive way of understanding or defining concepts such as skill, ability or knowledge. Different kinds of learning and research intentions require that different approaches be taken.[34] In professional cooking manuals, for example, the detail given as relevant to cooking methods and techniques can be extensive, the viewpoint and approach taken usually being very different to those of research and commentary referenced in this book. An article in a catering and hospitality journal, for example, uses 370 words to describe 'how to poach', a technique listed quite simply as a 'cooking skill' in recent surveys. For the trainee chef or catering student the skill of poaching involves knowing about complementary and appropriate garnishes and dressings for poached food, the usefulness of a 'resting period' and what foods are suitable for poaching. It entails being able to poach food to a correct or desired texture or consistency, to tell if the poached food is 'fork-tender', for example, and to make the remaining poaching liquid into a 'suitable' sauce.[35] Unlike for the home cook, perhaps, for the professional cook poaching is not a simple, 'stand-alone' skill but one linked to the numerous interconnecting methods, recipes and standards of a formalized craft. (That craft is for many catering colleges and cookery schools based on the French professional model. From the nineteenth century onwards a number of French chefs reorganized and rationalized professional and commercial kitchen practices into the 'parties system', a system usually credited solely to the most famous of them, Auguste Escoffier. An increasing desire for greater efficiency resulted in large kitchens being broken down into a number of sections. In each, a specialist and his assistants would deal with the particular, assigned tasks and dishes of that section. There could be up to ten or more sections, a kitchen with roast, vegetable, sauce, fish, larder and pastry sections being fairly typical, as is still the case today. Escoffier and other influential chefs of the time created new dishes but they also collated, adapted and classified existing hotel and restaurant favourites and regional recipes and cookery practices, arranging them into a whole and establishing, as they did, a formalized craft of cooking. Books such as *Le Répertoire de la cuisine*, which lists over six thousand techniques and dishes, catalogue the methods and terminology of the 'fonds de cuisine'.[36])

Another perspective on cooking skill can be seen in Gary Alan Fine's study of the culture of restaurant work, in which he describes the working practices, experiences and 'real lives' of kitchen workers, professional chefs and cooks. Though it is, at least in part, a study of their abilities, know-how and knowledge, Fine makes little mention of any of the kinds of cooking skills referred to previously in this chapter. The skills of working in a professional kitchen include, according to Fine, managing to cope with poor or broken equipment, the ordering and organizing of multiple tasks – 'it is almost as though the cooks are working on twenty assembly lines simultaneously' – and coping under intense pressure. They may include coordinating tasks with others as part of a team, 'toiling in an environment less pastoral than infernal' and, for those with supervisory responsibilities, orchestrating a team of cooks, waiters and porters. Fine also found that the required and displayed skills of the cook and the chef were very different. The understanding of those he studied is that a chef must have the skills to organize, manage and, if necessary or appropriate, be the creative force of the kitchen. The cook, on the other hand, is a line worker, a manual labourer, who must have the skills to cope with routine, work at great speed and take orders from superiors.[37]

The skills of the domestic cook and the professional or commercial cook can be seen as distinctly different. A professional cook and a domestic cook may both have and use the ability to prepare 'perfect' custard, debone a chicken, steam the rice to an agreed level of stickiness, make an apple tart or cut wafer-thin slices off a whole smoked ham. But an approach to skills that puts an emphasis on the context and the individual cook shows that they prepare food in different circumstances and with different resources and may have or use skills and knowledge that the other does not. A professional cook or chef may be more likely to have the skills necessary to prepare food to consistent standards day in and day out and to share tasks with others. A domestic cook may be more able to fit cooking around other tasks and activities, use up leftovers, improvise and prepare food to suit a range of tastes and dietary requirements.

To stand in a modern supermarket, look upon the rows and rows of ready-prepared foods – frozen mashed potato, chilled smoked salmon, stuffed ravioli, ready-basted, ready-to-roast chicken wings, pizza kits and ready-trimmed mangetouts – and judge contemporary cooking as being deskilled is understandable. Yet, if cooking skills are interpreted as contextual and as being related to the capabilities of the cook, then it is difficult to see 'cooking from scratch' and 'cooking with convenience foods' as requiring different kinds of skills. The deskilling theory becomes much more difficult to apply. For whether they are whipping up a favourite family recipe for chocolate brownies, mixing yesterday's leftovers into a can of soup with a spoonful of soy sauce and reheating it in the microwave, meticulously recreating a famous chef's signature dish for a romantic night in or hurriedly grilling some chicken nuggets before the babysitter arrives, home cooks use a whole range of perceptual, conceptual, creative, organizational and emotional skills. Moreover, the person who regularly reheats a ready meal for their dinner or enjoys a Caesar salad made from ready-washed and trimmed salad leaves, dressing from a bottle and a pre-cooked, barbecued chicken leg may be the same person who once a month, effortlessly and without recourse to any recipe, prepares a weekend lunch of roast lamb, potatoes and broccoli with fresh mint sauce and saffron rice pudding to follow.[38] People who cook may well have a more extensive range of cooking skills and knowledge, or will acquire a more extensive range at some point in their lives, than a 'spot check' of the contents of their shopping basket may suggest. Deskilled cooks and deskilled cooking tasks are two very different things. A busy, tired mother like Jules, alone for a Friday night and with the children finally tucked up in bed, may not think twice about popping a ready-made chicken curry into the microwave to heat up. She's happy, on occasion, to wait for the 'ping', to let someone else do the work. Jez, the student that regularly cooks frozen 'chicken Kievs' for his friends when they get together to watch football on television, may only exist on convenience foods during this stage of his life.

At pains to point out that she is quite capable of baking from scratch, Maureen says that she is far more likely to make a cake with her son if they use a pre-prepared mix. Cake mixes, she explains, suit his short, child's concentration span, mean less washing-up and provide lots of interesting little packages and sachets for them both to enjoy opening. Their way of making a cake together may be deemed a deskilled method by many but its difficult to see Maureen, who regularly cooks from scratch for both economic and health reasons, as a deskilled cook. And her son still gets to mix, spread, stir and fold ingredients. With a 'packet mix', just as with a more 'traditional' method, he can acquire cooking skills. He can learn how to appreciate different textures, become acquainted with using an oven, smell a cake cooking and judge when it is ready.

Microwaves and Mindless Chores

Microwaves erode society. Modern labour-saving machines leave only mindless chores in their place.[39] Kitchen technologies and their offspring, the trimmed, parboiled, floreted, deboned and ready-to-steam, are regularly proclaimed as the scourge of home cooking. Yet, despite the numerous commentators ever ready to poor scorn on the microwave, the deep-fryer and the bread machine, *how* they contribute to the deskilling of cooks and cooking has been far less a subject of attention.

Luce Giard is one of the few who has looked at their contribution, describing how today's cook has a wealth of 'tiny metal instruments' to help her – mixers, blenders, juicers, corers, electric knives and can openers, as well as hot plates with sensors, pans with non-stick coatings and the 'polyvalent food processor that shreds, chops, mashes, mixes and, beats'. The home cook has become, says Giard, an unskilled spectator who watches a machine whose workings she does not understand function in her place, pushing buttons when required and collecting the transformed matter. In contrast, the cook of yesteryear could apply her savour faire each time she cooked, 'she could perfect her dexterity and display her ingenuity'.[40] Yet Giard provides little more detail than this and doesn't employ any particularly rigorous skills analysis to tackle questions about what cooking skills are lost through the use of technology or how they are changed. Nor does she explain how, as she claims, domestic kitchen appliances do away so completely with the cook's creativity and manual dexterity. After all, food mixers and blenders, apple corers and processors, along with rice steamers, panini presses, waffle makers and electric woks do not perform a complete cooking task. They all require complementary 'by hand' tasks as well. Certainly, none are machines into which you can place a collection of indiscriminate, raw, unprepared ingredients and remove a fully-fashioned and cooked meal or dish.[41]

Making pastry, whether it is done by the 'food processor method' or the 'by hand method', both of which are described in 'The perfect pie crust', an article in a UK-based food education magazine, requires the collection, measurement and preparation of ingredients. Both methods require that the fat is cut by hand, that judgement is made on the best point at which to add sufficient water to make a dough of 'correct' consistency and that the dough is formed into a ball and rolled out. Apart from 'rubbing the fat into the flour' and 'pulsing the processor to mix the fat and flour', the skills and techniques referred to for both methods are the same.[42] Just as with cooking from scratch and cooking with pre-prepared foods, conventional 'by hand' methods of cooking and cooking with modern kitchen technologies do not require wholly dissimilar or different levels of skills and knowledge. Scrambling eggs in a jug in a microwave and scrambling them in a pan on the hob, both ways of cooking eggs used regularly by the people I spoke with, require that eggs are broken and mixed together, seasoned and stirred. Both require that the cook judges when they are 'done', cooked to the desired or requested consistency. It could be argued, too, that it's a task that demands greater skill to carry out when unseen and happening at a much greater speed in the microwave. As Elizabeth Silva has pointed out, microwave ovens have never replaced thermostatically controlled gas or electric ovens as was originally intended – being used mainly only as 'reheaters' or 'defrosters' – perhaps, she suggests, because cooking from scratch with a microwave, as opposed to re-heating or defrosting, requires greater skill and/or a more skilled cook than cooking with a more 'traditional' oven.[43]

In *Can She Bake a Cherry Pie?* Mary Drake McFeely makes the point that technology in the kitchen can save the cook precious minutes and even encourage them to be more ambitious in their cooking forays. The bread maker (one of the few pieces of kitchen equipment into which you *can* place raw ingredients and remove, with the press of a button, a finished dish or foodstuff) is a gift for those, she suggests, who are unsure or uninterested in the pleasures of digging their hands into soft, silky dough but who like to know how their bread is made and want it packed with health-giving ingredients. The food processor, on the other hand, is, she feels, an invaluable and ever reliable sous-chef for the home cook who's grown tired of those mundane and tedious everyday tasks of mixing and squeezing, grating and puréeing, slicing and chopping. 'Suddenly home made mayonnaise seemed like a good idea,' thought McFeely on acquiring her first food blender. 'Then it was on to the aioli'.[44]

Not only do 'improved' kitchen technologies give the cook the chance to be more ambitious, they can also, argues Ruth Schwartz Cowan, a historian of technology and science, require that the cook is more ambitious, that they take on more complex tasks. As milling equipment modernized in mid-nineteenth-century America, says Schwartz Cowan, fine white flour became more widely available and increasingly more popular. It had only ever been used by the city rich – for it was only they who could afford both the financial cost and the time to prepare it – and it was as a consequence associated with wealth and status. Home cooks, stretched already to feed and clothe their families and keep their houses clean, now had to make complex yeast breads, cakes and pastries rather than simple maize and rye porridges, griddle cakes and spoon breads if they were to acquire that status. They had to churn butter, pound sugar from loaves, maintain yeast cultures and plan bread rising and proving around their numerous other daily tasks. Also contributing to the spread of more complex cooking, Schwartz Cowan continues, was the arrival of the stove in place of the hearth. For, once she had mastered the skills of regulating the dampers and moving her pots to different places on the stove so that they cooked at different temperatures, the cook could accomplish far more. She could boil potatoes, simmer soup and bake a pie all at the same time. The stove heralded the death of one-pot cooking and one-dish meals and increased the amount of time women spent cooking and the variety of skills they needed to do so. Technological change, Schwartz Cowan argues, has led, not to easier cooking lives, but to ever greater demands on the cook.[45]

Measuring Cooking Skills and Cooking Ability

Cooking skills can be seen as far more than the practice of putting a steak or Vegeburger under the grill, the stir-frying of egg noodles, the making of a cake or the ability to poach, casserole or whisk. There is obviously a lot of sense in health experts measuring people's ability to use the types of healthier foods and cooking methods they espouse. The findings of my research, however, show that it may not be that appropriate to regard techniques and simple manual tasks such as these as synonymous with home cooking in its totality. They suggest that it may not be that useful to take this approach to cooking skills when appraising people's cooking ability or examining the state of home cooking and any implications for family, gender or civic relationships. Finding out about how cooking abilities relate to food choices, beliefs and practices, gaining insight into whether cooking really is in decline or judging who can and who can't cook – all require a more detailed and flexible approach to the concept of cooking skill. As those who have studied skill in the workplace point out, finding the most informative approach and level of detail for the study in question is critical if the research, and any debate or policy that follows, is to be useful.[46]

Following chapters will return to look again at cooking skills, focusing in turn on how they influence our food choices, how we can gauge who is able and who is unable to cook and whether theories about deskilling are at all relevant to the state of contemporary home cooking.

–5–

What is a Cook?

Gods on Earth

Cooks, concludes Michael Symons as he writes on their history, are 'gods on earth'. Professional, folkloric, prehistoric or domestic, 'they are nurturers, sharers and minders ... They are the practitioners, creators, observers and thinkers. They are the food-getters, distributors and story-tellers.[1] Symons's image of the cook is one that can be glimpsed too in Luce Giard's portrayal of them in her study of domestic cooking in France,[2] though for Giard it is the anonymous, inglorious and unglamorous, unpaid cooking of the home and everyday, the cooking of women, that merits most acclaim. It is women cooks 'who fashion the world'. It is they 'whose gestures and voices make the earth liveable ... Doing cooking is the medium for a basic, humble, and persistent practice that is repeated in time and space, rooted in the fabric of relationships to others and to one's self, marked by the "family saga" and the history of each, bound to childhood memory just like rhythms and seasons.' The 'Kitchen Women Nation', says Giard, share ways of doing things, they have their own language, methods and points of reference. In interviews, she explains, they are excited to find an ally, eager and relieved to talk with another woman who understands, someone who speaks their language: '"You know how we do it right?" and "you see," "you understand," "I don't need to explain that."'

The depiction of women cooks as a collective bound together by shared knowledge and experiences is far from rare;[3] but that collective is not always marked by a need to care, sustain and nourish. Women cooks can be shown as a reluctant, even recalcitrant, group too. In service to their families, says food historian Laura Shapiro, 'women cook because they're expected to and because the people around them have to eat ... Happy is she who also enjoys the work.'[4]

Women do the food work, research consistently tells us, because it is their responsibility to do so. They may enjoy it, they may not, they may be good at it, they may not, but they generally feel obliged to feed the household and 'do the cooking'.[5] But what of men who cook? Rarely are they found to be, or presented as, competent everyday cooks recumbent in their nurturing role and ability to feed the family. Nor are they generally seen as the kinds of cooks who prepare food day in and day out, begrudgingly and out of a sense of duty. Rather, the male cook is the inept helper, the understudy who enters the kitchen to cook only when pressed to do so. Or he is the hobby cook, the artist in the kitchen, the amateur chef.[6] Men, it appears, find the label of home cook and feeder of the family a difficult one to attach. Introducing his study of professional kitchen work, Gary Alan Fine, for example, describes how, when his wife began to work full time and asked him to take on more domestic responsibility, he chose cooking. Yet, despite the fact that he chose the household task most associated, he felt, with creativity and personal satisfaction, he found he needed a rationale to avoid feeling that he was 'wasting time' in the kitchen. So he decided 'as a sociologist interested in art' to learn to cook and to study the world of chefs and restaurant cooking as he did so. By aligning it with the real world of food and cooking, he explains (writing, it has to be said, knowingly and with a degree of irony), he made cooking at home acceptable. His role as home cook now had real value because he had elevated it into the world of artistry and professionalism.[7]

When men cook, their masculinity must not be diminished, says Sherrie Inness. Their choice to cook and the food they produce should be just cause for applause. They cook difficult dishes and recipes. They become, she claims in an article that explores 'the male cooking mystique', artists, experts and creators.[8] 'It is I who scrape carrots, cube beef, weep over onions and peel potatoes,' wrote Evelyn Humphreys in *House Beautiful* as long ago as the 1950s. 'It is my husband who, with the preoccupation of a florist at work on an orchid corsage, compiles the bouquet of herbs and tosses it into the pot.'[9] Jamie Oliver – or at least his media persona – may cook at home and for the family but his food is entertainment. Cooking has 'gotta be a laugh'. Those for whom he cooks are always seen to wait in anticipation. And though he may cook everyday food he 'cooks it really well', better than his 'missus' or his mother-in-law, who 'boils the hell out of spinach'.[10]

Corrine and Mick, People who Cook

Can we really all be bound into these two or three limited and very gender-specific identifications? And is there really something as solidly determinate as a 'home cook'?

When Corrine was younger, she used to chat about cooking with her friends. They would swap recipes they'd cut from magazines, she told me, tips about feeding their families and hints on how to make good pastry. She only ever had a couple of cookery books but there was one, now well worn and food-spattered, that she used regularly to check methods and ingredients. And she used to cook all sorts of things – soups, stews, pasta dishes, pancakes, bread, curries, spaghetti bolognese, pies, 'anything really'. But, though keen to point out that she still likes to spoil people and think they've been well fed, Corrine felt she ought to tell me, 'I'm afraid I cheat now.'

Corrine is a tired cook. Now in her fifties, her children are older, have their own social lives and are always coming and going. Sitting down to a meal with mother and father isn't high on their agenda. Her husband too is an unreliable diner and has got 'finicky' and choosy, she says, in his later years. When people either don't enjoy or don't have time to eat the food you cook them, when they don't particularly notice how much work you have put in, Corrine was at pains to explain, then it's difficult to remain inspired or find the need 'to cook':

> I used to do a lot more cooking when the children were younger but I've found as they have grown up and left home I don't do as much. Everyone grabs something for themselves more these days, I think ... I would make stews, curries, spaghetti Bolognese – well, I still do that. I would try out anything really, shepherd's pies, roasts ... especially when the kids were younger and there wasn't much money around. Then you made use of what you could. (Corrine)

Its difficult too, she added, to remain confident about your cooking. These days she finds it unsatisfying a lot of the time and mostly a chore, only enjoyable or worthwhile when she's got all her housework finished, is doing something new or making a special meal. 'If I'm trying something that's quite interesting, then its exciting to see if it works. If it turns out nice then I'm on a roll for it, it gives me a bit of encouragement. If it goes disastrously wrong I don't ever want to cook again.'

Corrine is also a somewhat guilty cook. With her children now in their teens, Corrine has taken on two part-time jobs and cooking is now 'something to be fitted in':

> Do you know, I've got myself into such a spin some days. I've gone to put the washing in the dishwasher and vice versa because I'm not thinking about it, I'm on autopilot. My hands are everywhere like an octopus. Sometimes you're just not concentrating on what you're doing. I'm always doing other things and trying to fit everything in at once. (Corrine)

And, though Corrine said she imagined that she probably feels guiltier about doing so than many people these days, she explained she feels she is more likely to turn to the freezer or a packet than 'cook properly from scratch'.

When I asked Mick 'how much cooking do you do?' his reply was blunt. 'None,' he said. But it became apparent that Mick, in his early thirties and living alone, does in fact 'cook' quite a bit. He could describe making a pizza 'from scratch' quite happily and spoke of the occasional roast Sunday dinner he has made for friends. He had done a lot more cooking in the past, he told me, when he lived with his last girlfriend. He'd experiment and try things out then. Now he's living on his own, he doesn't feel there's an incentive to cook. Indeed, his 'new favourite meal', introduced to him by a colleague who brought some to work for lunch, is roast vegetables and couscous. Just a kettle to boil and lots of vegetables chopped up and roast together, as Mick joked, it couldn't fail to find favour. Mick, however, didn't seem to feel that he really 'cooks' as such, rather that he 'makes food'. In fact, he appeared almost proud that he has no basic ingredients (including salt and pepper) in the house, just some bread, spread and a packet of cereals. Most often he picks up (he doesn't really consider it shopping as such) food for his evening meal on the way home from work: perhaps some chicken, a few vegetables and a cook-in sauce to 'throw together', as he put it. Mick definitely likes to see himself as a non-cook, a non-foodie. He is definitely 'not interested' in food and cooking and quite dismissive of those who are. He just can't imagine, he said, spending hours in the kitchen or 'arriving home and thinking, "ooh, I'm going to make seafood and rocket risotto. Unplug the telly. Unplug the phone. Let's get going!"' Some people take it all too seriously, he thinks, endlessly talking about it, watching cookery programmes on television and commenting on and judging other people's food. 'I like to have people round to eat something together rather than to want *my* food', he explained. 'I want the food to taste nice but I'm not really interested in thinking I'm a great cook.' However, Mick doesn't feel under any particular pressure to be a good cook, he explained, adding that 'socially there are some nice skills to have [and] as a bloke you think it might be nice to be a good cook because it shows you're a bit sensitive'.

Finding Out More about People who Cook

Studies have begun to show that people approach cooking in very different ways. Market researchers talk of how we may be 'confident cooks', 'foodies', 'always on the goers', preferring to do something other than cook, or even 'Kitchen Castaways', willing to do anything other than cook.[11] Then again, we may fall into the 'basic but fearful' or 'useless and hopeless' categories identified by public health researchers.[12] We might be grouped in even more divergent and numerous groups if we were differentiated in the way done by an American study that aimed to establish which types of 'good cooks' have most influence on their family's food preferences. Then we could be classified according to personality (are you a giving, innovative, competitive, healthy or methodical cook?), to food choices (are you meat, vegetable or tradition focused?) or cooking behaviour (do you create your own combinations of foods, prefer to use recipes or cook to facilitate acceptance and affection?).[13]

A scrabble round the literature reveals famous cooks with very different approaches. The modernist Poppy Cannon, famous for *The Can-Opener*

Cookbook, for example, loved technology, boxes, jars and experimentation and eschewed tradition and grandma's recipes, says Laura Shapiro. The realist Peg Bracken wrote the *I Hate to Cook Book* for women who did just that. She encouraged the use of convenience foods and set out to dispel culinary myths. 'Never believe the people who tell you that pricking potatoes with a fork keeps then fresh and flaky,' she counselled. 'And if a somewhat soggy potato is the worst thing that ever happens to you, you are Lady Luck's own tot. The butter and salt will make them taste good anyway.' The technical specialist Julia Child, on the other hand, writes Shapiro, thought anybody could learn to cook, and cook well, if they had a thorough knowledge and understanding of the methods and techniques, the whys and wherefores.[14] The cooks I have watched on television over the last few years, too, have their own very different approaches. Delia Smith can only be associated with precision, accuracy and structure, Jamie Oliver and Keith Floyd with spontaneity, resourcefulness and the mercurial. And, moving away from the famous, M.F.K. Fisher warns 'loving cooks beware'. People don't necessarily cook so that they can gather their friends and family at the table and enjoy watching them eat the food they have prepared. They also cook to feel powerful – the professional cooking for the inner satisfaction of turning out the perfect dish, perhaps, the amateur for the praise and envy that can be accrued.[15] Meanwhile, John Thorne debates the merits and otherwise of fat cooks and thin cooks. Fat cooks cook so that we eat with them, he claims, our appetite being only a foil for their own. Thin cooks, he goes on to argue, take pleasure in cooking only when it is for others. The aim of the thin cook, the artist as opposed to the artisan, is only to see us taste their food and proclaim it as good.[16]

People who cook, I found early in my study, do so in very different ways and with very different mindsets. For example, they enjoy cooking, if they enjoy it at all, for a variety of reasons. David, Patrick and Ash all said they have a definite interest in cooking, they like collecting recipes, articles, cookery ware and different gadgets and watch 'anything that comes up on the television'. Alec, on the other hand, went to quite some lengths to impress upon me that cooking 'was no interest of his'. He would go out of his way, he insisted, to avoid cookery programmes and celebrity chefs. He does like cooking with his one-year-old daughter, though, perching her on the counter so she can watch burgers change colour as he grills them or mix the filling whilst he makes a sandwich. Some, like John, who can only stop thinking about work when he gets his 'cooking head on', find cooking therapeutic. Others get enjoyment and satisfaction not from the process of cooking, what Mary called 'the actual preparation', but from the result of cooking. Liz, in particular, finds feeling she has been a good host and knowing her guests have enjoyed themselves far more satisfying than making the perfect soufflé. Dean is just happy if he manages to cook something 'without messing it up'. One of the most clear-cut differences in approaches to cooking is that, whereas some people like to cook spontaneously with few or even no rules, others such as Mrs Recipe (as Elspeth calls herself) prefer to cook dishes and stick to 'known' combinations of ingredients. Like Julian Barnes's pedant in the kitchen, for whom 'waltzing off with wicker basket over the arm, relaxedly buying what the market has best to offer, and then contriving it into something which might or might not have been made before' will always be too much, Elspeth likes to start with a recipe.[17]

Some of the people I spoke to found cooking a chore, even if only on certain occasions. Others described it as a source of great pleasure. For yet others cooking was thought of as 'just something I do'. Some cooks explained how they feel they have a duty to cook, maybe even a duty to prepare and serve food that is healthy. Others felt nothing of the sort, cooking being a chance to experiment, 'mess around' and show others what they can achieve. Two very different approaches to cooking can be seen in how Liz and Patrick described 'making a stew, casserole or curry' (as they were asked to do as part of the interview[18]). Liz, who sees cooking as 'just part of my life', chose to describe making an everyday casserole and seemed to be trying to show how she can cook creatively but without fuss, how she can feed her family both efficiently and economically. She spoke of unceremoniously 'chopping up' regular, unexotic ingredients like carrots, potatoes and onions to 'sling in' the pot along with the 'diced lamb or pork from the supermarket', dried herbs and the crumbled stock (bouillon) cube. No specialist shops or foods for her. Nor was her stew above the likes of some leftover soup or red wine. Both she would happily 'throw in' for flavour, she said. Patrick, on the other hand, in his own words 'a complete foodie', seemed keen to impress upon me his knowledge and understanding of professional cooking techniques and terminology. Patrick described how he would buy a piece of lamb, 'cube it' himself and then 'brown it off' in the frying pan before removing it so he can cook other ingredients in the juices. He'd then fry garlic, onion and flageolet beans or 'some kind of pulse' before adding the browned lamb, some red wine (which, unlike Liz, he would open specially) and, rather than dried herbs, 'a little bouquet of parsley, thyme and bay leaf' before letting it 'all cook through'.

Determining who the home cook is and finding cooks with a shared craft and/or work identification are dependent, of course, on how 'cook' is defined and what credentials are stipulated. Do we have to 'cook properly' with fresh, raw ingredients, follow recipes or work within a cuisine to be a cook? Or is a cook simply someone who makes food, either occasionally or regularly, for others or just for themselves, with pre-prepared foods or without. With my research I took the latter definition. I understood cooks to be 'people who cook', whether for themselves and/or for others, frequently or infrequently, with great technical expertise or without. In doing so, I found it wasn't possible to view them as a collective of cooks, working within a clearly identifiable craft with set skills, rationales and standards. Nor did I find I was able in my small study to fit the thirty cooks I spoke to into any neat categories of types of cooks (though that's not to say that a larger study wouldn't be able to do so). What I did find was that they each had, alongside those beliefs and ideas they shared, which are described in Chapter 3, very different and very individual approaches to cooking. Jez, for example, a hospitality and catering student, could talk in detail and at length about many aspects of cooking and restaurant service. But he also, without any sense of guilt or irony, described how he usually only buys ready-prepared food when he cooks for himself at home, 'frozen chicken Kievs' being a favourite. He sees himself as a chef, albeit a trainee one, rather than a home cook. Indeed, it seemed that in the kitchen at home he identified entirely with the 'teenager who has better things to do than cook' and didn't appear to find it the least bit notable that he doesn't 'cook properly' at home. Debora, a lone mother in her late twenties with a nine-year-old son, has to manage her household and food provision on a strict and tight budget. She nearly always cooks 'from scratch' because she finds it cheaper and she quite consciously set out to present herself, it seemed, as a resourceful, pragmatic and somewhat 'resigned to manage' cook. Debora enjoys occasionally cooking for her friends and cutting out recipes for quick, cheap meals from weekly magazines. But she appeared very aware, I felt, that she can't really afford to buy the often expensive ingredients and equipment used by celebrity chefs or participate fully in the current fashion for cooking. In contrast, Claire, a young woman of similar age to Debora who lived with her young daughter and partner and also had a low – though not state-supported – budget, rarely 'cooked'. She lacked confidence, she said. Claire told me how she finds pre-prepared foods more reliable because when she cooks for friends she has fewer worries about 'getting it wrong' and when she cooks for her family there is less waste (which she can't afford) because they are more likely to eat everything. They like to 'know what's coming', she explained.

The personal approaches of four of the people I spoke to in the second stage of research are described in the following paragraphs. Along with those of Corrine and Mick described above, they show how very different these approaches can be. (These particular six people – this I felt to be about the right number to emphasize the point without overlabouring it – were chosen for no other reason than to illustrate these varying 'personal approaches'.)

Stacey, a Learner Cook

Ooh one day [I'd like to be thought of as a good cook] but I haven't had enough experience yet. Although I've had three or four dinner parties since the beginning of the year so I'm really getting into them. Like I say, when I have the time I love cooking, I really enjoy it. But after work when you get in at eight o'clock you don't fancy doing a nice dinner, do you?

(Stacey)

As a young, professional woman – a clerk in a Barrister's chambers – commuting into the city, working long hours, spending weekdays at her mothers and weekends at her boyfriends, Stacey's idea of a cook is hardly that of the nurturer and feeder of the family. The good cook to which she aspires is the cook who arrives home late but manages nevertheless to whip up a gourmet evening meal for two as she drops her laptop on the sofa and kicks off her court shoes, the cook whose dinner guests talk of the food she cooks effortlessly and serves enchantingly for days afterwards. And, despite the fact that Stacey quite obviously regularly prepares food for herself, her mother and her boyfriend, she told me that she has only cooked a few times in her life. Stacey does not consider baked potatoes, pasta dishes, sandwiches and things she 'can just chuck in the oven' as really cooking and quickly discounts the cookery classes she had at school. But things are looking up. Her recent experience at hosting dinner parties has given her opportunities to practise, she explained. Just a few weeks ago she cooked – with the aid of a collection of recipes and a few phone calls to friends and her mother – 'stuffed mushrooms and peppers and chicken marinated in orange, lemon, honey and garlic with pan-fried potatoes, steamed carrots and mangetout'.

Stacey sees herself very much as a learner cook and looks forward to the day when she can cook 'nice dinners' without relying on a recipe or ringing her mother. Yet there is no particular plan or structure to her learning and despite the fact that she often looks at food articles in magazines and cuts out things that appeal to her 'for one day in the future' she hasn't used any as yet. Stacey would like to learn to cook the kind of food that you have at dinner parties and that impresses friends. But she doesn't want to devote too much time to doing so. Cooking is important, she thinks, but not as important as things like reading and writing, because 'you can always get by'.

Kate, a Cook who Hates Cooking

Kate's account of her 'cooking life' is interspersed with sometimes detailed but always very able descriptions of making such things as apple pie, pizza, beef in red wine, quiche and leeks in cheese sauce. She took domestic science at school, she told me, did lots of cookery and even has qualifications. A mother of two in her mid-thirties, she loves going to restaurants and buying 'nice stuff' to eat at home. She also enjoys looking at food magazines and has been known to take one of her fourteen or more cookery books to bed for a good read and perhaps a jolt of inspiration. But, though Kate is, as she said, very interested in food, she isn't interested in cooking particularly: 'I'm very into looking at food magazines. I mean most of the time I don't want to or find time to eat but at weekends I find it quite recreational to eat nice food. I love going to restaurants and looking at menus. I'm very interested in food but I'm not interested in cooking it.'

Like Mick, she has few basic ingredients in the kitchen cupboards because breakfast is yogurt or cereal, lunches are mostly eaten out and for the evening meal she pulls out 'something pre-prepared from the fridge or the freezer'. Usually there is a pasta ready meal for her husband and 'some sort of low-fat food in a tray' for herself that she can 'just stick in the oven' and eat with her children, who have 'mundane food like sausage and chips' or 'something from the freezer'. Although she still cooks the occasional family meal or for a very occasional dinner party, she said, since she has had children Kate's enjoyment of cooking has plunged. Now she finds it 'a complete and utter chore' for she's always having to think about food, wash-up and shopping:

> I feel like I'm constantly thinking about food, about what we need in the house. I spend a lot more time shopping now than I did before I had children. There seems to be a lot more time thinking about food although at any one time I'm not spending large amounts of time preparing it. It's the regularity of it. Even on holiday … you're there, clearing up after one meal and somebody else needs something. (Kate)

Not only that but with two small children in the house cooking has inevitably become 'yet another thing that has to be done after they go to bed', which she finds stressful because, as she put it, 'there's only so much that you do between eight and eleven'. Kate is quite blatant in her admission that she 'doesn't feel that any link with domesticity is particularly good'. Before she had children, she told me, she had never thought of herself as the slightest bit domestic. Now she finds herself in that situation, she wants to disassociate herself from it as much as possible. And that means disassociating herself from cooking and from being a 'family cook'.

Cooks and People who Cook

Mine was a small study, admittedly, but I didn't find any real evidence that women had any kind of shared, collective cooking identity, never mind a mutual group image of themselves as 'cooking woman', keeper and teacher of culture, family and tradition. She who 'fashions the world from the kitchen epicentre' may be, just as Jean Duruz, author of 'Haunted kitchens: cooking and remembering', suggests, little more than part of our nostalgic culture for home making and kitchen tables, for traditions and rituals of eating together.[19] Nor did I find anyone, for that matter, who neatly fitted the role of the ironic domestic goddess, the Nigella Lawson-type cook who plays at being the nurturer, the keeper of family customs and the enchantress before returning to her book, office or computer.[20] There was no indication that the young, contemporary 'anti-cook' identified by Hermione Eyre – she who is keen to be 'clueless in the kitchen', who brags about not knowing a colander from a courgette – is an especially prevalent 'type'.[21] Indeed, the cooking approaches of Kate, Stacey and Corrine, as well as others like Debora, Elspeth and Claire, show that, though it is possible to see a little of the scullion, nurturer and disinclined cook in them all, women who cook rarely conform to any given set image or role. However, they do have distinctly contrasting approaches and identifications to men. My findings entirely supported research that has shown men and women have completely different relationships to each other with regard to the selection, preparation and consumption of food.[22] Unlike the men, none of the women I spoke with tried to professionalize their role as cook, none saw it purely as a leisure occupation and none had entirely opted out of doing the cooking. For the most part, women did not use phrases like 'my speciality' and 'my recipe for' or refer to friends and other home cooks as being 'good chefs'. It was only the men who took part in my study, I found, who saw themselves as having a real choice of whether to cook or not, hence it was only men who could see cooking purely as a hobby or as something they were definitely 'not interested' in. As Alan Warde and Lydia Martens also found, women's contribution to food and cooking tasks, unlike that of men, is not dependent on and does not vary in respect of their more general interest in food.[23] In both the most egalitarian of households and those where more traditional views of male and female obligations and responsibilities hold sway, there is an implicit understanding that, whilst men can 'take on' cooking and being a cook, women have to reject or 'offload' it.[24]

Mick's 'personal approach' to cooking doesn't neatly fit the role he, as a male home cook, is often assigned either. He is neither a wholly disinterested nor an amateur chef in his own kitchen. There are, though, more suggestions of these approaches in him than there are in his female counterparts. The same is true of David and Dean.

Gadget-mad David

David is in his mid-fifties. He didn't really cook until he was well into his forties, he said, having been cooked for, in turn, by his mother, his landlady, servants and then wife and servants. Then, when he got divorced, he found he had to feed his two children and make sure he provided them with a varied, vaguely nutritious diet. Now he loves to cook, particularly for friends and his now 'grown-up' children when they come to stay. He avidly follows cookery programmes and has 'thousands' of cookery books, so many that he doesn't know what's in most of them. He's also 'gadget-mad' and using his huge range of kitchen equipment forms part of his enjoyment of cooking. He considers his bread machine 'the greatest invention known to man':

> You just put in your flour and your yeast and a bit of water and butter maybe. Perhaps olives and raisins if you want to make that sort of bread. Switch it on and four hours

later you have a loaf of bread, You can even set it so that it takes thirteen hours so you can put everything in the night before and you can get fresh bread for breakfast. It's wonderful … amazing. (David)

David spoke at length about the different ingredients he likes to use, the chefs he enjoys watching on television and the 'known only to a few' places he goes to shop for food. He described as he did so how he once spent a whole day making his partner a Japanese meal with nine or ten different dishes. He delighted too in describing to me a meal he might make for friends: bruschetta or salad to begin with, lamb tagine for the main course and then a soufflé omelette or cherries baked in custard to follow – a meal in which, although he isn't averse to using convenience and pre-prepared foods when he's eating alone, everything would be made 'properly from scratch'.

Despite the fact that he loves cooking and relishes it as a challenge, David is not always particularly confident about his own abilities. He feels that he's 'not a natural', follows recipes 'religiously' and uses them 'virtually all the time'. A good cook would have 'no need to follow recipes, of course', he told me. David has set himself some high standards and feels he is 'constantly faced' by people who are better cooks than he is. In fact, he asked me on finishing the interview whether I thought him a good cook, even though I had explicitly told people that the study was not an appraisal of their skills and knowledge. But at least my response left him upbeat: 'I've come out of this thinking I'm actually a rather better cook than I thought.'

Dean, a Non-cook

Dean is in his early twenties and defines himself as a 'non-cook'. He did cookery at school but since then he said, he hasn't 'done much cooking'. He makes the odd sandwich but he doesn't 'do any of the dinners or anything'. His girlfriend does that. Not that he hasn't watched the occasional cookery programme on television or seen something that he's thought he'd like to eat in a magazine or newspaper, he explained, but it never occurs to him to want to try and cook it.

Dean clearly remembered, he said, the last two occasions on which he cooked. (It is clear though, from what he said, that he often 'made food' like sandwiches and simple snacks.) The first was a dinner – a dinner about which he didn't want to talk, although he was grinning from ear to ear. The second time was when he baked a cake: also a disaster, he said, not even the dog touched it apparently: 'the cake was too dry and it just didn't taste very nice. I don't know what went wrong.'

Though a very different cook from David, like David, Dean sees cooking very much as being about success and failure. But, unlike David, Dean wears his lack of success as a badge of honour. Failure, though amusing, is also his reason for not cooking. 'If I was any good at it,' he told me, 'then possibly I might be a little more interested … If the end result was worth going through all that for and I could be proud of it then I would probably do more cooking.' Cooking for Dean is very much something you have to opt into, it's a choice. It's something that people do as a hobby, an interest if you want it to be, but one that he personally has no wish to take up: 'It all depends on what your outlook is. I personally think it's great if you make you own stuff but for me it's convenience stuff straightaway. It's easier. I'd rather go home and just flake out than carry on in the kitchen.'

As for his son, nine months old at the time of the interview, Dean said he wouldn't mind if he got interested in cooking but nor would he encourage it: 'swimming and things are higher on the agenda'.

Cooking and Identity

As was discussed in Chapter 2, studying the relationship between what food people eat and their self-identity, or the groups and institutions with which they identify, is gathering increasing popularity. Meat confers strength on the individual who eats it, vegetarianism hints at a political consciousness, a liking for dark chocolate shows good taste, perhaps even elevated social status.[25] Hermione Eyre's contemporaries, who want to be 'pathetically, curdlingly bad at cooking' so as to deny what they feel to be an imperative to 'make home' and lay greater claim to the more important world of men, suggest that there might also be a relationship between our approach to cooking and who we are or would like to be.[26] Yet the connections between the individual, how they cook and with what or with whom they identify remain largely unexplored. The work of Gill Valentine and Gerald and Valerie Mars, however, suggests that it may be useful to do so.

Valentine describes, amongst others, Colin and Wendy Webb, a couple who, not too unlike Mrs Recipe and her husband, cook in very different ways, one adventurously and one more conservatively:

> When Colin is in charge he invents new dishes for himself and Wendy, throwing in leftovers and any ingredients which come to hand, to create unique meals. In contrast, Wendy has very set ways of preparing food and always sticks to tried and tested convenience foods. She has strong opinions about which combinations of foods should go together. Colin claims it took him years to convince her that fish did not always have to be eaten with chips, but could be enjoyed with a baked potato too.

Colin and Wendy's different cooking styles, says Valentine, correspond to the way in which they see themselves. Colin's more daring and sophisticated take on food and life can be seen in his creativity as a cook and his enjoyment of more unusual food and ethnic restaurants, as well as in his going to university and travelling before settling down. In contrast, Wendy's more traditional approach to cooking, her belief in 'foods that go together' and set ways of doing things, mirrors her description of herself as 'working class, conventional and mildly xenophobic'.[27]

The aim of Gerald and Valerie Mars's study was to explore how two couples from the same social class and income group both construct and make known their very different social identities – as suburban conformists and urban individualists – through the manner in which they entertain and cook for guests. They found that the more conservative couple, the Browns, and the other couples (no single people) in their social circle invited each other for dinner in a strict rotation system. The Browns were careful to observe formalities and pleasantries, hang coats properly and served either red or white wine, whatever was 'appropriate', with each course. They prepared established dishes, like beef Wellington, and adhered to tradition and familiarity by cooking with well-known and long-established brand names like Mattesons and Bisto. The Joneses, on the other hand, they found, shopped eclectically and looked for foods they particularly liked to create an innovative and spontaneous menu of Greek sausages and champ (an Irish mashed potato dish) for their guests, guests who didn't conform to any rules of gender and marital status. The more idiosyncratic and impulsive approach to life and social relationships taken by the Joneses, explain the researchers, is reflected in their cooking practices and choice of fellow diners.[28]

An original intention of my study was to examine, in a similar way to Gill Valentine and Gerald and Valerie Mars, whether people have cooking identities – approaches to food and cooking that might be linked to their more general sense of who they are or wish to be. Though I did find that people who cook have a personal approach to doing so that is related to their cooking responsibilities, daily routines and household circumstances, a link with self-identity proved too ambitious an aim for the study I had designed and the resources available to me. It would be misleading, therefore, to make any firm claims in this direction. I would like to be able to declare, for example, that I found that confidence in cooking doesn't just stem from experience and acquired know-how, that it comes also from our general confidence, the confidence that we acquire from our social status, gender, position in the household and work identity or that is perhaps simply part of our personality – it being easier to be confident about cooking if you are an all-round confident person or if you have a valued career, job or position that provides alternative self-validation. I would like to be able to say that I found that men find it difficult to take on the role of home cook and family food provider because of their lack of other domestic identifications and suitable role models. Unfortunately, despite strong indications of both, I didn't feel I gathered quite enough evidence to firmly posit either as being a definite finding. The extent and nature of the relationship between our attitude towards and style of cooking and our social world, self-identity and social relationships will have to be the subject of further study.

Margaret, an experienced cook, admitted to me that being someone who is both a perfectionist and someone who enjoys fiddly, practical tasks (not necessarily cooking-related, but she enjoys things like removing the meat from crab and lobster claws and skinning tomatoes) means that she finds cooking with her children rather tiresome. She feels rather guilty about it but she finds it difficult 'not to mind about doing it properly' and is loath to share what little cooking time she has with them, being both 'a bit of a foodie' who loves to cook and a full-time working mother. Margaret, the 'good cook' who regularly cooks 'properly and from scratch', may not be that good at passing on her abilities to her children. There is nothing straightforward about cooking or being a cook, and that we have a 'personal approach' adds a further layer of complexity. For our personal approach, alongside our skills and abilities and the values and beliefs about cooking we share with others, is connected with what we cook, whether we use convenience foods or cook 'properly', how often we cook and even, perhaps, in the case of Margaret, who we cook with. The next chapter explores this relationship.

–6–

What do Cooks Cook, and Why?

What We Can Cook, What We Do Cook

People who can't cook buy convenience foods. They don't have as much control of their diet, but they have no choice. And, not being able to cook, they cannot teach their children to cook, so they'll have to use convenience foods when their time comes too. 'Domestic food consumption begins with what is bought; what is bought and what is served are in turn circumscribed by the ability to prepare food'[1] is how the oft-quoted Paul Fieldhouse puts it. It is a simplicity of approach that suggests an equally straightforward solution teach people to cook.

That there is a relatively straightforward set of connections between people's cooking ability, the foods they eat and cook (whether they use 'pre-prepared' products and ready meals or cook 'from scratch') and whether they have learnt or been taught to cook is usually taken as fairly implicit. 'Countries such as Britain where the teaching of food skills in the classroom has declined', warns the Scottish Child Poverty Action Group, for example, 'have seen a greater increase in reliance on convenience foods and a measurable decline in the health of the population'[2] – the answer being, they argue, to reintroduce nutrition and cooking skills into the school curriculum. Other commentators have suggested that consumers who can't cook risk their health and the chance to enjoy home-cooked food. It is essential, they claim, that children be taught food skills if they are to follow healthy eating advice and take control of their diet rather than succumb to the will of manufacturers and grow ever more dependent on their products. They argue, too, that, for the benefit of the eating habits of their families, women who can't cook be encouraged to attend cookery demonstrations and classes and be provided with free, simple recipes.[3]

Many of those involved in community food initiatives have become increasingly aware over the last few years that practical cooking skills classes can do more that 'just help you keep the lumps out of your custard' or instruct you in the ways of a low-fat chicken pasta recipe. 'Heightened self-esteem', 'confidence' and 'sense of purpose' have all been noted as outcomes that encourage people to make more informed food choices.[4] Recently, too, food policy experts have also begun to question the straightforwardness of the relationship between people's cooking skills and their cooking practices. Research has tended to pay little attention to people's attitudes towards cooking, they point out, to how confident they are in their cooking skills, for example, and how they feel about the task of feeding their family. Choosing 'not to cook from basics' might not be related to a lack of skills after all, it has been suggested, but to aspects of food culture.[5]

People who can Cook but Choose Not to

All the cooks I spoke with used pre-prepared foods at least occasionally, even Jez and Eamon, whose professional training and experience suggest their technical ability can go relatively unquestioned, Jez, as I've mentioned before, being very partial to frozen chicken Kievs and Eamon fond of buying dinner guests 'something splendid from the patisserie' or using ready-made pasta sauces when he's rushed – though he is often, he said, disappointed with the result and wonders why he didn't 'just use some crème fraiche, Parmesan and fry off a few mushrooms'. Two of the informants said that they didn't use pre-prepared foods, yet in both cases, from where I sat in their respective kitchens during the interviews, I could see things like packets of dried pasta, crackers and what was obviously factory-produced bread. Geraldine loves to use prepared, convenience foods, she explained, seeing them as a blessing after forty years or more of cooking for others. She may have a shelf stacked high with preserves and chutneys she makes herself but her kitchen also has cupboards full of store-bought jam, pickles and relishes lined up alongside a mixture of tins, jars and packets and 'basic ingredients' like rice, pasta, flour, sugar and dried yeast. Her fridge and freezer too reveal a selection of different ice creams, both home and commercially made, frozen chips and vegetables, individual pots of yogurt and other desserts, trays of ready-prepared salads from the deli section of the supermarket as well as fresh meat, cheese, vegetables and fruit.

Many of those I interviewed had practical cooking abilities they didn't always use. Liz, for example, was obviously quite adept at making pancakes and surprised at being asked to describe something so simple. Despite her confidence, though, using a batter mix is one of two perfectly acceptable alternatives: 'Well, I'd either make a batter or I'd buy an instant batter mix. I mean it's just flour, egg and milk isn't it? And a bit of salt? Then I'd put some vegetable oil in a pan and make it very hot and then put it [the batter] in ... drizzle it in.' Elspeth used to make pizzas from scratch but gave up when she found, she said, that they didn't really taste any better than those she could buy ready prepared. Debora, cooking on a tight budget, usually makes economical things like pies and stews but 'because they don't like the kind of food we eat' dishes up chicken nuggets and chips when her son's friends come round. Often, it seems, people who cook buy and eat pre-prepared versions of foods and dishes they are quite capable of cooking from scratch for reasons that have nothing to do with their skills or ability. Claire used to enjoy baking and considers herself pretty good at it but now she has children, she said, she often buys ready-made pastry: 'I used to make steak and kidney pies, apple pies and crumbles and stuff. I think now I buy ready-made pastry due to time constraints I suppose. I was actually rather good at making pastry.' Ash is just relieved that, because shops now stock it, he no longer has to go through the long and convoluted process of making paneer cheese: 'Paneer was something that you had to make at home ... because it just wasn't available. Now paneer is available in almost every shop and supermarket ... which is surprising ... and so I think there is a tendency to mix and match, not to cook everything yourself, but just to cook certain parts.'

There are also fluctuations in how much cooking people do at different stages of their lives, variations that, again, have little to do with ability. Kate accepts that her dislike of cooking is probably just a 'stage' linked to her having two small children and a busy job. But it is a stage of her life that she is certain she will move on from. Others too spoke to me of how there were times in their lives when they had 'done more cooking', though this could mean either making food more frequently or doing more 'proper cooking', than others. Mick used to 'progress a bit further into experimenting with different things' when he had a flat with his girlfriend. He rarely bothers now, he said, because he lives alone. Amrit too used to cook more frequently and 'properly' when he lived with friends in a shared house. Short of money, if he wanted to eat anything vaguely interesting or tasty, he explained, then he had to do it for himself, and, because he did, he inadvertently became the household's cook. Yet, despite the fact that he acquired lots of new cooking skills and knowledge as a result, now he's financially better off he's more likely than ever before, he said, to eat out or buy something to heat in the microwave. People who cook, it seems, don't necessarily 'do more cooking' as their experiences and skills grow.

Influences on What, Why and How we Cook

In this book I've looked at different aspects of cooking in the home and the different approaches of the cooks who do it. I've tried to show how current debates fail to fully acknowledge the varied experiences people have of cooking and of being cooks, the divergent meanings and understandings that they bring to those experiences, and the different kinds of abilities and know-how they develop as a result. In this chapter it is argued that, likewise, there is nothing simple about the relationship between a cook's ability and how much cooking they do or what kinds of food – pre-prepared or otherwise – they cook with. Drawing on the three previous chapters, this chapter looks at how the cook's individual approach to cooking (discussed in Chapter 5), the beliefs, values and opinions they share with others (in

Chapter 3) and their cooking skills and knowledge (in Chapter 4) relate to their food choices and practices. It examines these different influences separately before turning to focus on how, on any one cooking occasion, they converge, are reconciled and work together to determine what, why and how people cook.

Food Practices, Food Choices and Individual Approaches to Cooking

Kitchen-castaways, a cooking 'type' identified in market research, consider themselves incompetent cooks and prefer to eat out or use convenience foods, anything other than 'cook'. 'Always-on-the-go'ers too, rarely 'cook'. However, they use convenience foods because there are other things they would rather do, not because they have doubts about their cooking abilities.[6] Kate also explains her use of ready meals and commercially prepared foods as being because of her lack of desire to be seen as housewifely and domestic, not because she can't cook or is unsure of her ability to do so. Her personal identification as a cook, her individual approach, has an influence on her food practices, her use of fresh and pre-prepared foods and how she 'cooks'.

'Uninterested cooks' like Alec, Dean and Mick are perfectly happy to use convenience foods because they neither cook recreationally for enjoyment and 'success' nor see themselves as household cooks, responsible perhaps for their family's food. Debora, on the other hand, has taken on the role of the efficient 'real cook' who makes healthy, home-made food as cheaply and resourcefully as possible and she usually cooks with 'fresh', 'raw' ingredients. Corrine has a similar personal approach to Debora's in that she sees herself as the feeder and food provider of the household, but Corrine has been cooking for others for much longer. She is very aware of her weariness with cooking and that perhaps she shouldn't rely on the standardized, neutral qualities of 'convenience' foods to keep everyone in the family happy, but as a 'tired cook' she does nonetheless. Jules and her partner, meantime, have a kind of informal policy by which they aim to eat with their children and cook from scratch as much as possible. They've changed their working lives and routines in order to do so and gain a great deal of satisfaction from achieving their goal. In contrast, Ash is fully aware that his identification is that of a 'hobby cook'. He appreciates that he is not the 'family cook' responsible for the weekly shopping, everyday meals, packed lunches, the washing-up and so on. He knows he can cook what he wants when he wants, choosing recipes and ingredients as he wishes. For Ash, cooking is all about enjoying the process and getting satisfaction from the challenge and others' appreciation of his technical skills. He neither uses 'pre-prepared' foods nor, even though he speaks of 'tackling' new recipes and dishes, takes on anything that he feels he won't enjoy making, that is too complex or convoluted:

I would never attempt to cook those things that I think are just too complicated or can only be done in certain quantities because it is just not worth it. Not because I wouldn't like it at all but because it is just not worth me taking the trouble. If I was in a position where I had to [cook] and if it was required of me ... but I don't see myself in that way in the family ... then I would do, yes. Because I'm only doing it because I like it, then it's just too much trouble. (Ash)

Food Practices, Food Choices, Shared Values and Beliefs

Perfectly capable of making a pizza (she can easily describe making bread dough and tomato topping), Jules has various ways of doing so depending on when she is cooking and who she is cooking for. For Jules, making a pizza has different forms and different arrangements. It can take on various meanings. A pizza for an evening meal with the family or a weekend lunch may well incorporate a halved French baguette or ready-made pizza base. On a Friday evening 'making a pizza' often becomes 'having a pizza' and taking a commercially made, frozen pizza from the freezer or, for more of a treat, a better-quality but still ready-made, chilled pizza from the fridge, and quickly cooking it in the oven. (When we spoke, reheatable, microwaveable pizzas had yet to make a proper appearance.) Only on certain, more special occasions would she bother to prepare a bread base and tomato sauce 'from scratch':

I suppose if I'm honest I haven't really made pizza for quite a long time, since we discovered those ready-made bases probably. Some of them are so good. We generally would just use one of those but if we were having a picnic with friends then maybe we'd make it from scratch, make a bit more of an effort. (Jules)

For people who cook there are times to use 'prepared convenience foods' and times to use 'raw ingredients and fresh foods'. Convenience foods are generally thought wholly appropriate for particular kinds of meals and snacks, albeit that the occasions considered suitable and the amount used may vary, even considerably, between individuals. Stacey, though fond of giving quite lavish dinner parties for her friends, thinks ready meals are perfect for those times when she and her boyfriend just want to eat something before they go out. Pasta sauces, cooked meats and prepared salads are useful when she's in a hurry to get the train round to his house for the weekend. As was explained in Chapter 3 people who cook all share ideas about when to 'cook properly' or 'make an effort' (dinner with friends at the weekend, perhaps), when 'the odd jar or packet' is fine (maybe midweek dinner for the family) or 'when not to bother at all because it's not worth the effort' (midweek breakfast being typical): ideas or guidelines that are in turn underpinned by a belief that the effort put into cooking should equal the reward received. 'We'd rather sit down and watch a bit of TV, have a chat or play with our son than stay in the kitchen and cook,' said Dean. With neither him nor his girlfriend having taken on an approach that says 'it's better to cook with fresh ingredients', like Jules and her partner or Debora, say, their cooking-related reward on an occasion like this can come straightforwardly from their not having to. Corrine is more likely to go to the effort of making an evening meal from scratch if there is some reward. For her that means getting all the housework done and being able to relax and enjoy the process. Ash, on the other hand, a father of two teenagers, would 'be bothered to cook them something nice for a weekend breakfast' if they 'would just sit down for an hour or so rather than be finished in fifteen minutes'.

There are numerous shared approaches to cooking – beliefs and values like the creative ideal, the concepts of success and failure, the endless search for the interesting and the different – that have a part to play in both the perceptions of the reward offered and the effort involved, approaches that have in turn an influence on how often people cook and what kinds of foods they cook with. Chapter 7 will take a look at how these more oblique, abstract shared approaches have an equivalently indirect and complex influence on domestic food choices and practices. There's also washing up, of course: 'Making something like mash, veg and gravy you're talking more than an hour and a pile of washing up. With a pizza you just throw it in [the oven] and throw away the bit of foil and hey, it's all done.' Mick's words sum up the view of many. Few of those I spoke with failed to mention tidying and cleaning up as being an effort and as being a direct influence on their cooking habits. The effort of tasks like washing up discourages cooking. Porridge on a weekday is out of the question, unless it's made in the microwave, for many of those I spoke to because of the mess factor and having to clean the saucepan. For Claire, despite the fact that she enjoys making pies and quiches, it's pastry making that's a clear no-no. She can't bear 'all that scraping the gunge off the surface'. Similarly, Liz hates cleaning her food processor, so, although she feels it does encourage her to 'cook more' for special occasions, she rarely uses it for every day.

There are many foods, often considered 'pre-prepared' by writers and experts, which people who cook treat as 'basic provisions' – never mind having the cooking skills to do so, the approach of those I spoke with to foods like mayonnaise, passata, biscuits and cookies, vegetarian sausages, burgers and fruit yogurts (obviously these foods varied slightly between individuals) being, 'Well, they're just not foods you make are they?' Now and then, on special occasions, perhaps, or when using cooking to unwind or impress, they may well do things like make stock, 'real' custard or paneer, bake bread or grind fresh spices. On an everyday basis, however, even experienced cooks and keen cooks who like a challenge think it perfectly acceptable to use things like bouillon cubes, custard powder and tinned tomatoes.

And therein lies an inherent problem in examining, not only how cooking abilities, attitudes and approaches influence our food choices, but the wider meanings of cooking in the home, the difficulty being (again) clearly defining and differentiating between 'raw, natural foods' and 'pre-prepared, convenience foods'. As Rachel Laudan asks in her plea for culinary modernism, does food really fit into these two nice, neat groups?[7] It's easy to appreciate how a frozen pizza or a ready meal that only requires reheating can be judged as being a 'convenience' food. Yet 'raw, basic ingredients' like fresh fruit and vegetables are often cleaned and trimmed, meat butchered and dressed, fish skinned and filleted. White flour has undergone a long processing treatment but is rarely thought of as being a 'processed food'. A sachet of instant cappucino is very definitely a convenient, pre-prepared food in most people's minds, but what about a vacuum-packed carton of ground coffee? Why is it thought of as being more of a 'proper fresh, raw food'? (Notably, informants in the first stage of the study who kept cooking diaries gave information on making fresh coffee but not on making a cup of instant coffee.) Rice can be bought parboiled or converted for quick, final cooking. It can be ready-cooked, frozen and ready for the microwave or mixed with roast chicken or garlic and butter flavouring.[8] Yet the staple, 'real' rice of the 'good cook's' cupboard – brown, Arborio, basmati, Thai jasmine – is also heavily processed and way past its truly natural state.

Food Practices, Food Choices and Cooking Skills

Not only are 'prepared', 'convenience' foods and 'raw' foods frequently regarded as entirely different and opposite, so too are the skills used in preparing them. Raw foods require skill to prepare them, pre-prepared foods don't. 'Cooking from scratch' is associated with some sort of traditional set of skills, 'using pre-prepared foods' with assembly only. These phrases are part of a meaningful, shared language amongst people who cook. They are also laden with a conceptual ambiguity that makes it difficult to examine not only the meaning and state of cooking in the home but also, more simply, how people choose between these 'different' types of foods and why even 'skilled' cooks only choose to 'cook' on certain occasions. My research showed that it can be insightful to step back from value-laden interpretations of cooking skills and take a more analytical and dispassionate perspective. A perspective that acknowledges that all the different kinds of foods used today are pre-prepared outside the home to different degrees and that they all involve overlapping and interchangeable selections of a whole range of cooking skills and practical knowledge to prepare.

Cooking skills, I found, do influence food choices and cooking practices. But it is not mechanical abilities to perform practical tasks and techniques like roasting, deep frying or making a white sauce (which are frequently referred to as 'cooking skills') that have the key role. She finds it a struggle to express, but Jaclyn is reluctant to make pastry just as Ash is to make bread, not because she is unable to knead, weigh out ingredients or roll dough but because she's concerned about 'mixing in the water and everything else'. She finds it difficult to know what consistency she is looking for and how it relates to the final product. Similarly David said of following a recipe for spinach soup that I gave him to look at: 'I'd be quite happy about actually "doing it" but I'd just be a bit worried about the result.' Like Jaclyn's with the pastry, David's problem with making the soup does not lie in the application of practical techniques but in envisioning the process and understanding how the soup takes form. In both cases it is not mechanical skills but tacit perceptual and conceptual skills that are of prime importance, the skills that would give them greater confidence to make pastry or to try the soup recipe[9] – the kind of adaptable and transferable abilities that might, as wider skills research suggests, give them greater confidence in carrying out comparable tasks or cooking with similar foods, abilities that might encourage them to make other kinds of soup, perhaps, cook with spinach more regularly or take up baking.[10]

Just as a lack of a clear appreciation of these kinds of tacit skills makes it difficult for researchers to explore how skills relate to practices and where cooking confidence comes from, it also makes it difficult for cooks to voice where their concerns about cooking lie. As he reads the recipe, Ash knows that he isn't particularly sure about making a quiche but he can't find the words to express what it is that makes him lack confidence:

> There are so many ingredients and then there's the pastry ... which is always supposed to be tricky. Maybe it isn't, I don't know. But there are some dishes that you never try simply because you think they're too tricky and you don't know. This bit about 'knead the dough very quickly and lightly until it is ...' and then 'wrap in cling film and chill for half an hour ...' Well, that must be a very important part of how the recipe will come out, I would think. (Ash)

Ash's words also show his lack of knowledge about why certain techniques and methods are applied, why it's best not to knead pastry dough for too long or why you might leave it in the fridge to chill. Amrit too (like Ash, not one of the study's least knowledgeable or least confident cooks by any means) seems baffled by certain aspects of cooking:

> You've got this floury, powdery stuff and you've got to add an egg and a bit of water and it suddenly becomes a cake or something. I don't get that. I understand that it rises but ... And then people talk about making a white sauce, making a roux or whatever, and it's 'how can a solid go to a liquid?' ... that's what gets me about cooking. (Amrit)

Amongst the cooks I spoke to uncertainty about cooking, and often the crux for not doing more cooking, came from not knowing what to expect and from not understanding why and how the consistency and appearance of food changes when it is mixed, heated or chilled. In other words, uncertainty about cooking came from both a lack of secondary, tacit skills and a lack of academic knowledge about the science of cooking.[11]

Rather than practical, technical cooking skills, it is tacit skills and practical knowledge, along with academic knowledge, which are the main skill-related influences, I found, on what we 'cook' and how often or how regularly we do so. These abilities influence our approach to cooking. Knowing what to expect and an acquaintance with different ingredients, textures, smells and appearances increase our confidence. They also decrease the effort we perceive as being involved. 'There's always been [for me] a mystique about baking, making scones and bread,' explained Ash. 'I think "Oh it's going to take ages" and "I'm going to make a mess of it." But now that I've actually made them I realize that it's not that difficult at all. It's just knowing what to do and things.' Jaclyn has similar views about all kinds of cooking but in particular a 'pine nut and spinach salad with Thai flavours' she recently made. She'd eaten it at her friend's house and thought it too glamorous and complicated for 'her kind of cooking'. Urged to borrow the recipe, however, she found it disarmingly quick and easy to make, she explained. It didn't require anywhere near as much effort as she thought it would.

How much someone cooks or whether they take up a particular cooking task is dependent not just on their confidence in doing so but also on how much they think it an effort – and how much effort they want to go to. (For, as we have seen, there are occasions when cooks want to or feel they should make an effort and occasions when they don't. There are cooks who often like to make an effort and cooks who rarely do.) Dean's account of his 'failed' attempt at making a cake that 'not even the dog would eat' shows how his experience has not only lowered his confidence about doing so again but has also made it seem like just a little bit too much of an effort. Has he made a cake since? 'I haven't been brave enough to make a cake again. Well, not brave, I've just not really tried. I gave up.' Dean made the cake alone and by following a recipe. Lacking the academic knowledge and the experience or tacit skills that would enable him to understand the process and where he 'went wrong', he is left uncertain and unsure about 'going to the bother' of making another.

The Food Choices we Make, the Cooking we Do, and Why

Yet Dean said he would bake a cake again, at least 'if it was just a case of "oh let's make a cake"'. Dean is no achievement-oriented cook and has no particular interest in making a beautiful, praiseworthy cake that says 'look what I can do'. But he might, he said, enjoy messing about in the kitchen one afternoon. He would be hesitant about making a cake for a special occasion, however, an occasion where it would be important – perhaps for others, if not for himself (he had his son's first birthday party in mind, I think) – that his cake 'worked' and was deemed a 'success'.

There is nothing straightforward about cooking ability, the way people cook and the type of food choices they make. Confidence in cooking, for example, can come from experience and secondary tacit knowledge and skills, but it doesn't necessarily do so. Being a confident cook or being confident about a particular cooking task can result from being a generally confident person. Twenty-three-year-old Amrit, for example, though he did once live in a shared house where he was responsible for the cooking for a year or so, is not an especially experienced cook in the way that, say, Eamon, the ex-chef, is. He takes an unemotional and intellectualized position on cooking, however, especially on it being something that relies on 'natural ability' and that can be 'successful', which enables him to read between the lines and be confident:

> [Reading] 'Add the spinach and simmer for thirty seconds,' well, that's presumably to slightly cook the spinach and soften it. And if the spinach is softened whether it takes ten minutes or ten seconds then it's done the job. When someone writes a recipe they want to make sure that the basic thing is done. Obviously it's not vital that it's thirty seconds, what they mean is 'soften the spinach'. Some people will think 'well, it looks soft but is it soft enough yet?' So they say things like thirty seconds so you'll guarantee it'll be soft by then. I wouldn't sit there with a stop-watch, no. (Amrit)

Amrit's confidence in cooking may also arise, at least in part, from that fact that he doesn't feel any real obligation to cook 'from scratch'. He feels that as a young man living on his own he is at the stage of his life where he can eat what he wants and cook only if he so wishes. Ash too, despite having two children, doesn't feel particularly burdened by any obligation or responsibility to cook. He only cooks for his family now and then, he explained, at the weekend, for special occasions or because his wife isn't there, so he can treat them as much as he likes. Debora, however, has the responsibility not only to cook for herself and her nine-year-old son on a very limited budget, but to cook, she felt, healthy and nutritious food and to do so 'properly and from scratch'. Debora lacks Amrit's critical, detached stance and, as a woman and lone parent, Ash's ability to walk free from cooking and only be involved when he chooses to be. So, despite the fact that she's an experienced cook, well used to cooking with fresh, raw foods, her concerns that she 'won't be able to follow a recipe or get it right' and that friends won't enjoy the food she cooks mean she often seeks 'help' from pre-prepared foods. After all, they're there:

> I'm not very good at making lasagne. I just can't get the sauce right. I've tried it a couple of times. I'd like to be able to make lasagne because everyone loves it but the last time I made it, it came out bland and tasteless even though I followed the recipe. I actually got a friend of mine who's a chef to tell me what to do with the minced meat

and what herbs to put in and how to make the cheese sauce up. I was thinking of making it with a ready-made cheese sauce to see how that goes because the sauce I made was such a disaster. (Debora)

Rather than our technical skills, it is our approach to cooking that influences what and how we cook, 'approach to cooking' being made up of the attitudes and beliefs about cooking that we share with others, our personal identifications as people who cook and our confidence in cooking and the degree to which we find it an effort, arising in part from our tacit, unseen skills and academic knowledge. (There are, of course, wider and more numerous influences on our approach to cooking and the food choices we make. These include the financial and practical resources and access to different kinds of foods, shopping facilities and sources of learning available to us. They also include life stage, income, religious and cultural background and social and economic grouping, as well as agricultural and food distribution, retailing, town planning and educational, transport and health policies. These influences were not specifically researched in the study upon which this book is based but they are a main and very accessible focus of other research and debate.[12])

For any one cook or person who cooks, on any one cooking occasion, a myriad of different influences – confidences, uncertainties, attitudes, beliefs, perceived rewards for perceived efforts, abilities and indentifications – come into play. In many ways, Kate and Jules, for example, have very similar lives. They are both in their mid-thirties, have two young children, live with partners who work full-time and work part-time themselves, Kate as a lecturer and Jules as a journalist. As cooks, they both agree that they have reasonable access to food, financially and practically, but feel pushed for time. Yet for Kate and Jules cooking means very different things and they are two very different cooks.

Kate is 'the cook who hates cooking' that we met in Chapter 5: the skilled and seemingly capable cook who prepares and provides food for her family from 'when she wakes to when she sleeps', as she put it, the cook who, in a bid to distance herself from any 'offending' link with domesticity, relies heavily on pre-prepared foods and ready meals.

Kate places a higher value on dishes and recipes than on what she calls 'made-up' food. She's not very sure about combinations of ingredients that haven't been tried and tested. For her, good cooking is not about looking through the fridge and making something from 'what you've got':

There are all sorts of dubious practices going on here [in the first of two descriptions of making a one-pot stew, or something similar, in the oven], I mean, I wouldn't make anything with an Oxo cube because I think they taste really salty and I don't particularly like casseroles with potatoes in. It all sounds a bit like you've bunged your leftovers in. If I was doing a casserole, it wouldn't be to use up anything that was left over, it would be because I wanted to create something nice. (Kate)

It's not likely anyway, she pointed out, because she only ever buys specific ingredients for specific dishes and recipes she's planned to cook. There aren't any leftovers to use up, she laughed, because she always cooks with jars of ready-to-heat sauces, chilled pasta, bags of prepared salad leaves and ready-made dressing, individual yogurts, cakes, sliced bread and cartons of juice. She doesn't 'keep much in' in the way of rice, beans and pulses, oil, sugar, dried fruits, spices and herbs. Kate's 'not very sure about spontaneity in any form', she said, and likes to be planned, to always know where she'll be and what she'll be doing. A Saturday shopping trip (and a once-a-week shop goes unquestioned as being socially conventional and entirely normal) relies on the diary for the week ahead and involves picking foods for each meal. She likes to plan and know in advance exactly what she will serve her son's friends when they come to tea on Tuesday, what is for lunch on Sundays and that she has enough packed lunch goodies or breakfast cereal for the week ahead. Neatly categorized and identifiable pre-prepared foods fit her needs to designate and allocate perfectly:

> Two or three weekends ago we ended up with friends arriving on Friday [who] left Saturday morning and within an hour some more friends arrived with their two children. So I had meals to think about for the Friday night, Saturday and Sunday night. And when I have to factor in multiple meals I would tend to prepare less and buy things from Marks and Spencer, say … everything, lock, stock and barrel. (Kate)

'Ready meals' and 'convenience foods' also help her get over the hurdle of wanting to be able to enjoy a wide variety of foods and cuisines without actually having, or having to be able, to cook them.

Kate is fully aware that she uses pre-prepared food in a climate where they are seen as the scourge of good diet and family health and unity, but food is not that high on her priority list, she explains. She likes it over and done with so she can relax with her husband or go out with her boys, to the park or to play rugby. Spending time with her family is far more important, she feels, than standing in the kitchen and cooking for them.

Jules is a very different kind of cook from Kate. She generally dislikes using recipes, except perhaps on special occasions, and is extremely confident about either cooking without them or adapting them and making do. She is also far less likely to meal-plan than Kate and usually 'makes it up', designing and cooking spontaneously from a wide-ranging store of provisions and frequent, sometimes daily, shopping trips. She doesn't tend to buy food with a dish, recipe, particular meal or even occasion in mind but looks for what is fresh, what might be a bargain. 'We always buy lots of vegetables and if you've got those and you've got your staples like rice and pasta in the cupboard, which we invariably do, then you can always make a risotto or something.' Though it is Kate who gained a cookery qualification at school, Jules is a relatively experienced home cook who appears to have the tacit skills that, along with her non-prescriptive approach, allow her to adapt, improvise and substitute, recreate food she has eaten elsewhere and meet the taste preferences of her family:

> If I said to my sister 'oh this is really nice' she's the sort of person who would tend just send you the recipes. She's a very organized person. But if it was someone else I might just say 'ooh, what's that flavour?' I mean it's not everyone you would want to say 'oh, will you write the recipe down?', particularly if it's someone you don't know that well. It's a bit of an imposition! I'd just quiz them about what was in it and try and have a go. (Jules)
>
> [On reading a recipe for soup] I wouldn't bother pushing it through a sieve. Well, I'd probably do it pretty much like this. Yes [reading], that's how I make soup. I don't think I'd be bothered about it being smooth and things like that. I wouldn't put flavours in I didn't think the children would like ... the spices and that. (Jules)

Food and cooking are a priority for Jules and she and her partner prefer, whenever possible, to use 'fresh', 'raw' foods. They also like to eat with their two young daughters and usually make sure that one of them is home in the evenings to cook – during weekdays at least. At the weekends they like to 'go to a bit more of an effort'. They might make something that involves more complex techniques, perhaps, that is new or a little different. (If she is alone, though, say, on a Friday evening, Jules said she probably wouldn't bother cooking and would happily get a takeaway.) Jules also uses the weekend to cook with her daughters. They often help out with the evening meal during the week but when there is more time on a Saturday or Sunday they cook more for fun, making things like cakes and jelly. Maybe they would make a pizza together for a picnic, she said. It would be fun and it would make her proud to see them cut it up and serve it to their friends.

Despite her dislike of domesticity, Kate insists that she does enjoy cooking when she has time and is left alone in the kitchen. She doesn't necessarily see weekends in themselves as time to 'make an effort', as Jules does, but she does enjoy cooking for guests (though cooking for guests doesn't necessarily mean cooking 'from scratch') and will often spend time beforehand thinking about what she will make or browsing through her cookbooks for recipes she hasn't made for a while. She may even look for inspiration to try something new. On the whole, though, Kate prefers and feels more confident about serving things she has made before, dishes or foods that she is confident her friends or guests will like. Knowing that they have enjoyed the food and their evening together is important, she feels, but she doesn't like that enjoyment to be dependent on her cooking, on what she cooks or how well she cooks it. It's a sentiment felt also by Jules, despite the fact that she's a very different cook. The food isn't the only part of an evening with friends, she explained to me: 'it's a vehicle for having a nice time'.

If there is no simple, straightforward relationship between cooking ability and food choices and practices, then there are clearly implications, as will be discussed in Chapter 8, for policies and campaigns that seek to promote or encourage cooking through teaching cookery skills. There are implications too for theories about the deskilling of domestic cooking and hypotheses about its decline – the assumption being amongst proponents of such theories that if people don't have the skills to cook something they won't cook it and therefore won't acquire the relevant cooking skills to do so even if they so wished. 'It seems unlikely', says Paul Fieldhouse, 'that consumers will buy foods which they do not know how to prepare or that they will attempt to prepare dishes which make undue demands on their cookery skills.'[13] Yet the cooks I spoke with do just that, and sometimes very purposefully. Cooks like David and Ash love a challenge. They like to stretch their skills and learn something new: it is often their very reason for cooking. Indeed many people who cook, like Jules at the weekend, make an effort in this respect at least occasionally. Experimentation and trying out new foods, ingredients and recipes is a well-loved and well-accepted pastime for people who cook.[14] The next chapter looks more fully at theories about the decline of cooking and asks, 'Are we really being deskilled?'

So How is Cooking?

Can We Cook?

Working out whether today's cooks can really cook, whether the skills and knowledge of previous generations have been lost to us, requires that we come to some sort of conclusions about the kinds and levels of cooking skills and knowledge people had and used in the past. Perhaps, for a point of comparison, we need to assess the skills of a specific population at a particular place and point in time. Certainly we have to decide what we mean by 'being able to cook', 'having a cooking skill' or 'being a skilled cook', definitions that take into account not only the many different approaches towards skill and ability that there are but also the numerous ways in which both the verb and noun cook can be interpreted. After all, 'to cook' can mean anything from 'adding heat' to 'making food' to 'cooking properly from scratch'. 'Being a cook' can refer simply to 'someone who prepares food' but it can also be loaded with certain values to do with nurturing and caring or with talent and professionalism. And different interpretations of cook will lead inevitably to different definitions of related concepts like 'skilled cook' and 'cooking ability'. Taking the verb cook to mean the everyday task of preparing and providing food for the household or family, for example, will result in some very different conclusions about who can cook or who does cook than if its meaning is associated with contemporary ideals of 'proper cooking' and all the connotations that has of effort, technical expertise and 'important' meals.

So what does 'being able to cook' mean? Does it refer to an ability to prepare healthy food that fits dietary requirements? To be 'able to cook' does someone have to be able to cook effortlessly with all the different kinds and types of foods available to them in the locale in which they live or shop for food? There are many shops where I live in London that sell foods I have absolutely no idea what to call, never mind how to cook – any number of sauces and condiments, dried and fresh vegetables, cuts of meat and types of fish that I have never encountered on cookery courses or made use of in any of the restaurants and kitchens I have worked in. Food critic Dara Moskowitz writes of a similar unfamiliarity with the products sold on the South-East Asian stalls of her local farmers' market in Minneapolis. 'I know my collards from my kale from my chard, celery, celeriac,' she says, 'yet even with such vegetable skills ... I'm stunned speechless more than I care to admit ... There they are mocking me: two dozen types of greens arranged in a green-on-green rainbow ... Greens with tendrils. Greens with flowers. Greens with silky leaves, with stubby spines, with hollow stems.'[1]

'Being able to cook' with these greens might mean knowing how to prepare them in a 'traditional' manner, how to do so for the greatest nutritional benefit or in ways that are most appealing for the whole family. It might also mean 'cooking them well', reaching a particular level of technical standard. But whose standard? Presented with a chicken on holiday in Malaysia once by the family who ran the little guesthouse I was staying in (wanting to offer something in return for their hospitality, my friends had suggested that I, 'a chef back home', cook dinner one night), I was appalled. Old, stringy and with a few feathers still attached and looking nothing like the chickens I was used to, it came accompanied by a bunch of tired, limp greens that owed little to the 'rainbow' described by Moskowitz, a huge cleaver and a single wok over a precariously positioned gas cylinder. I managed to cook something vaguely edible, I believe, but I had no idea how to make the most of those greens, or, in truth, whether to use the leaves or the stalks. As for the chicken, I knew it had to be sliced thinly if anyone was to be able to chew it, but I no more knew how to handle the cleaver without risking the removal of my fingers than I had the physical, manipulative skills to do so.

As can be seen clearly in a report from the UK's Food Standards Agency on a government-supported evaluation of the 'food and nutrition competencies' of young people, the consideration of 'reaching a standard' adds a further layer of complexity and ambiguity to any understanding of what cooking ability means. The agency's researchers found that respondents who did food technology at school or who cooked at home had greater confidence in using raw ingredients and kitchen utensils. 'However,' they argue, 'this did not always mean that their meal [cooked as part of the evaluation process] turned out better.' The authors of the report provide no further comment on this judgement, one that immediately raises the question, by what or whose standards? And, reading between the lines, despite diet and healthy eating being the overriding point of the study, it doesn't seem that their verdict on which meals were best was made with regard to the nutritional status of the meal.[2] However, a hint as to where the basis of their appraisal lies may perhaps be glimpsed in the words of celebrity chef Gary Rhodes writing in *Cook School*, the magazine of the Food Standards Agency-approved Focus on Food campaign. 'Young people should be taught to make and cook well-crafted, good-quality dishes,' writes Rhodes, his particular standard, even for children and learner cooks, it seems, resting unhesitatingly with technical ability and prescriptive, set combinations of foods[3] – presumably, considering his highly trained, professional background, those that come from what food historian Christina Hardyment calls the 'French gastronomic tradition'.[4]

There is a further layer of complexity still with regard to the concept of 'being able to cook' – understanding, at a more precise level, what is meant by 'being skilled'. To explore the idea of 'being able to cook' it is necessary to think about how and when someone can be said as having reached a point where they have acquired a cooking skill, an ability to use a certain technique, maybe, or to carry out a particular cooking task. What do surveys mean when they ask their respondents about their confidence or ability to, for example, fry, bake, microwave, cook white fish or make a sponge cake? Take frying fish, for example, frying often being used alongside grilling or roasting in research trying to assess cooking skills and abilities to follow dietary guidelines. How does an individual qualify as 'being able to fry' fish? Are they required to have an understanding of the chemistry at work, knowledge of the best kinds of equipment to use or types and cuts of fish that are 'better' fried rather than baked or steamed? Does 'being able to fry fish' refer to an ability to cook fish in the style or to the degree of doneness that those for whom you cook prefer? Or does it refer to more external standards of good cooking which demand that for fish to be cooked 'properly' it must be almost opaque in appearance and just beginning to flake easily?[5] (In my time cooking professionally, I found that many people prefer fish to be drier and 'well cooked', crispy even.) A more person-centred and domestic approach to understanding cooking skills may suggest, on the other hand, that in order to be thought 'skilled' the cook has to be able to fry fish with one eye on the three-year-old, whilst getting rid of the salesman on the doorstep, or timed to perfection with the arrival of guests at the dining table.

Cooking ability, as I have pointed out on a number of occasions in this book, has, to date, rarely been associated with this level of complexity. And conclusions and treatises on the deskilling of cooking in the home have similarly and accordingly been treated as simple and straightforward.[6] George Ritzer, for example, argues that, in pursuit of contemporary, Western ideals of convenience, efficiency, predictability and control, home cooking is being deskilled through the use of ready-made foods, recipes and technologies such as the microwave. Ritzer's explanations and conclusions, however, arise from a very task-centred, technical approach. Based on pre-prepared foods, packet mixes and step-by-step instructions, cooking today, he argues, 'requires few and easy skills' and resembles little more than a 'game of connect-the-dots or painting by numbers'[7]. Ritzer is, of course, using home cooking symbolically and looking at overall trends rather than specifics related to individuals, but it is still worth being aware that he doesn't approach cooking as an activity that takes place within different contexts and for different reasons. Nor does he see cooks as having different and very varied approaches or cooking skills as personal and value-laden. His use of home cooking to illustrate the increased rationalization and deskilling of the tasks of everyday life is immediately made problematic by the cook who reheats ready meals during the week but makes an effort to 'cook properly' at the weekend. (My research found, as does other research, that few people rely solely on 'pre-prepared' foods.[8]) Like the post-war cooks Laura Shapiro describes, who might at times cook grand dishes like coq au vin or oysters Rockefeller 'from scratch' but at others 'put curry powder, canned grated Parmesan and bacon into a dish called Zucchini Creole' or create 'Gourmet Pate de Fois Gras out of cream cheese, liverwurst and a can of bouillon', Aidan, one of the cooks who took part in my research, used two cookery books and three different types of fish to make fresh sushi, the same Aidan who the next day made a chicken casserole from a frozen, ready-jointed chicken and instant gravy granules.[9] Ritzer and many others who argue that cooking is being deskilled – whether as a consequence of modernity, as a purposeful practice of a power-hungry food industry or as a dismissal of 'proper' cuisine by the masses – tend to fit food into two nice, neat groups. On the one hand are 'pre-prepared' and 'ready-made' foods and on the other are the 'fresh', 'raw' and 'unprepared': two types of food that employ two different sets of skills. Nor do they seem to easily acknowledge the cook who enjoys the challenge of new foods, recipes and dishes, who consciously attempts to push him- or herself and acquire new skills.[10] The challenge-driven hobby cook for one can easily be presented as sitting uncomfortably alongside theories of the demise of home cooking.

The deskilling of domestic cooking can, however, be interpreted very differently. For Les Gofton writing on consumer culture, in an era when convenience foods are becoming ever more popular and cooking is being squeezed out of the everyday (as he sees it), the cooks' only chance to demonstrate their abilities and skills has become limited to times of recreation, play and leisure, times when what they do can easily be viewed as trivial and of little consequence. This, Gofton says, is the much overlooked, debasing and dehumanizing aspect of deskilling.[11] Yet not everyone would agree. A Marxist perspective that links self-worth and self-identity only with what is 'useful' misses the point, say Betsy and Stephen Wearing, for example. Leisure, serious leisure like mountaineering or being in a book club rather than hedonic, casual leisure such as walking in the park or watching a firework display,[12] even if not self-defining, can enhance our sense of who we are.[13] As food historian Mary Drake-McFeely suggests, cooking can readily 'be made complicated enough to provide intense challenge'. No longer only seen as family-centred and domestic, cooking has become, she argues, 'a challenge for over-achievers and an area of competition for people who have become accustomed to constant striving at work or play'.[14]

Leon Rappaport has made the point that for most of history meals have consisted of whatever meagre foods are available boiled in a pot over a fire or stove. Indeed, he explains, even in twentieth-century America, high cuisine for his East European immigrant parents meant 'nothing more than a boiled chicken, with feet, neck and liver included'.[15] Likewise, the older cooks in Luce Giard's study in

France in the 1980s can remember times when there was no talk of dishes, recipes and cuisine, times when food, cooking and eating amounted to little more than buckwheat porridge and buckwheat pancakes, with the occasional bit of salt pork or potato at the weekend – a variety so limited that, even if cooking skills are understood as complex and person-centred, surely the range used was severely limited. Maybe not, for Giard also describes how cooks of the past – who cooked in times before food was sorted, graded, cleaned, deboned, parboiled and pre-baked, carved, sliced, diced and pre-packaged – would have required a whole range of abilities that most today would probably not even recognize. They had to squabble over prices with market stall and store holders and work out whether the food they bought – vegetables, eggs, milk, flour and butter as well as meat and fish – was fresh. Through endless techniques of plucking, singeing, skinning, filleting, salting, smoking, drying, soaking, roasting, peeling, pickling and poaching, they had to clean, dress and preserve food as well as cook it. They had to learn too how to keep ants, weevils and roaches from the stored food and stop it rotting and spoiling. 'One examined each jar closely to detect the beginnings of mold,' Giard writes, 'one tested with a finger the firmness of the paraffin wax that plugged the mouth of the jar, one tightened the paper that closed off the jars of jam.'[16] Similarly, Ruth Schwartz Cowan describes how making something as 'simple' as pottage (a one-pot, boiled mixture of whatever grains, vegetables and meat were available) on a farm in America in the mid-eighteenth century might utilize any number of long forgotten skills. Water would have to be collected from streams and external wells and carried in buckets made at home and by hand. The fire built and maintained throughout the day would require both gathering wood and storing it in such a way that it would not ruin. Any meat used would have to come from pigs and cattle raised and butchered on the farm. Vegetables, fruit and herbs would have to be grown. Grain would have to be both grown and milled. There would be wooden spoons for skimming and stirring and trenchers for serving only if someone could make them, utensils that would then have to be cleaned, along with the blackened iron pots and kettles that sat on the stove all day, with sand, rags and twigs.[17] The histories of cooking for the urban and rural poor are a litany of coping skills, of feeding families while contending with cramped, poorly lit and poorly ventilated conditions without sufficient healthy, unadulterated or hygienic food, resources or facilities. Those of the middle classes are concerned with budgeting and etiquette, managing staff and keeping up with fashions, fads and 'the Joneses'.[18]

It seems there are skills we haven't lost but cannot seem to see and skills we may have lost but don't seem to mourn. The focus of those who, for whatever reason, rue the decline and deskilling of cooking is far more strongly placed on 'end' tasks, like making dough and baking bread, than on less obvious tasks, like growing grain and turning it into flour or keeping yeast or a fire alive. As Ruth

Schwartz Cowan points out, 'if a resistance coil comes loose on a twentieth-century electric oven, no one in the household is likely either to know what to do or to have the appropriate tools at hand'.[19] This is alienation from the tools that cooks work with, but seems to instil far less worry than an 'inability to bake'. My own brother (a frozen pizza devotee) on hearing about the subject of my doctorate study was quick to remark that washing your clothes on the stones down by the river was probably very skilful and socially bonding but it's not something we feel we should miss. Shouldn't we be thankful, asks Rachel Laudan in her plea for culinary modernism, for the processing of grains and other foods that has removed the need for any number of thankless, back-breaking tasks?[20] Or for the kitchen equipment like dishwashers and extractor fans that, as Luce Giard puts it, 'make the stench of cold grease disappear'?[21]

Some may argue that new skills have simply replaced old skills. We may no longer be able to judge the heat of a stove or store apples so that they don't rot but cooking, feeding and eating today, says Mary Drake McFeely, means ceaselessly keeping up with 'the science of nutrition' and the 'business of consumerism'.[22] Likewise, Luce Giard sees new knowledge in the 'hermeneutics' of label reading and in the blenders, pressure cookers, coffee grinders, espresso makers, deep-fryers and 'hot plates with sensors, inductive heating surfaces [and] sequential burners' that come with no one to demonstrate or explain how to use them.[23] Technologies like the industrial mills of nineteenth-century America, which helped shift 'home baking' from the production of simple spoon breads to more complex yeast breads and cakes,[24] and the food processor, which allows Mary Drake McFeely to ignore the tedious tasks of chopping, slicing and squeezing and concentrate instead on making mayonnaise and aioli,[25] may encourage, even demand, more ambitious cooking. Today's cook, it has been argued, must know a lot more 'about the composition of meals and techniques of preparation'. They must 'be able to follow manifold fashions'. Cooking for a family is now, rather than routinized and relatively skill-less, a far more demanding task than it ever was,[26] a social pressure that can be seen even in the responses of schoolchildren, who, when asked what they would like to be able to make by a study for the journal *Health Which?*, didn't suggest breakfast for mother, cookies, burgers or TV snacks. They wanted to be able to make 'roast dinners with all the trimmings', 'authentic Indian and Chinese dishes' and 'luxury cakes and puddings'.[27] This social pressure is apparent too, perhaps, in the numerous different ways respondents who took part in a study of eating out associated with preparing and serving steak. It wasn't just keen cooks and foodies who casually identified that steaks could be 't-bone, rib, burger, sirloin, rump, fillet or Chateaubriand' and that they could be accompanied by 'mushrooms, peppers, mushroom sauce, onions, mustard, or barbecue relish' and served 'rare, medium rare and well-done' and as steak Diane, steak with baluchi dressing and tampquina steak with chilli.[28] The different kinds of foods, dishes, meals and so on mentioned by the thirty people who informed my research covered, single spaced, roughly six sides of A4 paper.

Home cooking from this perspective can look anything but routinized and deskilled. Conscious of the rise of cooking for leisure alongside pre-prepared foods and convenience eating, Tim Lang and Martin Caraher have put forward the theory that, rather than a deskilling, recent years have seen a revision of culinary skills as both lifestyles and home cooking practices fragment and are restructured.[29] Though they too highlight the individualist nature of cooking, the findings of the study upon which this book is based add a yet further layer of complexity to the cooking skills debate. For, rather than a deskilling or reskilling, they highlight the potentially changeless and constant nature of many kinds of domestic cooking skills: the skills which cooks use whatever the generation or society, the foods available, the current fashions and compatibility rules and whether they are cooking with 'raw' or 'pre-prepared' foods: abilities to design, plan, manage, evaluate and meet others' needs. It is notable, I think, that the community cookbooks written by women in early twentieth-century America and described by Mary Drake McFeely provide favoured combinations of ingredients and instructions for such things as bread making techniques far less often than they do 'helpful suggestions about fitting the baking into the day's work'.[30]

Appreciating the Cook

For those I spoke with, good cooks are those who make interesting and different food, food that is good to look at. Good cooking means 'proper cooking', guests and technical ability. Creativity is highly valued, but for the most part only if it is connected with professional, glamorous and sophisticated cooking and titled dishes from recipes and cookery books. It is seen as having little to do with the school cook's inventiveness with leftovers and the daily special, or the hospital cook's ability to conjure up new combinations daily within a strict budget. Nor is it associated with the home cook who appears to effortlessly summon up a meal from the nearly expired 'best by' tubs and packets in the fridge. That's just 'throwing things together'.

If only certain kinds of cooking and certain types of skills are associated with 'being able to cook', then those who don't measure up on those given terms can easily be judged deskilled, unable or 'not very good', even if they do have other kinds of cooking abilities. Somebody who can prepare food that will appeal to the whole family or manage to cook a full meal with two gas rings and a couple of dilapidated pans may be judged as 'incompetent' if cooking skills are only being taken to refer to technical competence, nutritional knowledge or the ability to make 'good to look at' weekend-type food. Research has shown that the less well off are better equipped with the kinds of managing, budgeting and organizational skills that are,[31] it seems from the research upon which this book is based, less socially recognized as being 'of value'.[31] I found the people I spoke with had a whole range of cooking skills and that individual cooks had very different kinds of expertise. Bearing in mind that I did not design my study to appraise how skilled cooks today are, I would say from the accounts informants gave me that Debora managed wonderfully to prepare healthy food – none of it exactly haute cuisine, as she said – that appealed to her friends and family. Liz was expert at fitting food provisioning around her other daily, household work. Patrick and David had excellent technical skill and knowledge of worldwide cuisines and food practices and Amrit had a uniquely methodical and rational approach that gave him a highly confident take on cooking. I would suggest that, at least in part, both declarations from food writers on the death of cooking and academic and policy allegiance to the deskilling argument result from a recognition of only certain types of cooking skills.

Despite their range of abilities, however, the cooks I spoke with did not acknowledge cooking in the home as a 'skilled' occupation or activity. The notion of home cooking and household food provision as a task or recognized craft with its own set of skills and standards was nowhere to be seen in their accounts of their experiences and approaches to cooking. For Luce Giard, Bravermanesque in her approach, it is not so much the disappearance of certain techniques or ways of doing things but the demise of the craft of home cooking – the loss of the love of the materials involved, pride in what is produced and appreciation of it as skilled work – that is what makes for its deskilling.[32] Yet cooking, Veronica Beechey argues, has never been defined as 'skilled work', unless, that is, it is the cooking of chefs who work in glamorous restaurants and who cook commercially for wealthy and high-status paying customers. Their work is more likely to be seen as 'skilled', not because anyone has sat down and analysed the difficulty of what they do and compared it with that of other people who cook, but because those for whom they cook have greater social power and are involved in the visible circulation of money.[33] Whatever their ability the, usually female, home cook involved in the domestic and the everyday 'that has not market value, that has neither profit nor glory'[34] can never be seen as being similarly 'skilled'. A capitalist-oriented society, sharply divided as it is into public and private sectors, simply does not allow it.

Not all surveys or studies of cooking have been as limited and culturally specific as that which asked its respondents how confident they would feel about frying an egg, baking a cake, making a white sauce or cooking a Sunday roast.[35] (And note that these were the *only* tasks about which it enquired.) Yet many,[36] like a recent food skills initiative,[37] focus on some very 'Western', often French professional-cooking-based, techniques. Roasting, blanching, braising, seasoning (with salt and pepper?), poaching, baking blind, folding in and creaming ('to beat butter and margarine and sugar together until fluffy and light-coloured, usually when making a cake') being regularly mentioned. Stir-frying is often included, admittedly, but in a singular, 'added on' way – what about pot-stewing, red-cooking, splashing, clear-simmering, cold-mixing and sizzling?[38] A nod to external, 'foreign' influences that brings to mind home economist Mary Leah de Zwart's argument that her subject has often taken a somewhat racialist, 'Cook's tour' approach to including foods and cooking methods from different nationalities and ethnic groups.[39] In a socially and culturally mixed society it does not seem entirely appropriate for the Cook Club page of the British Nutrition Foundation's website, like many other surveys, campaigns and interventions referred to in this book, to concentrate on culture- and possibly generation-specific 'basic cooking skills', like making shortcrust pastry, mashed potato and a roux sauce and lining a Swiss roll tin.[40]

Nostalgia for Home Cooking

Perhaps it is too cynical to suggest that recent declarations from food writers and campaigners that people cannot cook any more because they no longer know how to boil an egg, cook brisket[41] or 'make the simplest dishes [like] Shepherd's Pie'[42], are little more than a way for certain social groups to discriminate themselves from others and assert their 'good taste' and status of 'being knowledgeable'. Maybe conclusions like these are little more than the protestations of a group whose previously dominant food tastes and ways of cooking have been supplanted by those of another, the incapable objects of their concern being in fact quite capable cooks, but cooks who make quite different kinds of foods. Gauging 'cooking know-how', as the authors of a French study of food attitudes and behaviours point out, is reliant on the kinds of foods chosen to do so, the findings of their own study being weighted, they felt, by their use of 'traditional French dishes' like vegetable gratins, home-made cakes, beef bourguignon and cottage pie as a point of measurement – foods, they concluded in the end, that 'may not be fully representative of contemporary consumption and culinary trends'.[43]

Popular fears over the death of cooking may be more nostalgic than they are cynical. As Eric Arnould and Linda Price found in a study of home-made food traditions, 'cooking from scratch' and 'homemade meals', vague though those concepts are, readily produce childhood memories and evocative, idealized images of mother, grandparents and the family.[44] When everyday life has become ever more hectic, technology-driven and urbanized, are our quests for rural idylls, proper food and family meals and our 'celebration of the labor-intensive cooking processes of the past', asks David Sutton in his anthropology of food and memory, simply a nostalgia for something we feel to be 'real' – romanticized and ultimately unreal nostalgia that we can easily adopt because we don't have to clean the grate or blackened kettle with twigs and because we have the choice not to 'cook'?[45]

There is nothing new, as I said in Chapter 4, in worries about the state of cooking. Laura Shapiro has described, for example, how 'when stoves were first introduced a feeling of unutterable repugnance was felt by all classes toward adopting them'. For a whole generation, she explains, they were used solely in schools, shops, courtrooms and other public places because only the open hearth, it was felt, could be the true centre of home life. Later, in the 1950s, she continues, food writers and media presenters like James Beard would spend years 'gloomily monitoring the disappearance of old-fashioned good cooking'. Beard, like many today, she writes, 'believed the housewife was losing her way, forfeiting her skills, mindlessly surrendering to packaged foods whenever they beckoned'.[46] The deskilling and downfall of home cooking has been here before. Like Anne Murcott's remarks on the disappearance of family meals (referring to a 1920s study in Indiana, which found that people had similar concerns), 'it is exactly parallel to Pimlott's observation that it is "part of the tradition that Christmas is never as it used to be"'. Every generation looks back on the one before and 'not only finds it altered, but judges it wanting'. 'It is a constant', Murcott writes, 'that the past is mourned, the golden age feared lost.'[47]

The grandmothers who feature in Carol Field's book on Italian recipes and traditions, however, as David Sutton explains, can't help but secretly rejoice that they have found new, time-saving ways of preparing their 'traditional' dishes. Now, they say, they can cook flat breads on more efficient, metal rather than terracotta discs and buy puff pastry ready-made in the shops.[48] Would anyone really want to go back to a time when cooks were called upon to make flowers out of mashed potato spooned into the middle of tinned pears?[49] Surely no one would want to be faced too often with this recipe:

> For 1000 lbs of fresh meat use 40 lbs of salt, 10 lbs of sugar, four lbs of black pepper. Rub the meat thoroughly, using half the mixture … Pack in box or lay on table … Let lay ten days then rub the remainder of mixture into meat leaving at least 20 days or two days for every pound of meat for the larger pieces, such as hams. Brush off or wash off in warm water, hang up to dry and smoke several days with hickory or apple wood. Sack all hams, putting only one in each sack.[50]

The ham still wouldn't be 'cooked', of course. And, baking being seen by the author as superior to boiling, that would mean at least six hours in a stove that would have to be stoked throughout. It would also mean pounds of pastry, potentially far more difficult to make than it is today because flour types were not uniform, brands varied and therefore measurements could not be relied on. Deeply unfashionable though it seems, there must surely be a place for food modernism and a chance to embrace kitchen technologies – the technologies that mean the household cook no longer has to spend forty-four hours a week, as was general in the 1900s, or even ten, the norm in 1975, preparing and cleaning up after meals.[51] Do women really want to go back to a time when their identity and reputation were dependent on what or how well they cooked or attached to their recipe for cherry pie or chocolate cake?[52] Not for nothing did the editor of the Napton cookbook (from which the methods for preserving and cooking ham above are taken) interrupt the recipes with a quick and unknowingly prophetic paean to ready-prepared, 'convenient' foods:

> Oh weary mothers, rolling dough
> Don't you wish that food would grow?
> How happy all the world would be,
> With a cookie bush and a doughnut tree[53]

Much has been written, not only about the health benefits but also about the depth of experience and sense of well-being associated with cooking from fresh, raw and unprepared foods.[54] Yet all of those who took part in my research felt very strongly that pre-prepared and ready-prepared foods had a definite place in, and could even greatly enhance, their lives. 'They're good to fall back on ... and for lunch ... or if you just want something quick ... or for families,' said Claire. Acceptance and appreciation of 'convenience' foods came accompanied with an acknowledgement that they weren't as good as 'real' foods. 'I think they're good,' said Patrick, 'as long as you avoid the muck.' 'If they're not just taken as the be-all and end-all, I think they're wonderful. You can make a really interesting meal in just twenty minutes,' commented Kirsty. Margaret's doubts too, couldn't dampen her enthusiasm for the products of a modern food system:

> I love the variety and the wide availability of dozens of things, things you never used to be able to get. I think I'm fairly predictable really. I mean I'm not terribly thrilled with the amounts of processed stuff you can get but on the other hand, you know, I've no objection to going round Marks and Spencer for something ready-made! I love the choice, the wide availability and I love the constant new things. (Margaret)

Even those who purported to dislike pre-prepared products couldn't help but 'admit' that they sometimes used, enjoyed eating and welcomed the variety. As John said, 'Occasionally I try something and I'm disappointed by it but on the other hand if I've got a sore throat or something ... would you include things like baked beans and tinned tomatoes? I'm happy with those as long as you can buy the low-fat versions and the rest of it.' 'Ready-made' and 'prepared' food was seen as an intrinsic part of contemporary lifestyles, where there is little time to 'spend all day' cooking or shopping. Martin explained that he felt 'you can eat well and healthily without cooking' but that 'there's a large part of our lives with pre-prepared foods'. He still felt 'it was cheating' but, comparing his life with that of his parents, he said he preferred having a more challenging job and a 'bigger and better social life' than they did and spending time making his house look nice. 'My mum cooked,' he said, 'but our house looked the same for years.' The people who took part in my study accepted that fresh foods were probably more nutritious and that baking a cake or sitting down with their family to a freshly prepared meal was sometimes enjoyable and worthwhile. Few, however, could see anything life-enhancing in substituting their free time for tasks like 'washing potatoes', 'growing your own lettuce' or 'plucking a chicken'. As Liz commented, 'I think the more choice the better basically. I'm impressed by people who make everything from scratch but I wouldn't demean people who eat prepared foods occasionally. I always use frozen veg. I'm not going to shell my own peas, am I?'

History is populated by people who eagerly abandoned the cuisine so valued by today's 'culinary Luddites', as food historian and writer Rachel Lauden calls those who are prone to disparage today's types of foods and production methods. Those who long for the 'real food' of the past, she goes on to say, but who fail or choose not to see that without processing, pre-preparation and industrialized global methods there would be no Thai fish sauce, udon noodles or estate-bottled olive oil – only endless hard work, illness and upset stomachs, warm milk, tough or rank meat, barely digestible grains and insect-ridden fruit and vegetables, when they're available.[55]

The Cooking Myth

My study revealed that it is not only the reality of cooking in the past that is often obscured by selectivity, lack of analysis and value judgements. Though the people who contributed to my research rarely appeared overtly anxious about cooking (anxiety, following the breakdown of the grammar and rules of food choice, is often seen by scholars as an overriding feature of contemporary food practices[56]), it does appear that some kind of mystique or myth surrounds cooking today: a set of images and ideas that frequently turns cooking ability from what could be an accessible and reachable goal into something that is confused, intimidating and even inhibitory, a myth that arises from the creative cooking ideal and the high value placed on professionalism, variety and natural ability, from stylized and quantified media representation and a lack of any real appreciation of the range of skills and knowledge involved in cooking in the home. Cooking and 'being able to cook' have taken such a direction that, though there are those occasions when we may be inspired by the myth and love to meet a challenge or make an effort, there are plenty of other times when we feel that cooking is so much of an effort that we lighten our load. On at least some occasions and to some extent, people choose and use the kinds of 'prepared', 'convenient' foods that can alleviate the organization and technical skills required, that can hand over the responsibility for their family appeal or 'success' to others.

The cooking myth is one that has emerged in earlier studies. The confident, fearful and hopeful cooks who took part in a Scottish food skills initiative, for example, found it difficult to put into words but felt somehow 'disempowered by the process of cooking': 'I'd love to be able to cook lots of things from scratch,' said one, 'but I just haven't attempted it.'[57] The stakes of 'being able to cook' are high. A 'housewife' who took part in Anne Oakley's study of housework regrets that she is probably trying to be better at cooking than she really needs to be. 'I feel I've got to cook something interesting,' she explains, 'and the effort that goes into that every night is a bit much really.'[58]

Experiential and, in particular, situated learning theories suggest that skills are best learned, practised and improved on incidentally rather than purposefully and in authentic contexts as part of everyday life. Confident practice and learning of a craft or activity are dependent on observation of others at work, the imitation, application and adaptation of what has been observed and the chance to collaborate, discuss and assess experiences. In other words, learning requires social relationships and interaction, a 'community of practice'.[59] Yet representations and meanings of cooking in contemporary Western societies are regularly removed from recognizable daily experiences. In the words of Oakley's cooks and the accounts of those who took part in my study, allusions to the 'different' world of professional cookery and the creative cookery ideal – the image of cooking as good to look at, technically competent, interesting, sophisticated and requiring effort – are frequent. These are representations often seen in the media too. Alan Warde's comparative study of food columns in women's magazines in 1968 and 1992, for example, shows that, whereas cooking in the earlier period was most usually associated with family food and family care, in the latter 'the food stands for itself, the result of effective performance, a demonstration of culinary expertise or knowledge about food'.[60] The image of cooking so often given to us today is that of special occasions and dishes, guests, historical and geographical knowledge, glossy, beautiful pictures, restaurant-style food, technical achievement and professional, highly experienced cooks. We are encouraged to constantly try out new foods, methods, recipes and combinations of ingredients, moving on before we have any grounding or depth of knowledge and understanding. Rarely are we presented with the mundane, daily reality of cooking. And, when we are, it is deemed deskilled and skill-less in comparison. Therein, perhaps, lies the true debasement and degradation of home cooking today.

Julia Child was a popular cook, famous in part for the numerous errors she made on television, dropping food or flipping a pancake onto the stove and then putting it back in the pan, writes Laura Shapiro. Yet these 'mistakes' were purposeful, a means of instilling a sense of approachability and 'oneness' and belied the fact that she spent hours preparing for each programme.[61] I've seen many a television chef pass a huge twelve-inch knife to a participating 'civilian' and watch them struggle whilst they show off their own superlative, super-fast chopping skills to the camera, a state of affairs that would be much altered with something smaller and less weighty, a couple of sacks of carrots and an impatient head chef – speedily chopped and perfect slices of carrot being based, I would argue, not on some kind of special, gift-like talent or dexterity, but on plenty of practice and a correctly sized knife. These are the images, though, that media theorists believe shape the 'logics and perspectives we use in perceiving reality' and our 'expectations of everyday life'[62] – unqualified and decontextualized images that most usually place cooking firmly, not in the world of the everyday and the low-status work of the hospital cook, the fast-food grill chef and the put-upon parent, but in a glamorous world of professional artistry.[63] Even children, asked in a UK study to draw a picture of someone cooking in their kitchen and a meal they would like to share with Grubb when he visits them from his planet, came up with 'lots of drawings of celebrity chefs'.[64]

Some of the cooks who took part in my research, like David, Patrick, Ash and Margaret, sometimes enjoy rising to a cooking challenge but 'fear of failure means a lot of young women don't even begin cooking', says cookery writer Jill Dupleix. 'They want to do things very well or not at all.'[65] Today, cooking, even if it is something you are not overtly nervous about, can often be disconcerting and 'not worth the effort'. Part of the cooking myth is that 'being able to cook' is not about feeding work and healthy, enjoyable eating, it is about good cooking, success and failure, 'getting things right' and 'getting it wrong'. Eating out and ready meals offer Anne, who took apart in Alan Warde and Lydia Martens's study of eating out, the opportunity to eat lasagne, something she feels she's not very good at making because 'the pasta is never right'. They also offer her the point of comparison by which she judges the 'success' of the lasagne she cooks herself (and invariably considers wanting),[66] successful cooking being linked, so the myth goes, with the achievement of the variety and invariability offered by pre-prepared foods, the technical and presentation standards of professional chefs and media representations and the emphasis in contemporary, Western society on set methods and established, 'expected' outcomes. Warde and Martens themselves tell us that 'when people talk of cooking it usually connotes combining and assembling ingredients to *create a dish*'.[67] Elsewhere, an investigation of community food initiatives in Scotland based its appraisal of its informants' cooking ability on their 'repertoire of dishes' whilst also concluding that 'the anxiety of not knowing whether a dish would turn out properly appeared to play a large part in discouraging respondents from trying new techniques'. A lumpy cheese sauce or stodgy rice, say, would reinforce the respondents belief that they weren't very good at cooking and encourage them to use 'easy cook' products like dried packet sauces and boil-in-the-bag rice.[68]

With their ubiquity and our understanding that they are part and parcel of cooking, recipes too contribute to the myth.[69] Their titles, decontextualized yet highly prescriptive and quantified approach, lack of emphasis on tacit knowledge and perfected illustrations of 'correct' dishes suggest, albeit subliminally, that cooking is not about practice and experience. They add to the 'why didn't it work?' intrigue and the culture of 'successful' and 'unsuccessful' cooking. Further, recipes are synonymous with cooking alone, an accepted and desired feature of contemporary cooking practices. And people who cook alone tend not to see the differences and discrepancies that occur between cooks and cooking occasions. They have no one with whom to 'mull over' and disassemble their cooking 'triumphs' and concerns. They can only compare the food they make with the standardized products of the food industry and the perfected culinary images of the mediated society in which they live.

Domestic cooking culture, however, is not just disengaged and 'mythical'. It is also intricate and individualized, with a wealth of different meanings, approaches and abilities. If cooking practices and food choices are to change, then it is to that complex and meaningful cooking culture, not an indeterminate and oversimplified set of cooking skills, to which we must turn. The final chapter looks at what can be done about cooking.

–8–

What to Do about Cooking

The Dichotomies of Cooking

Culinary Luddites, writes Rachel Laudan, regularly attempt to convince us that there are two kinds of food, the pre- and post-global and industrial: 'On the one hand are the traditional and ethnic foods, fresh and natural, local, slow, rural and artisanal, diverse, old, tasty, healthy and authentic. Hurrah! Hurrah! On the other are industrial foods, processed, preserved, global, fast, urban, industrial, homogenous, bland, unhealthy, and artificial Yuk! Yuk! Boo! Boo!'[1] It's a kind of cleaving into two that is also evident in the debates and discourses that surround home cooking today, dichotomies that are stressed perhaps, albeit without clear intention, to strengthen the positioning of the 'good' and the 'bad' and add weight to arguments: real food versus processed food, the fresh and raw versus the pre-prepared and convenient. We either eat alone or with our families. We cook properly by hand or we cheat with gadgets. We use legitimate technologies like the gas oven or modern abominations like the microwave. We cook from scratch or assemble and reheat. We use real, learned, traditional cooking skills or simply join the dots.

Unlike the antinomies of economy and extravagance, health and indulgence, novelty and tradition, care and convenience that Alan Warde found to problematize our food choices,[2] the presentation of cooking in the home as dichotomous – real, traditional and skilled versus artificial, technologically reliant and unskilled – isn't evidentially based. It's an easy picture to present, though, because few of the terms and concepts related to cooking have been defined or analysed in the kind of thoughtful and systematic manner that would allow it to be discussed in a serious, scholarly way. Pre-prepared and ready-prepared are not descriptions based on any set or agreed-upon level of pre-preparation. The verb cook, as Michael Symons says, is frequently used with 'conceptual sloppiness' as 'we slip unthinkingly from "cooking" as in heating food to something much, much more'.[3] Cooking may be described using terms like 'recipe' and 'dish' but lemon meringue pie, chicken zorba, salmon coulibiac and pork chops charcutière are less of a feature of contemporary cooking than instruction- and title-free combinations like ham salad, rice with coconut milk and lime leaves, steak and chips, egg mayonnaise sandwiches and baked potatoes with tuna. Cooking today means a heterogeneous mix of the fresh, the raw and the pre-prepared, the new and the traditional, the techno-logical and the manual. As Tayla described, fresh eggs, white granulated sugar, pre-weighed butter and a packet of biscuits, a hand-held electric whisk, by-hand lemon squeezer and state-of-the-art convection oven combine to make lemon meringue pie 'from scratch'. John bakes a piece of gammon and then slices and serves it with pre-washed salad leaves, pre-graded but home-boiled eggs and store-bought pickled beetroot from a jar for a ham salad. Jaclyn makes speedy salmon coulibiac from organically produced, fresh salmon, filleted in the supermarket, and a packet of frozen, 'bought' puff pastry, which she cuts beautifully into leaf shapes for decoration.[4]

There's So Much More to Cooking

As more studies are carried out and more thought is applied, more and more people are becoming aware that cooking cannot be viewed as neatly fitting into two 'traditional' and 'modern' types, that cooking skills are complex and that cooks are more than just the executors of practical tasks and techniques. The authors of a much referenced paper from the UK think tank Demos, for example, write that it is time to acknowledge skills like 'how to stretch the most basic of ingredients' (though I wonder what they mean by basic ingredients).[5] Researchers in Scotland conclude that greater insight into cooking practices in different cultural and social settings may come from defining food skills more broadly than just 'cooking from scratch'.[6] Others have begun to acknowledge the importance of approaches to cooking and the influence of context and situation. The Cookshop Program, a study of 590 children in New York, found that their diets improved most dramati-cally when cookery classes were, rather than taken separately, combined with eating together and advice about healthy food.[7] Studies in the UK have begun to notice that the benefits of cooking skills classes have as much to do with their being a facility to bring people together who have similar experiences and instil in them a sense of purpose and confidence as they do with the straightforward passing on of recipes and technical skills:[8] the effect, perhaps, of providing some sort of community of practice.[9]

The aim of my research was not to appraise the state of home cooking at a par-ticular place and point in time and measure skills against people in different social settings (according to age, income, gender and so on) in order to come up with specific policy directives. Rather, its aim was to be informative, to provide frame-works for thinking about and fresh ways of looking at cooking, to stimulate con-tinuing thought and discussion. In the following paragraphs I have summarized the issues and themes that, following the study, I feel should be borne in mind by anyone who seeks to promote, improve or encourage cooking.

The Ambiguous Meaning of Cooking

Cooking has ambiguous meaning. Some commentators and researchers use 'cooking' to refer to 'the preparation of raw foods only',[10] others have interpreted it as the household task of food preparation.[11] Cooking has also been explicitly defined by those in education as the process of 'designing and making something to eat'.[12] Others in the same field, however, see it more prescriptively, as 'following a set recipe: the exact measurements and ingredients are given in order to produce a successful outcome',[13] a process that 'often has to follow some predetermined stages if it is to come out right'.[14] For people who cook, cooking can mean both 'doing the cooking' or 'making something to eat' and some kind of more highly valued, but not necessarily 'from scratch', 'real cooking'.

Though they are not often made particularly clear, the reasons behind the promotion of cooking can vary too. Health promotion and public health specialists seem largely to be concerned with teaching people healthier cooking techniques and getting them to prepare nutritional, 'fresh' food more regularly. Others appear to want to promote cooking and culinary ability for more aesthetic, social reasons. One UK magazine for teaching cooking in schools has a section called 'Masterchef', which looks at ways of achieving 'a high quality product'.[15] They're concerned that food is becoming homogeneous and cuisines are disappearing. They're concerned too about the standards of cooking. As one food writer coined it, rather flippantly maybe, some campaigners are worried about biscuits being made with margarine and not butter, pizza with scone bases instead of proper yeast dough.[16]

The debate about why and how cookery should be taught in schools has recently begun to gather momentum. Ali Farrell of the Food Forum has argued that teaching children to cook should be about understanding food and making choices based around a healthy diet and value for money. But they should also, she believes, centre on developing 'the knowledge and skills to problem-solve, create and innovate as opposed to just being taught to cook a standard range of dishes which may or may not prove useful in the future'.[17] The findings of my study suggest that this type of approach to cooking – the ability to design, adapt and cook 'off the cuff', to work out 'what kind of soup could I make with these special-offer sweet potatoes?' or 'it was pasta last night so what about rice tonight and what have I got in the fridge that needs using up?' – comes from thinking of cooking along 'process' rather than 'result' lines.

Rather than being based on following recipes and set, perhaps titled, dishes, a process approach to cooking involves knowing how and being able to make 'generic' foods like soups and pasta sauces. It means being able to decide on 'suitable' methods for cooking different combinations of available foods and being confident about using, say, rice to make pilaf, biriani, congee and risotto.[18] The process approach lessens perceptions of the effort involved, allows for spontaneity and flexibility and gives control to the cook. Not forgetting that, repeated use of the same or similar recipes can help in perfecting skills or that for certain cooks and occasions, recipes, dishes and a desire to make an effort inspire 'more cooking', the process approach can, I believe, encourage cooking on an everyday basis. The difficulty, of course, is that this is not really how cooking is generally presented or perceived today. People do not set out to learn to cook and to be food providers, they do not clearly appreciate or value the skills involved in this kind of everyday home cooking. Methods used to promote or encourage children to cook are likely to be along the lines of giving them a toque and letting them be 'little chefs' for the day or presenting them with celebrity heroes who 'make cooking cool'.[19] Cooking is often sold to people along the lines of the gourmet model, as being about fine foods, entertaining and the creativity of the five-star restaurant chef. The danger is that this approach may promote cooking as a fun, achievement-oriented and even identity-fulfilling hobby or pastime: which is fine if that is what you are setting out to do. (Though, if we aim to make people better cooks and teach them how to prepare certain dishes 'properly', let's at least make people aware that 'standards' and 'correct' cooking are the result of different cuisine histories and cultures, professional job differentiation and pay. It may be preferable to have a concept of 'perfectly cooked' or 'skilfully made' to mark out who is good at their job and who isn't, but it could be argued that it's not really a necessary part of making breakfast or something to eat in the evening.) The associations this kind of gourmet construction has with concepts of 'professionalism', 'success and failure' and 'making an effort', however, are not necessarily going to encourage more frequent and/or healthier cooking or, for that matter, the passing of skills from one generation to another. We saw earlier that it is the cook who wants to make an effort and show off their skills or unwind whilst they make dinner who is most likely to be the first to 'kick the kids out of the kitchen', so to speak. For useful, successful campaigns, those who seek to promote cooking – be they teachers or writers or in connection with food research and community initiatives – should have a firm idea of what they mean by cooking and clearly drawn-up, complementary plans.

Policymakers and others who wish to promote home cooking should also be aware that cooking means both different things to different people and different things on different occasions. It's not simply a case that teaching in schools, for example, must challenge the very different gender roles connected with domestic cooking, though it obviously must, as researchers and writers like Rachel Dixey and Dena Attar have argued.[20] Cooking is individualistic and multifaceted. Cooking can mean 'just something you do', a dish to be mastered or the occasional recipe to be tried out. It can be a way of being a good host, a means of providing a balanced diet, a way of showing others you care, a source of self-identity and self-worth or something definitely to be avoided. Even if there is an intention to give people the option to cook by helping them acquire what are thought to be the necessary skills, their approach to cooking may mean that they choose not to. Some people don't want to cook at all or don't want to cook all of the time, some don't have to, and some will always be pleased of the occasional chance not to.

Cooking Skills are Complex

Cooking skills are complex and diverse. They are much more than the vague, non-specified list of technical abilities often collated together under the banner of, say, 'basic cooking skills'. Cooking promotion has the challenge of finding out what kinds of practical techniques and technical skills are most empowering for different aims: which are most helpful in assisting the cook to reach exacting standards, perhaps, most useful in the quest for a healthy diet, most likely to get reluctant, nervous cooks cooking. It also needs to examine the role that tacit skills can play in changing domestic food and cooking practices. For, as I found in my study, it is the secondary, tacit skills of perception, conception and planning, acquired from the application of mechanical skills and techniques and enhanced by academic knowledge, that are most likely to lessen the effort perceived as being involved, increase confidence and 'get people cooking'. This immediately raises questions about when to teach cooking. At what age is it most useful to learn to cook? It would be ill considered to dismiss teaching young children to cook too hastily (and this is where campaigns often focus) but it may be worth bearing in mind that there could be more helpful times to learn to cook, times when cooking has become more a part of life, is actually practised and skills can be acquired *in situ*. It may be worthwhile considering the relative appropriateness of, for example, lessons for young children, young people who have just left home or are just setting up their own home, or new parents.

It is also important that policy and campaign bear in mind that cooking skills can be viewed as either task-centred or person-centred and as specifically domestic or otherwise. The findings of my research certainly support the view of P.A. Street when she says that policies that seek to increase the use of fresh, raw foods should seek to educate everyone – not just those who cook – about the time, effort and range of skills involved in home cooking.[21] There is an unevenness, even within domestic cooking, with which we acknowledge and appreciate skill. The 'daily grind of frying sausages and mashing potatoes' is, as Vicki Swinbank says in her analysis of culinary hierarchy in Western culture, far less likely to be credited as difficult and skilled work than cooking for a dinner party.[22] Real appreciation of food cooked and the range and depth of skills that have gone into the cooking of it may well be a first step in encouraging people to 'cook' or to 'cook' more frequently.

It probably doesn't help that we are constantly being told that the kinds of foods we use do not require any real cooking skills to prepare, that we cannot cook and are being deskilled. It is important to remember that, just as pre-prepared foods and raw foods cannot be absolutely differentiated, neither can the skills used to prepare them. Cooking skills are transferable and therefore 'workable on'. As an illustration, some of the participants in a Scottish 'food skills initiative' were categorized as 'basic but fearful' cooks because they were found to have only 'limited abilities' and only made things like sausages and chips, chicken nuggets, mince and boiled potatoes and 'simple' pasta meals.[23] Yet in order to prepare these foods and dishes, they would have had to apply technical abilities like frying, boiling and grilling, chopping and slicing, as well as perceptual skills relating to such things as timing and judging when food is cooked. They may have had to cook the foods in ways that others like or require, manage with poor resources or cope with a strict schedule and a kitchen full of children or even no kitchen at all. In other words, the 'basic but fearful' cooks would probably be found to have a number of existing skills that could be developed.

Cooking is Cultural

A final policy point concerns the general understanding that food choice is 'circumscribed by the ability to prepare food'[24] and the straightforward response that calls for practical cooking classes in schools and various sections of local communities.[25] The study I carried out revealed practical cooking skills to be just one of a whole range of influences on what and how often we cook and even perhaps on how 'well' we cook. As was shown in Chapter 6 cooking skills do have an impact on food choices and home cooking practices but only as part of an intricate set of relationships and influences. People's cooking lives cannot be separated from their wider lives, from their access to food and information about food, from the social and cultural settings in which they live and their generation and gender, from mediated constructions and shared beliefs and values, from their religious and ethnic background, from their personality and from the responsibilities they have for providing others with food. Like food, cooking is cultural. In order to change food and cooking practices, it's necessary to focus on the food and cooking culture in its entirety rather than on particular and discrete aspects of it like practical cooking skills. This change in focus has already been endorsed in some quarters, where there is a growing belief that effective strategies and programmes come from working *within* the food experiences of the people concerned.[26] Tailor-made cooking skills sessions for different kinds of groups and communities have been suggested as the result of one project.[27] A report of another concluded that it had more success with recipes and foods considered normal by the group. Soup, for example, had to be 'ordinary' and not include anything considered exotic,[28] the writers noting wider research that has found that successful interventions are usually the result of working around and within existing community projects and 'avoiding a "top down" approach'.[29] Work from the Joseph Rowntree Foundation, too, has found that schemes to improve cooking skills and nutrition knowledge benefit hugely from involving local people and treating then as equal and active partners.[30]

It shouldn't really have been a surprise that teenagers who took part in a cooking initiative in Wales enjoyed making familiar foods like brownies and pizza more than foods like Cornish pasties, fish pie and Spanish omelette, which they had perhaps never seen before.[31] Yet there is often, as a flick through a few project recipe sheets quickly reveals, a tendency to want to teach people things like sausage stretch, tuna pasta bake and beany pasta bake, Chinese soup and fruit trifle, foods that no one really eats and that don't really belong to anyone's cooking culture – foods and dishes reminiscent of what food writer Jeffrey Steingarten calls the 'weakly flavoured mock-ethnic dishes that American dieticians love'.[32] They remind me very much of the kind of neutral, one-size-fits-all foods that I have been called upon to cook in many a staff restaurant and canteen.

It is often said that people today don't feel they have the time to cook. But that, of course, depends on what they feel cooking is. If we want to 'get people cooking' or 'make them better cooks', then we must break down the myth that cooking is difficult and requires a great deal of effort. We must move on from seeing cooking in a dichotomized and limited way and unpack the social constructions and value-laden judgements that surround good cooking and good cooks, skilled cooking and skilled cooks. It is time to appreciate the continuities and changes, the diversities of approach and the different meanings of cooking.

Appendix: Extracts from Interviews

Making Pizza

Frances: Do you like pizza?

Claire: I don't mind them but I don't go out of my way to get them to be honest. Apart from the one I do like, which is plain cheese and tomato thin crust from Sainsbury's, which is really, really nice. It's the nicest pizza I've ever had yet it's got hardly anything on it.

Frances: Have you ever made a pizza?

Claire: I did when I was at school. We made pizza but we used bread. I can't really remember how we did it but somehow we had to wet the bread and sort of mash that into a base with something else. I can't remember what it was but this was in 8G many years ago. I've also more recently bought pizza bases and sort of chucked everything on. I've done that once or twice. It's just that I never know what goes with what and whether to chance it and poison everyone. I suppose if I put my mind to it, yes, I could make one.

Frances: You've sort of answered this a bit but would you feel confident about making it ... to make everything?

Claire: Oh God no, not unless I had a week to try ... Maybe if I was having a go with someone else at trying to make one. Then, you know, I wouldn't take all the blame if it was absolutely awful or ... well, I wouldn't feel so let down in myself if it was a complete disaster. But yes, yes, I suppose I would.

Frances: What would make you feel uncertain about making one? After all, you say you've made bread before and you've made similar things to the tomato sauce.

Claire: The toppings perhaps, I don't know. I mean I used to do more cooking when I was at home and didn't have any responsibilities and didn't have to watch the clock. But now I suppose I'll make whatever is there when I get in. I don't experiment as much as I used to, although I still like to. I don't know, I suppose I'm quite insecure in some ways, always looking for people to see me in a good light or whatever. So I suppose if don't do anything disastrous then they can't criticize me for it!

Frances: Would you use a recipe if you were going to do the whole thing?

Claire: Probably yes. Or I'd get someone else to just tell me what they tried and then go by what they ...

Frances: Would that make you feel more confident ... using a recipe?

Claire: In some ways, yes. But I've used recipes before and its never turned out how I expected it. I suppose it's down to individual interpretation in a way and, well, what you expect and what you get are not always the same. Yes, I think I would probably use one and I think there's more chance of me feeling confident that I had done something well using a recipe than just trying it myself.

Frances: Would you feel confident about making the bread dough bit … the bit you've done before?

Claire: Um, probably, not a definite yes.

Frances: What would make you hesitant?

Claire: I don't know, to be honest, I haven't tried it for years. It's not the actual kneading, I don't mind that, I get plenty of practice on my husband! I suppose it's mixing the water in, putting too much or too little in, and everything else.

Frances: What about the tomato sauce?

Claire: I wouldn't have the first clue how to make it, to be honest. It would probably have to be from a tube, either that or I would ask my friend Anne because she does it. If someone told me what to put in, I'd probably know how to do it. But it's the sort of not knowing where to start and everything. And if you're talking about taking ripe tomatoes and all that and doing it from there, I'd probably panic.

Frances: Would you have any of the ingredients in the house?

Claire: Onions I'd have. I'd have fresh tomatoes, not tinned ones. Cheese I'd definitely have, yes. Probably those three.

Frances: Would you have any flour?

Claire: I haven't bought any flour for a while, I must say. So probably not flour, no.

Frances: Are there any circumstances when you might make one spontaneously? You might use a pizza base, but would you ever go home and think 'I'll make pizza tonight'?

Claire: I probably will, now you've mentioned it! I mean, sometimes I'll get sort of three-quarters of the way through the afternoon and I'll think 'ooh, what should I make for dinner tonight?' Sometimes I'll think 'oh, I'll go to the supermarket on the way home and I'll buy some ingredients and I'll have a go at making something.' But by the time I get out of the door I think 'I'm too tired for that now' and I don't want to drive to the supermarket and queue up with millions of people who have just finished work … A few months ago I did use the pizza bases. I think I just did something plain because I was just doing it for me and my daughter, not my husband. Me and her … we did it together one weekend. It turned out quite well. I wouldn't exactly rush to make it again but I suppose it was quite nice if I think about it.

Frances: Have you ever made a pizza?

Eamon: Yes.

Frances: And when was the last time you made a pizza?

Eamon: That's a good question. I think it would be earlier this year, probably some six months ago now. I made it with my godson and his family.

Frances: Would you feel generally confident if I said 'go and make a pizza'?

Eamon: Yes I would, yes.

Frances: What would you do, then?

Eamon: I would start off by making a bread dough for the base and that would be the very first thing depending on how much time I'd got to make the whole dish. I'd use easy-blend yeast and things like that probably to get it going quickly and rather more yeast than I would use to make a bread dough because I'm assuming that I would want it done quite fast. So I would make the dough and get that started and leave it to rise. Then I would start thinking about my tomato sauce for the topping. I'd fry off some onions and garlic and olive oil – extra virgin for flavour. I'd use a tin of chopped tomatoes probably, add that and reduce it and then think about what herbs I'd got and whether I'd got fresh herbs. I've got some basil on the windowsill at the moment and that would be very nice, thank you. Then I'd forage round for things to put on top, mushrooms and things like that, and cheese. By the time my sauce had been cooking away and reducing, the dough would have shown some indication of actually rising and I would knock that back and shape it. I would prefer that to have two rises but it would depend on how fast I needed it. Usually I would make a circle but I have made oblong pizzas, it depends on the size and shape of the oven. Then I'd season the sauce and put that on top and garnish it with whatever vegetables and things I'd found, mushrooms, peppers, olives and a few capers from the fridge, and cheese. And then I would cook it.

Frances: Would you use a recipe for any part of that?

Eamon: No.

Frances: Would there be any part of that you would feel uncertain about?

Eamon: No.

Frances: … the dough, texture …

Eamon: I would hopefully be quite happy about all of that. I like making bread and I'm fairly good at that. The only thing that might bother me slightly, depending on how much tomato sauce you put on top, it can be quite difficult to judge when your pizza is cooked I find. If you overdo the tomato sauce you can get a bit of a soggy base. That's the only thing I can think of.

Frances: How long would you say that it takes to go through that process, making the pizza, the dough and everything?

Eamon: I mean you're talking two hours possibly. You'd be pushed to do it in less than two hours, I think. An hour and a half maybe.

Frances: When would you be prepared to spend an hour and a half or two hours making a pizza?

Eamon: Like I said, the last time I made one was with my godson and his family. They really enjoyed it because they helped in the process so it was kind of an entertainment. He's now twelve and it's quite fun because he can come and chop a few mushrooms and help. He can see that he's created something, that we've all created together and we can chat about it. We don't see each other that often and I find it good from that point of view. It's a social event in a way. And I'm okay with 'chop that mushroom'. When it comes to 'I'll chop this mushroom' it's a case of 'no you won't dear'.

Frances: Have you ever made a pizza?

Kate: ... er yes ...

Frances: Can you remember when you last made pizza?

Kate: It might have been for my O level cookery course! Let's face it, nobody makes good pizza, do they? Well, somebody somewhere makes good pizza but it sure as hell wasn't me.

Frances: And you made it from scratch and everything?

Kate: Oh yes.

Frances: And that would be the last time you made one?

Kate: No, probably not. I think I have made something more recently but it must be in the region of eight years ago.

Frances: If somebody asked you to make one now, would you feel confident about doing so?

Kate: Yes. Well, if I had a day to work on it.

Frances: How long do you think it would take you?

Kate: Possibly about, I don't know, an hour and a half? I don't think it takes quite as long as doing bread dough. I don't think it needs two lots of rising.

Frances: Are there any occasions when you'd be prepared to spend that hour and a half?

Kate: Well, I haven't very much experience of making it and I think somebody put me off once when they suggested you could make pizza with a scone base. I mean, my general sort of memory of home-made pizza is not brilliant. So no, I don't think I would. I think you can buy too many good pizzas out there. You could phone someone up and have them deliver one to your house. So I don't think I would ever do that, no.

Frances: If you did find yourself making a pizza would you use a recipe?

Kate: Absolutely, yes. Definitely.

Frances: How would you use a recipe?

Kate: Word for word. I wouldn't remember how to make a good pizza base without a recipe and I would want some ideas on different toppings. I think the topping would be quite crucial. It would have to be something a bit different than that you can buy ready-made. In fact, I was looking at a recipe recently for ... I don't know how you pronounce it [pissaladierre] I was looking at that with a view to a friend coming up this weekend and I did look at it and think 'that looks nice'. But it wasn't a traditional pizza, I think it actually had a pastry base. I might consider that.

Frances: You mentioned the topping being crucial ...is there anything you would feel uncertain about doing?

Kate: I suppose getting the tomato sauce right. I think they're quite highly sweetened, the ones you get delivered and the ones you buy. I don't think you would do that at home really. I think that would be quite a key ingredient. And making the dough I would want to follow a recipe, by the letter really ... I don't do any yeast baking. I don't ever make bread so I'm not that comfortable with using yeast, fresh yeast or dried yeast. That's the part I would really want to follow some instruction over. The actual mixing of the ingredients and the kneading are not a big deal.

Frances: Would you feel confident about knowing it was cooked, it was done?

Kate: I would feel quite confident about pulling it out. If I'd used a recipe I would have that as a guideline. But I would also look. In fact we've got a new cooker that's been passed on to us by my brother-in-law so I'm not one hundred per cent sure about it. It's a fan oven so it tends to cook quite quickly so I would always look and check.

Frances: Which of the ingredients would you have in the house?

Kate: We would have plain flour. We wouldn't have the yeast. We'd have butter and tomato purée. I wouldn't have onions if we were going to need onions for the topping. I would probably do something with fish if I was making pizza. But I probably wouldn't have any fresh fish and if I was going to go to the trouble of making a pizza I would prefer to use fresh fish rather than frozen. Very few of the ingredients, I suppose.

Frances: Are there any circumstances when you might cook something like that spontaneously, you know walk in from work and ...?

Kate: ... never, no, no.

Frances: What about making one with a pizza mix?

Kate: I'd think of that as being a bit naff really. I wouldn't do that. I certainly wouldn't. I don't like the idea of cake mixes and things, I associate them with poor cakes. I think of pizza dough in the same way. I would almost rather buy the whole thing completely made up than do that.

Frances: What about those bases you get, do you ever use those?

Kate: I think on occasion I have done that, but again it's going back a long way. I think there was a time when I would make things for my brother when he came back from university. I used to cook some things then because it was fun to cook at home and I think maybe I probably did something like that at that stage. But I don't remember that being particularly good either. I think it ended up being a bit crisp. I don't think it was really very successful.

Doing the Cooking

Frances: How much cooking do you do?

Ash: Um ... I help out really because my wife is here and I sort of help her. I'm like an assistant in the family so I probably do a couple of hours a week, something like that. There's weeks when I may not do anything but lately I've been doing lots. I've been doing some cooking classes to regenerate my interest.

Frances: Are there any particular kinds of meals that you help out with?

Ash: Usually things that are very basic, like the other day we did snacky type foods. Anything to do with bread, cheese, eggs, stuff like that, falafal or chapattis and things like that. And pasta sometimes.

Frances: ... and with meals?

Ash: Yes, I suppose so. We don't really eat too much at lunch. Lunch is really treated just like ... well, it depends on the moods of people and who's at home. If somebody all of a sudden feels hungry they may cook something, otherwise it's just sandwiches and snacks or something that was cooked the previous night, we might have some of that.

Frances: And what about breakfast?

Ash: I'm the only one in the family who eats breakfast. And I literally just have cereals and toast, no cooked breakfast.

Frances: Have there been times in your life when you have done more cooking, would you say?

Ash: Yes, when either my wife has been away or the children have asked me to experiment or something, some dish they've read about maybe, then I would get involved. In general, since I got married twenty years ago, there hasn't been that ... well she does the cooking and she actually loves cooking as well. She doesn't like people working with her, she's a little bit of a tyrant! So generally speaking it might go a long time between me doing anything in the kitchen, that's how it works.

Frances: What about before you were married?

Ash: Well, then, obviously I was living with my mother. We certainly used to help her a lot because she used to go through periods when she wasn't well. It wasn't always successful because there were too many people who wanted to help. My sister and my brother ... we would all get involved, we'd do simple things, nothing too complicated. It would always go wrong because it was the more old-fashioned, traditional sort of food, which is about marinating and all that. We're not into that any more.

Frances: Do you enjoy preparing food?

Ash: Yes. I think I enjoy preparing food because of that sort of ... it's like anything you do where you work with your hands and it comes out the way it should do, it's very satisfying. ... And the way I look at it, when you get visitors to the house it's like in a restaurant, they comment. And I think if somebody else appreciates it as well ... I don't know, it's just a personal thing.

Frances: Would you ever say it's recreational, a leisure type of thing?

Ash: Yes, I'd say it is, because recreation is something you enjoy and cooking is enjoyment for me.

Frances: Are there occasions when you feel more that way, when you enjoy it more?

Ash: Yes, sometimes at the weekend when you're cooking not just for yourself but doing it for more people and it's going to be appreciated more. I don't think I would cook anything unusual for myself, more for somebody else.

Frances: What do you mean by unusual?

Ash: Something you would experiment with out of a recipe book, something which the family hasn't eaten for a while. Something you wouldn't normally get in a restaurant perhaps. It would be something unusual because of the nature of the ingredients. You do it yourself and you think 'well, that's not so complicated as it looks'. That's the pleasure I get from it, anyway.

Frances: Do you ever find it's a bit of a chore?

Ash: Sometimes it is, yes, if it's a lot of ingredients. But I think in general I don't pick on things that are going to be that complicated. If halfway through I think it's going to be something that will put me off ... well, I wouldn't pick that recipe at all. I would rather pick something I know I'm going to go through and enjoy.

Frances: How much cooking do you do?

Amrit: In a week? Say, four nights a week probably. I only cook at night. So, yes, four nights out of seven I'll cook.

Frances: What kinds of things do you do?

Amrit: The easiest stuff to do is obviously the pasta and rice dishes, pseudo-Italian-type things. I enjoy cooking Thai and Indian and Chinese the most. I have the odd cookbook but not many. Thai curry, like a green curry, is probably my favourite thing to cook at the moment. And just making stuff up, trying new things, which is probably going to be tomato, based Italian dishes with bits and pieces.

Frances: What do you do about breakfast and lunchtime?

Amrit: I don't have breakfast. For lunch I usually just make a sandwich or I go and buy a baguette down the road because they're a bit nicer. So, as I say, the only time I cook is in the evening.

Frances: Does it vary between weekends and weekdays?

Amrit: [He explains that he works a lot in the evening and often gets home at twelve or two in the morning.] After a three hour gig, I'm far to knackered to cook so it's Mr Pizza company. Weekends ... well, if I had time to cook on the weekend, which I never do, I would. But, as I say, because I've been working all night, there's no way I'm going to start chopping onions when I get back.

Frances: Do you enjoy preparing food ... cooking?

Amrit: Yes I do. I enjoy trying all the new herbs and spices and seeing what happens. Sometimes something comes out well, sometimes it doesn't. Once in a while, I'll treat myself to fresh herbs and stuff. I've got some fresh coriander and basil in the fridge now.

Frances: What will you do with the herbs, do you think?

Amrit: What I was trying to do was just take advantage of the fresh coriander to make a nice Thai curry. I'll try anything with the word curry in it. And with the basil just make a simple Italian thing. You know, shove in loads of garlic and you're away.

Frances: Are there any occasions when you most enjoy preparing food?

Amrit: When there's a group of people coming round. If we're having friends round for dinner, it's really nice to make my one dessert rather than buying in a chocolate mousse or whatever ... to actually sit down and smugly know that you've done it all and they've got to pay you back, sort of thing. Perhaps it's the class conscience type thing where you've actually cooked something and it's nice, rather than going down to the supermarket for a quick and easy [meal] or you go and get fish and chips. I really don't like doing that, partly because it's so expensive and partly because it tastes nothing like something you have prepared. I'm sure, though, it's like everything in life, if you actually spend time over it, chopping away and all that and you run out of olive oil and have to run down the shops ... you're going to appreciate it a lot more than if you just get by with a couple of sausages and some Smash [instant mashed potato].

Frances: Do you think it ever becomes recreational, a hobby, say?

Amrit: A hobby, yes, I think so. I go through different periods of cooking and not cooking quite so much but when I'm cooking a lot I do enjoy it. I'll go out and get interesting things because I enjoy preparing and cooking interesting dishes. But then again, I can easily slip into being a bit lazy.

Frances: Does it ever become a chore?

Amrit: It only becomes a chore when I'm really knackered. If the pizza places are closed and I can't get any food and I have to cook, though that's only a result of other things. It's not because I don't enjoy cooking, it's because I've just come home from work and it's really late. In fact, it's not actually the cooking, anything would be a chore, even walking down the stairs. So yes and no.

Frances: When did you last feel like that, do you think?

Amrit: Oh, last weekend. It was Saturday night and we'd had a gig and got back here at two in the morning or something and everywhere was closed so I had to make something. Mary had flu so I thought it would be nice for her to have a proper meal. Luckily I had onions and mushrooms and other vegetables and crème fraiche and a tin of tomatoes. I didn't really enjoy that.

Frances: Let's start by looking at the food diaries you kept. Would you say this was a fairly typical few days?

Liz: Yes, absolutely.

Frances: I noticed that you did everything that's on here ...

Liz: Yes again, absolutely. Alec's out all day, all week and he doesn't get back till eight o'clock so by then I've prepared the meal if we're going to eat. So yes, it's completely typical.

Frances: Did this just come about or did you sit down and decide or ...

Liz: No, not at all. I mean, the thing is, when I used to work full-time before we had the children, I would do most of the cooking. Then, when I used to work full-time and we had one child, I would do all the cooking. Then, after I had the second child I stopped working but of course I still did all the cooking. There's been no difference whatever in our lifestyle.

Frances: Would you change things?

Liz: I think I'm a bit of a control freak really, about the shopping anyway. I don't really trust Alec to go and do the shopping. He's no interest in doing the shopping anyway. And I suppose I prefer my cooking to his cooking, at least for evening meals. I would be happy for him to cook breakfast, like a fried breakfast, or a basic lunch. Though even sandwiches he would defer to me because he makes crap sandwiches. He really does. He's really lazy about it, he doesn't butter to the edge of the bread and he doesn't think about what he'd put in it. He'd just put cheese in it. Just cheese! I've no interest in eating a plain cheese sandwich. And the thing is, if he was to cook an evening meal, I'd have to be in the kitchen giving him directions. You know, put this on now, do that, cut that, do that first. And if I have to manage his time about it and everything I may as well do it myself, I think. He never knows where all the ingredients are either, so he'd just be saying all the time 'where's the pasta?', 'have we got any pasta?', 'where's the mushrooms?' After I've looked after the children all day I can't be bothered taking anyone else through the steps of doing anything. I've had it by then. I'm much quicker than he is as well.

Frances (Looking through Jean's cooking diary): It looks like you do all the cooking ...

Jean: Yes, that's right.

Frances: Is that typical?

Jean: Well, it is ... though if I'm out or working or something and I come in late then Seth will do it. But that doesn't happen very often. Yes, I always do the cooking.

Frances: Are you happy about that?

Jean: Well, in a way! I don't think a lot of people like cooking, do they? But you've got to do it, someone has to. I find it easier now there's just me and Seth, now that the children are gone. We can have something simple like, like bacon ... or we eat a lot of pasta and all. I said to him the other day, 'I prefer pasta now to potatoes and things.' I like spicy dishes too. So does he, but he's a bit fussy, you know. Tomatoes, say, you've got to make sure you don't put them in but other than that ... It seems quite easy now for just the two of us. I just cook it and dish it up now. I mean, I have made quite a few mistakes. I mean, we've sat there and tucked into it and then at each other and 'urgh', you know, 'you've done that wrong'. But other than that, as long as I don't put tomatoes in. I mean, I do sometimes without him knowing because like I say 'if you've never had tomatoes how do you know you don't like them?' I try and get him used to them that way. There's a load of salad stuff he don't like much too and he's gradually got used to it. And cheese he don't like. But now he does eat a little bit of cheese every now and again. When my kids was small I sort of made them eat everything, whatever I put in front of them they had to eat. But I think on his side when he was small, you know, if he didn't want it he didn't eat it. That, why he don't like half the things he don't like. But, like I say, he's getting used to cheese and salads and things. If I had my way I would live on salads. Less cooking! Maybe not in winter though. I do a lot of stews in winter ...

Frances: Do you ever try anything new ... think 'oh, I haven't done anything like that'?

Jean: I did go through a phase of making cakes ... coconut cake, currant cake and all the puddings, suet puddings and all that. I mean, Seth will tell you, I used to put them on the tray and they looked so nice. I thought, I'm not going to let the kids touch them! I used to take photos they looked so nice. I know it sounds silly but they looked so nice. They'd demolish them when they come home from school, that's how long ago that was. That went on for a few months and then all of a sudden I just stopped. And now I wouldn't really bother just for me and Seth. Though there is one I want to do and that's bacon suet pudding ...

Frances: Is that the sort of rolled up ...?

Jean: No, its like spotty dog, you know? Only instead of putting currants in you put bacon in. It's gorgeous, it's really nice. I know Seth will eat that anyway. You sort of cut up onion very fine and put it in ...

Frances: And do you bake it?

Jean: Steam it. Steamed pudding, that's what it is. It's funny because I often say to Seth, some of my Mum's puddings and that ... I did try them when the kids were little but they don't taste half as good as your Mum's, I don't care what anyone says. She used to do a lovely pudding like that, we was talking about it the other night. I want to try and do that. I haven't done it yet but I will have a go. I will, yes.

Frances: Do you ever do anything else when you're preparing food …

Jean: No, no.

Frances: Not like the putting the washing out or …

Jean: Oh yes, I do stuff like that. If the washing's on the side, I'll hang it out. Or if it's out in the garden, I'll get it in, fold it, put it in the airing cupboard, that sort of thing. If I've got washing in the machine and it's finished, then whilst the dinner's cooking I'll get that out and hang it up. I feed the dogs and things like that.

Frances: How much cooking do you do?

Jez: Well, not much, to be honest. I mean, you learn all that stuff at college and everything but I don't generally put it into practice when I get home. My Mum does most of the cooking when I'm at home … I mainly cook frozen foods and easy stuff.

Frances: What sort of frozen things do you make?

Jez: Let me think … well, things like … well, not exactly frozen, I suppose, but things like pasta that comes in the packet, things you can heat up in the oven or something. I suppose I might make a sauce to go with that, with some tomato things or something … I just cook to eat really. I mean I do have some favourites. Sometimes I'll think 'oh, I'll have chicken Kiev tonight, that sounds nice'. But it's not like I'm inspired and think 'oh, I'll make up a really nice dish'.

Frances: How much cooking do you do?

Jaclyn: Oh, it varies. Probably every other night I will try and cook something from scratch but then on other nights I'll use what I made the night before, have a jacket potato or I'll buy some sort of, you know, precooked thing. I tend only to cook things from scratch, you know, soups, stews and I don't know, say, lasagne, at the weekend. Hours-wise, I don't spend long cooking during the week.

Frances: What about things like breakfast and lunch?

Jaclyn: Oh, I don't always have breakfast, I might have it two or three times a week. I always have it at the weekend but it will only be something like toast or cereal. And lunch … I often have the good intention of pre-making sandwiches but don't, I buy sandwiches. At the moment, I've got time to actually come home so I may have toast or something like that.

Frances: Have there been times in you life when you have done more cooking perhaps … or less?

Jaclyn: Yes, if I'm on holiday and at home, I will cook more. I'm probably cooking a bit more at the moment because my boyfriend is staying here. We're taking it in turn a bit and I suppose between the three of us [she has a flatmate] we're probably eating better. I don't know. I think I've become more aware of my diet and trying to cook more from scratch than ever before. Like I say, when I've got time, I love it. I love all the preparation and I actually really enjoy spending time preparing food, it's quite a relaxing thing to do then, when you've got time. But I find if I come home, and I'm not home till half past seven or eight, the last thing I want to do is start cooking. I don't actually find it that relaxing then, I just want to eat something straight away.

Frances: You think it something recreational, then?

Jaclyn: Yes ... and it has done more so every time because I have got more confident in trying different things. I still have to use recipes but I've got more confident. Though, you know, there are some recipes that I don't have to use any more because I know them and I find them quite easy. But I do find I can get quite stressed with cooking sometimes, the timing and all that.

Kitchens, Microwaves, Mixers and Other Equipment

Claire (2): At the moment, it's a bit odd in here because we've got two ovens ... cookers ... stoves ... whatever you call them. That one's the new one that Aidan's mother gave us because this one's very dangerous. We're getting rid of it. Anyway, the fridge is round the corner in the corridor and away from the main bit of kitchen. It's a split fridge-freezer because we like to have lots of frozen stuff, although we don't actually buy that much, it's just nice to have the space. I hate those little fridges where you get a tiny little icebox.

Frances: So what do you keep in it?

Claire (2): You want to have a look? Well, in the freezer, we seem to have a couple of cans of beer! He must have just put them in. There are some things we've bought and some things that we've frozen just so they don't go off. Often we buy meat, like a joint, and freeze it. There's some bread. That was fresh, so it'll be nicer if we freeze it than if we just keep it. And there's always a bit of this fish-in-batter kind of stuff. It's a good standby. And I believe we have some mince that Aidan just put in there. Then there's some ice cubes and some fresh herbs ...

Frances: That's a good idea ...

Claire (2): Yes. I mean they're not quite the same but at least they don't go off. And that's about it, really. Well, maybe, you know there's a couple of pizzas in there or something, things to fall back on in case we run out of fresh food. And then in the fridge we have the usual things like milk and coffee. We have beans and ground at the moment. We bought this grinder so we're always doing ground beans. It's a bit of a pain, really, so we've got some ground coffee as well ... We usually get chicken, we eat a lot of chicken. And once a week or so we do a joint or something because we both like roasts. And there's eggs and bacon and sausage, sort of fall-back stuff, and cheese. And we've got beef dripping that Aidan uses to cook with.

Frances: That's quite unusual.

Claire (2): Yes, but he loves it. And there's Parmesan cheese, which I can't do without, and it's not quite the same if you get the dried stuff, is it?

Frances: You normally keep fresh Parmesan in, then?

Claire (2): Yes. We went through a phase recently of not having any and just getting that dried sort of tinned stuff but I'd much rather have a block of the fresh. We eat an awful lot of pasta, so it's worth it. We keep the fresh vegetables out here in this little red tray thing. We don't buy many vegetables at a time because they go off so quickly. That's something actually we usually have in the freezer, frozen peas.

They're the only frozen veg we buy but they're a good standby.

Frances: That's a nice coffeepot.

Claire (2): Yes, it is, we bought one of those espresso coffee makers. We've got a filter coffee one as well. I really like espresso but I like it watered down with a bit of hot water rather than having it straight, full strength.

Frances: And a salad spinner …

Claire (2): Yes, which we very rarely use now. It was a bit of a novelty when we bought it … And this is a little mixer. We used to have a blender as well but it broke. I used to use it quite a lot. I like making soups. I used to use that a lot for soups.

Frances: Did you use it for anything else?

Claire (2): Um, batter mainly, but not much else apart from that. It was just really handy. Oh, I'll tell you what we used to use it for too … milkshakes. Aidan went through a phase of making milkshakes in the morning when he didn't want to eat breakfast. He'd make himself a milkshake and put an egg in it. But the mixer, Aidan's Mum bought us that and I've made a few cakes with it but it doesn't really get used very often. I think we use the blender much more.

Frances: And what's that in the corner?

Claire (2): It's a chip fryer, a deep-fat fryer, but we don't really use it. I think my Mum and Dad gave it to us. I think Aidan's made tempura in it, that kind of thing, but he even when he made tempura on Sunday he did it on the hob. If it was me making chips, I think I would be more likely to use that just because it's safer but he doesn't like it.

Frances: What kind of equipment do you have?

Debora: Just a whisk and I don't know … the usual stuff, the normal implements.

Frances: Do, you have a toaster or anything?

Debora: No we just use the grill.

Frances: What about a microwave?

Debora: No, I haven't got a microwave. I did have a deep-fat fryer but I've gone off it. I use oven chips and things like that, just for health reasons really. If I'm making a breakfast at the weekend, say, I'll grill everything and just keep it warm in the oven.

Frances: Is there anything you wouldn't like to be without?

Debora: No, not really … because I just have normal things, I haven't got like a liquidizer or anything like that. I just have the normal tools that you use, casserole dishes and things like that.

Frances: Is there anything that you would really like?

Debora: A blender. I've got to get one of them! That would be really useful.

Frances: What would you make with it?

Debora: I would do a lot more soups and things like that because, I mean, you need one for those kinds of things. I would make a lot of fresh soup and things like that. It'd also be handy if I've got friends round with children and babies … for their food.

Frances: Would you ever attempt to make soup without one?

Debora: Er, no … my friend down the road attempted it once without one and it was just totally lumpy and everything. It just didn't taste like soup at all. So, no, I wouldn't attempt it without a blender or something.

Frances: I noticed that you did some scrambled eggs in the microwave ... do you ever do them on the stove, in a pan?

Mark: No, not for the kids and that. Basically all the stuff they have is, you know, microwave jobs ... see, I can't cook ... or just stick it in the oven things like pizza. I mean I can cook scrambled eggs in the saucepan and things like that. I do omelettes. The kids like their cheese and ham omelettes. I do those in a sort of omelette saucepan. But with their scrambled eggs and everything we just do it in a Pyrex pint jug. You just mix it all up and stick it in the microwave. It's the same with their baked beans and sausages and things like that. I do the same with them. Basically you don't touch the oven with the kids because they're so fussy about what they eat. If you put something in front of them and they don't want it, they don't touch it, well, then it's just a waste of time, isn't it? I always ask them 'what do you want to eat?' And then when they tell me, I ask them 'are you going to eat it or am I just going to waste my time?' If you cook for them and they didn't ask for it, they won't eat it, they're funny.

Frances: If you were cooking scrambled eggs for yourself, would you do them in the microwave ... do you eat scrambled eggs?

Mark: Well, I do eat scrambled eggs that are done in the microwave but, I mean, stuff they leave because it's no good chucking it away. I must admit, though, I prefer it done in the saucepan.

Frances: Do you use the microwave a lot?

Margaret: Yes, a fair bit. Well, I suppose we don't actually do very much cooking with it but it's very useful for reheating leftovers. Patrick will quite often make a curry in the morning or something, before he goes to work, and then we'll just reheat it in the evening. Some people say it's good for cooking vegetables but I haven't found that particularly. I find that when you actually look at the cooking times for them they're not really any shorter. It isn't quicker and therefore the motivation for doing it diminishes enormously. This is the oven we use. This is where the wok and the storage things and instruction booklets live. This is, well, I think they call it a cake carrier or something. It's just quite a useful, well, big, flat plate really, with a lid that flips down over it and a handle. You could use it the other way up and just carry things in it or you can carry a cake or a tart or something on it. This is just an oval casserole-type dish. And this is oddments of children's stuff and biscuits, raisins, cocoa, tea ...

Frances: ... those look nice (*looking at some bottles of oil, vinegar, etc.*).

Margaret: That's one of those things one gets given for a Christmas present. It's perfectly nice but isn't used that much. I have used the walnut oil and the balsamic vinegar but I haven't used the almond and hazelnut very much.

Frances: And what's this?

Margaret: That's very useful. Hannah's added a rabbit face, but it's a pepper grinder. For some reason the rice and the spaghetti and the flour live here, I don't know why. And then we've got cooking implements and saucepans ...

Frances: You've got lots ...

Margaret: Yes, probably. We don't actually use all of them, probably only half of them. We use this, for example, all the time. I bought that at IKEA, it's a sort of sauté pan. This is a toaster and this is Patrick's spice cupboard.

Notes

Chapter 1 Who Cares about Cooking?

1. See, for example, Lupton, D. (1996), *Food, the Body and the Self*, London: Sage Publications, and Rappaport, L. (2003), *How We Eat. Appetite, Culture, and the Psychology of Food*, Toronto: ECW Press.
2. From Press, J. (2002), 'Feeding frenzy', article in *The Village Voice* quoting Darra Goldstein, editor of *Gastronomica, The Journal of Food and Culture*, available www.villagevoice.com/issues/0212/press.php
3. From Dixon, J. (2002), *The Changing Chicken*, Sydney: UNSW Press.
4. See Telfer, E. (1996), *Food for Thought. Philosophy and Food*, London: Routledge.
5. Full titles are Lang, T. and Heasman, M. (2004), *Food Wars: the Global Battle for Mouths, Minds and Markets*, London: Earthscan; Nestle, M. (2002), *Food Politics. How the Food Industry Influences Nutrition and Health*, Los Angeles: University of California Press; Schlosser, E. (2001*), Fast Food Nation. What the All-American Meal is Doing to the World*, London: Allen Lane The Penguin Press.
6. See, for example, Mintz, S. (1985*), Sweetness and Power: the Place of Sugar in Modern History,* New York: Viking; and Kurlansky, M. (1999), *Cod. A Biography of the Fish that Changed the World*, Vintage: London.
7. See, for example, Warde, A. (1997), *Consumption, Food and Taste. Culinary Antinomies and Commodity Culture*, London: Sage Publications; and Kjaernes, U. (ed.) (2001), *Eating Patterns. A Day in the Lives of Nordic Peoples*, Lysaker: National Institute for Consumer Research.
8. See, for example, Fernandez-Armesto, F. (2002), 'Meals make us human', in the *Guardian*, 14 September; and Marcin, G. (2004), 'Food, love and the human animal', report in *IACP Food Forum. Culinary Trade Winds* on talk by Sydney Mintz given at the 26th Annual IACP Conference, Baltimore, 2004. See also, for a discussion, Warde, A. and Martens, L. (2000), *Eating Out. Social Differentiation, Consumption and Pleasure*, Cambridge: Cambridge University Press.
9. Briffa, J. (2003), 'Course and effect', in the *Observer*, 22 June, referring to Neumark-Sztainer, D., Hannan, P.J., Story, M., Croll, J. and Perry, C. (2003), 'Family meal patterns: associations with sociodemographic characteristics and improved dietary intake among adolescents', in the *Journal of the American Dietetic Association*, Vol. 103, No. 3, pp. 317–322.
10. Okada, M. (2003), 'Children's perception of dinner conversation with parents in

Japan', in the *International Journal of Consumer Studies*, Vol. 27, No. 3, pp. 190–199.

11. Valentine, G. (1999), 'Eating in: home, consumption and identity', in *Sociological Review*, Vol. 47, pp. 492–524.

12. Burchill, J. (2002), 'Just don't make a meal of it', in the *Guardian*, 7 September.

13. Bove, C.F., Sobal, J. and Rauschenbach, B.S. (2003), 'Food choices among newly married couples: convergence, conflict, individualism, and projects', in *Appetite*, Vol. 40, No. 1, pp. 25–41.

14. See, for example, de Certeau, M., Giard, L. and Mayol, P. (1998), *The Practice of Everyday Life. Volume 2: Living and Cooking*, Minneapolis: University of Minnesota Press; and Holm, L. 'Family meals', in Kjaernes, U., *Eating Patterns* (note 7), pp. 159–212.

15. Rowe, D. (1999), 'A brief history of mealtime', in the *Guardian*, 1 September, quoting psychotherapist, Susie Orbach.

16. From www.babycentre.co.uk/expert/554249.html

17. Jakeman, J. (1994), 'How food snobs guard the right to scoff', in the *Independent*, 29 August, quoted in Wood, R. (1996), 'Talking to themselves: food commentators, food snobbery and market reality', in the *British Food Journal*, Vol. 98, No. 10, pp. 5–11.

18. See *Eat Better; Eat Together* on the nutrition education website for Washington State University, available http://nutrition.wsu.edu/eat/why.html

19. Kjaernes, U., *Eating Patterns* (note 7), p. 7.

20. See, for example, Holm, L., 'Family meals', in Kjaernes, U., *Eating Patterns* (note 7); Morrison, M. (1996), 'Sharing food at home and school: perspectives on commensality', in *Sociological Review*, Vol. 44, No. 4, pp. 648–674; and Murcott, A. (1997), 'Family meals – a thing of the past?', in Caplan, P. (ed.), *Food, Health and Identity*, London: Routledge, pp. 32–49.

21. See *Eat Better, Eat Together*, available http://nutrition.wsu.edu/eat/why.html (note 18); and Murcott, A., Family meals – a thing of the past? (note 20).

22. Warde, A. and Martens, L., *Eating Out* (note 8), p. 217.

23. Jennings, C. (1999), 'Can I get down now?', in the *Guardian*, 25 June.

24. Holm, L., 'Family meals', in Kjaernes, U., *Eating Patterns* (note 7), p. 199.

25. A web search produces websites from, for example, the University of Hawaii, the University of California and the United States Department of Agriculture offering tips for eating together and family mealtimes.

26. Blythman, J. (1999), *The Food our Children Eat. How to Get Children to Eat Good Food*, London: Fourth Estate, p. 215.

27. See Lang, T. and Caraher, M. (2001), 'Is there a culinary skills transition? Data and debate from the UK about changes in cooking culture', in the *Journal of the Home Economics Institute of Australia*, Vol. 8, No. 2, pp. 2–14; and Leith, P. (2001), 'Choice for children', in *Resurgence*, Issue 205.

28. Lang, T. and Caraher, M. 'Is there a culinary skills transition?' (note 27), quoting a forecast from the Henly Centre given in Novartis (2000), *A Taste of the 21st Century*, Novartis: London.

29. Fort, M. (2003), 'The death of cooking', in 'Food, the way we eat now', in the *Guardian*, 10 May.

30. Marshall, D.W. (1995), 'Eating at home: meals and food choice', in Marshall, D.W. (ed.), *Food Choice and the Consumer*, Glasgow: Blackie, pp. 264–287.

31. Ritzer, G. (1996), *The McDonaldization of Society*, Thousand Oaks, California: Pine Forge Press. See also, for example, Fieldhouse, P. (1995), *Food and Nutrition, Customs and Culture*, London: Chapman and Hall; and Mintz, S. (1996), *Tasting Food, Tasting Freedom: Excursions into Eating, Culture and the Past*, Boston: Beacon Press.

32. The National Food Alliance's (now Sustain) 1997 publication, *Myths about Food and Low Income* (London: National Food Alliance Publications) talks of how 'there is a general deficit of cooking skills in the UK', p. 19. See, for other examples, Meikle, J. (1999), 'Poor to be offered cooking lessons to improve diet', in the *Guardian*, 12 May; and a consultation paper for the Food Standards Agency UK (2004), *Review of UK Work on Food and Low-income Issues*, which refers to 'the loss of cooking skills' without specific reference, available www.food.gov.uk/foodindustry

33. See Lang, T., Caraher, M., Dixon, P. and Carr-Hill, R. (1999), *Cooking Skills and Health*, London: The Health Education Authority; and Sorg, L. (2004), 'A lone star state of mind. Can you eat well on food stamps?', in the *San Antonio Current*, 9 September.

34. Ripe, C. (1993), *Goodbye Culinary Cringe*, St Leonards, Australia: Allen and Unwin.

35. Lang T. and Caraher, M. 'Is there a culinary skills transition?' (note 27).

36. Stitt, S., Jepson, M., Paulson-Box, E. and Prisk, E. (1996), *Research on Food Education and the Diet and Health of Nations*, Liverpool: John Moores University Consumer Research.

37. See, for example, Davies, L. (1998), 'Issues Facing Food Technology', in *Modus*, March, pp. 36–40 and April, pp. 80–83; Farrell, A. (2000), *Food in the National Curriculum: Balanced Diet or Seriously Malnourished?*, available http://www.food-forum.org.uk/hot/National_Curriculum-Tea-Fis.shtml; and Ridgewell, J. (1996), *Working with Food in Primary Schools. Design and Technology*, London: Ridgewell Press.

38. See, for example, Bateman, M. (2000), 'The cooking class war', in the *Independent*, 4 June; and Leith, P. (n.d.), *Goodbye Mr Chips*, available www.waitrose.com/food_drink/wfi/foodissues/children/0106023.asp supporting the Royal Society of Arts Focus on Food programme.

39. See for discussion, for example, Kjaernes, U., *Eating Patterns* (note 7); DeVault, M. (1991), *Feeding the Family: The Social Organization of Caring as Gendered Work*, Chicago: University of Chicago Press; and Mennell, S., Murcott, A. and Van Otterloo, A.H. (1994), *The Sociology of Food: Eating, Diet and Culture*, London: Sage Publications.

40. See Arnould, E.J. and Price, L.L. (2001), 'Bread of our mothers. Ruptures and con-tinuities in families and homemade food traditions', paper presented at the 8th Interdisciplinary Conference on Consumption, Paris, La Sorbonne; Rappaport, L.,

How We Eat (note 1); and Scruton, R. (1996), 'The way we eat: time to fight the fridge culture', in *The Times*, 17 June.

41. Fernandez-Armesto, F. (2001), *Food: A History*, London: Macmillan, pp. 22–23.

42. www.slowfood.com, www.slowfoodusa.com; and Jones, P., Shears, P., Hillier, D., Comfort, D. and Lowell, J. (2003), 'A return to traditional values? A case study of Slow Food', in the *British Food Journal*, Vol. 105, No. 4/5, pp. 297–304.

43. Fort, M., 'The death of cooking' (note 29); Grigson, J. (1993), *English Food*, London: Penguin Books; and Leith, P. (1998), 'Cooking with kids', in Griffiths, S. and Wallace, J. (eds), *Consuming Passions: Food in the Age of Anxiety*, Manchester: Manchester University Press.

44. See reports on both studies: Nicolaas, G. (1995), *Cooking, Attitudes and Behaviour*, produced on behalf of the Nutrition Task Force for the Department of Health UK, London: Crown Copyright; and Lang et al., *Cooking Skills and Health* (note 33).

45. Demas, A. (1995), 'Food education in the elementary classroom as a means of gaining acceptance of diverse, low-fat foods in the school lunch program', unpublished PhD thesis, Cornell University; Street, P.A. (1994), 'An investigation into the prevalence and degree of cooking skills in North Reddish, with particular reference to mothers on low income with young children', dissertation for the Department of Food and Consumer Science, Manchester Metropolitan University; Wrieden, W., Anderson, A., Longbottom, P., Valentine, K., Stead, M., Caraher, M., Lang, T. and Dowler, E. (2002), *Assisting Dietary Change in Low-income Communities: Assessing the Impact of a Community-based Practical Food Skills Intervention* (CookWell), Report to the Food Standards Agency.

46. Rodrigues, S.S.P. and de Almeida, M.D.V. (1996), 'Food habits: concepts and practices of two different age groups', in Edwards, J.S.A. (ed.), *Culinary Arts and Sciences. Global and National Perspectives*, London: Computational Mechanics Publications, pp. 387–397.

47. See report of study for BBC Good Food and the National Food Alliance (now Sustain), Lang, T. and Baker, L. (1993), 'The rise and fall of domestic cooking: turning European children into passive consumers?', paper for the 13th International Home Economics and Consumer Studies Research Conference, September, Leeds, UK.

48. See report of 1997 Food Survey for Sainsbury's by Innes, M. (1998), 'The way we eat', in *Sainsbury's The Magazine*, April, pp. 36–41.

49. See Holm, L., 'Family meals' (note 14); Morrison, M., 'Sharing food at home and school' (note 20); Warde, A. and Martens, L., *Eating Out* (note 8).

50. See Lang et al., *Cooking Skills and Health* (note 33); Ripe, C., *Goodbye Culinary Cringe* (note 34); and Stitt, S. et al., *Research on Food Education and the Diet and Health of Nations* (note 36).

51. See, for examples, Lang et al., *Cooking Skills and Health* (note 33); Rodrigues, S.S.P. and de Almeida, M.D.V., 'Food habits: concepts and practices' (note 46); and Warde, A., *Consumption, Food and Taste* (note 7).

52. Lang et al., *Cooking Skills and Health* (note 33).

53. Adamson, A. (1996), 'Food, health and cooking: why it matters', report from *Get Cooking!* in Newcastle, a National Food Alliance publication.

54. Lang et al., *Cooking Skills and Health* (note 33).
55. Nestle Family Monitor (2001), *No. 13, Eating and Today's Lifestyle*, research by Market and Opinion Research International.
56. Singleton, W.T. (1978*), The Study of Real Skills. Vol. 1, The Analysis of Practical Skills*, Lancaster: MTP Press; and Wood, S. (ed.) (1982), 'Introduction', in *The Degradation of Work? Skills, Deskilling and the Labour Process*, London: Anchor Press, pp. 11–22.
57. See Wellens, J. (1974), *Training in Physical Skills*, London: Business Books Limited.
58. See, for examples, note 41, and also Lang, T., Hitchman, C., Christie, I. and Harrison, M. (2002), *Inconvenience Food. The Struggle to Eat Well on a Low Income*, research for Demos, London: Demos Publications; and *Myths about Food and Low Income* (1997), a National Food Alliance publication, available www.sustainweb.org/publications/downloads/pov_myths.pdf
59. Braverman, H. (1974), *Labour and Monopoly Capital. The Degradation of Work in the Twentieth Century*, New York: Monthly Review Press.
60. See Gofton, L. (1995), 'Convenience and the moral status of consumer practices', in Marshall, D. (ed.), *Food Choice and the Consumer*, Glasgow: Blackie, pp. 152–182 and, on assembly skills, Mars, G. and Mars, V. (2000), 'The digest of memory: food, health and upbringing in early childhood', in *Food and Memory. Proceedings of the Oxford Symposium*, Totnes, UK: Prospect Books, pp. 163–172.
61. Innes, M., 'The way we eat' (note 48); and see Caraher, M. and Lang, T. (1998), 'The influence of celebrity chefs on public attitudes and behaviour among the English public', paper given at a conference of the Association for the Study of Food and Society, San Francisco, quoting figures from the Henly Centre, UK.
62. Wood, R.C. (2000), 'Is food an art form? Pretentiousness and pomposity in cookery', in *Strategic Questions in Food and Beverage Management*, Oxford: Butterworth Heinemann; and 'Make it convenient' (2003), in 'A survey of food', in *The Economist*, December, pp. 10–11.
63. Freeman, J. (2004), *A Cultural History. The Making of the Modern Kitchen*, Oxford: Berg.
64. Caraher, M. and Lang, T., 'The influence of celebrity chefs' (note 61).
65. Mennell, S. (1996*), All Manners of Food: Eating and Taste in England and France from the Middle Ages to the Present*, Chicago: University of Illinois Press.
66. For theme see Shapiro, L. (2001), *Perfection Salad. Women and Cooking at the Turn of the Century*, New York: Random House.
67. See Dickinson, R. and Leader, S (1998), 'Ask the family', in Griffiths, S. and Wallace, J. (eds), *Consuming Passions: Food in the Age of Anxiety*, Manchester: Manchester University Press, pp. 122–129; Warde, A. and Hethrington, K. (1994), 'English household and routine food practices: a research note', in the *Sociological Review*, Vol. 42, pp. 758–778; and James, W.P.T. and McColl, K.A. (1997*), Healthy English Schoolchildren*, a proposal for the Minister for Public Health, Aberdeen: Rowlett Research Institute.
68. Sutton, D. (2001), *Remembrance of Repasts, An Anthropology of Food and Memory*, Oxford: Berg Publishers, p. 142.

69. Murcott, A. (1995), 'Raw, cooked and proper meals at home', in Marshall, D.W. (ed.), *Food Choice and the Consumer* (note 30), pp. 219–234; and 'Is it still a pleasure to cook for him? Social changes in the household and the family', in the *Journal of Consumer Studies and Home Economics*, Vol. 24, pp. 78–84.

Chapter 2 Who Knows about Cooking?

1. See, for brief overview, Tangrob, N. (2002), 'A brief history of life before Delia', in the *Observer*, 10 November.

2. A viewpoint put forward by Symons, M. (1998), *A History of Cooks and Cooking*, Chicago: University of Illinois Press.

3. Theophano, J. (2002), *Eat My Words. Reading Women's Lives through the Cookbooks They Wrote*, New York: Palgrave.

4. As pointed out by sociologists and scholars of food. Both Stephen Mennell and Alan Warde have studied representations of domestic cooking in the written media. See Mennell, S. (1996), *All Manners of Food: Eating and Taste in England and France from the Middle Ages to the Present*, Chicago: University of Illinois Press; and Warde, A. (1997), *Consumption, Food and Taste. Culinary Antinomies and Commodity Culture*, London: Sage Publications.

5. Shapiro, L. (2004), *Something from the Oven. Reinventing Dinner in 1950s America*, New York: Viking, p. xxi.

6. de Certeau, M., Giard, L. and Mayol, P. (1998), *The Practice of Everyday Life. Volume 2: Living and Cooking*, Minneapolis: University of Minnesota Press.

7. Examples include Beardsworth, A. and Keil, T. (1997), *Sociology on the Menu. An Invitation to the Study of Food and Society*, London: Routledge; Germov, J. and Williams, L. (eds) (1999), *A Sociology of Food and Nutrition: The Social Appetite*, Melbourne: Oxford University Press; Gofton, L. (1992), 'Machines for the suppression of time: meanings and explanations of change', in the *British Food Journal*, Vol. 94, No. 7, pp. 30–37; and Mennell, S., Murcott, A. and Van Otterloo, A.H. (1994), *The Sociology of Food: Eating, Diet and Culture*, London: Sage Publications.

8. See Charles, N. and Kerr, M. (1988), *Women, Food and Families*, Manchester: Manchester University Press; Counihan, C.M. (1999), *The Anthropology of Food and Body: Gender, Meaning and Power*, London: Routledge; Ekstrom, M.P. and Furst, E.L. (2001), 'The gendered division of cooking', in Kjaernes, U. (ed.), *Eating Patterns. A Day in the Lives of Nordic Peoples*, Lysaker, Norway: National Institute for Consumer Research, pp. 213–234; and Murcott, A. (1985), 'Cooking and the cooked: a note on the domestic preparation of meals', in Murcott, A. (ed.), *The Sociology of Food and Eating*, London: Sage Publications.

9. Mennell, S. et al., *The Sociology of Food* (note 7), p. 99.

10. DeVault, M.L. (1991), *Feeding the Family. The Social Organization of Caring as Gendered Work*, Chicago: University of Chicago Press, back cover.

11. DeVault, M.L., *Feeding the Family* (note 10), p. 118.

12. Oakley, A. (1974), *Housewife*, London: Allen Lane, p. 119.

13. Douglas, M. (1975), *Implicit Meanings: Essays in Anthropology*, London: Routledge and Kegan Paul; and Douglas, M. (1998), 'Coded messages', in Griffiths, S. and Wallace, J. (eds), *Consuming Passions: Food in the Age of Anxiety*, Manchester: Manchester University Press, pp. 103–110.

14. See, for example, Barthes, R. (1972), *Mythologies*, London: Paladin Grafton Books; Harbottle, L. (1997), 'Taste and embodiment. The food preferences of Iranians in Britain', in MacBeth, H. (ed.) *Food Preferences and Taste: Continuity and Change*, London: Berghahn Books, pp. 175–185; and Warde, A., *Consumption, Food and Taste* (note 4).

15. Bourdieu, P. (1986), *Distinction: A Social Critique of the Judgement of Taste*, London: Routledge.

16. Bently, A. (2001), 'Reading food riots: scarcity, abundance and national identity', in Scholliers, P. (ed.), *Food, Drink and Identity. Cooking, Eating and Drinking in Europe since the Middle Ages*, Oxford: Berg, pp. 179–194.

17. See, for example, Mintz, S. (1985), *Sweetness and Power: the Place of Sugar in Modern History*, New York: Viking; and Koc, M. and Welsh, J. (2002), 'Food, identity and immigrant experience', in *Canadian Diversity*, Vol. 1, No. 1, pp. 46–48.

18. Goody, J. (1994), *Cooking, Cuisine and Class. A Study in Comparative Sociology*, Cambridge: Cambridge University Press.

19. Mennell, S., *All Manners of Food* (note 4).

20. Warde, A., *Consumption, Food and Taste* (note 4).

21. Willets, A. (1997), '"Bacon sandwiches got the better of me": meat-eating and vegetarianism in South-East London', in Caplan, P. (ed.) *Food, Health and Identity*, London: Routledge, pp. 111–130.

22. Miller, T. (2001), 'Screening food: French cuisine and the television palate', in Schehr, L.R. and Weiss, A.S. (eds), *French Food on the Table, on the Page, and in French Culture*, London: Routledge, pp. 221–228 – referring to Fine, B. and Leopold, E. (1993), *The World of Consumption*, London: Routledge.

23. Dusselier, J. (2001), 'Bonbons, lemon drops, and Oh Henry! bars: candy, consumer culture, and the construction of gender, 1895–1920', in Inness, S.A. (ed.), *Kitchen Culture in America. Popular Representations of Food, Gender and Race*, Philadelphia: University of Pennsylvania Press, pp. 13–50.

24. James, A. (1997), 'How British is British food?', in Caplan, P. (ed.), *Food, Health and Identity* (note 21), pp. 71–86, quoted from pp. 72–74.

25. Scholliers, P. (2001), 'Meals, food narratives, and sentiments of belonging in past and present', in Scholliers, P. (ed.), *Food, Drink and Identity* (note 16), pp. 3–22.

26. Scholliers, P. (ed.) *Food, Drink and Identity* (note 16), p. 5.

27. Mennell, S., et al., *The Sociology of Food* (note 7), p. 194, describe 'cuisine' or 'culinary culture' as a 'shorthand term for the ensemble of attitudes and taste people bring to cooking and eating' within a particular social group. Fieldhouse, P. (1995), *Food and Nutrition, Customs and Culture*, London: Chapman and Hall, p. 52, describes it as 'a term commonly used to denote a style of cooking with distinctive foods, preparation methods and techniques of eating'.

28. Sydner, Y.M. and Fjellstrom, C. (2003), 'The meaning of symbols of culinary rules',

in Edwards, J.S.A. and Gustafsson, I.-B. (eds), *Culinary Arts and Sciences IV. Global and National Perspectives*, pp. 363–371, a study of four residential homes in Stockholm examining how the meaning of food is expressed and presented by different social groups.

29. James, A., 'How British is British Food?' (note 24).
30. Mintz, S. (1996), *Tasting Food, Tasting Freedom: Excursions into Eating, Culture and the Past*, Boston: Beacon Press, p. 96.
31. Cook, I., Crang, P. and Thorpe, M. (2000), 'Regions to be cheerful: culinary authenticity and its geographies', in Cook, I., Crouch, D., Naylor, S. and Ryan, J. (eds), *Cultural Turns/Geographical Turns*, Harlow: Longman. See also Cook, I. and Crang, P. (1996), 'The world on a plate: culinary culture, displacement and geographical knowledges', in the *Journal of Material Culture*, Vol. 1, No. 2, pp. 131–153; and Cook, I., Crang, P. and Thorpe, M. (1998), 'Biographies and geographies: consumer understandings of the origins of foods', in the *British Food Journal*, Vol. 199, No. 3, pp. 162–167.
32. From a children's column in a Norwegian national newspaper and referenced in Bahr-Bugge, A. (2003), 'Cooking – as identity work', paper presented at the 6th Conference of the European Sociological Association, Ageing Societies, New Sociology, September, Murcia, Spain.
33. As it is described on their website, www.yosushi.com
34. Cook, I. et al., 'Regions to be cheerful' and Cook, I. and Crang, P., 'The world on a plate' (note 31).
35. Fernandez-Armesto, F. (2001), *Food. A History*, London: Macmillan.
36. The BBC News e-cyclopedia, available http://news.bbc.co.uk/1/hi/special_report/1999/02/99/e-cyclopedia/1285804.stm
37. Cwiertka, K. (1998), 'A note on the making of culinary tradition – an example of modern Japan', in *Appetite*, Vol. 30, No. 2, pp. 117–128.
38. Wildt, M. (2001), 'Promise of more. The rhetoric of (food) consumption in a society searching for itself: West Germany in the 1950s', in Scholliers, P. (ed.), *Food, Drink and Identity* (note 16), pp. 63–80.
39. Tellstrom, R., Gustafsson, I.-B. and Fjellstrom, C. (2003), 'Food culture as a political tool – meal contruction during the Swedish EU Chairmanship 2001', in Edwards, J.S.A. and Gustafsson, I.-B. (eds), *Culinary Arts and Sciences IV* (note 28), pp. 341–352, quote from p. 349.
40. Green, H. (1998), *Northern Exposure*, available www.waitrose.com/food_drink/wfi/foodissues/foodtrends/9808076.asp
41. Shapiro, L., *Something from the Oven* (note 5).
42. See, for further detail, Finkelstein, J. (1989), *Dining Out: A Sociology of Modern Manners*, Cambridge: Polity; and Warde, A. and Martens, L. (2000), *Eating Out: Social Differentiation, Consumption and Pleasure*, Cambridge: Cambridge University Press.
43. Caraher, M. and Lang, T. (1998), 'The influence of celebrity chefs on public and attitudes and behaviour among the English public', paper given at a conference of the Association for the Study of Food and Society in San Francisco.

44. See Corner, J. (1997), 'Television in theory', in *Media, Culture and Society*, Vol. 19, pp. 247–262. See also Altheide, D.L. (1997), 'Media participation in everyday life', in *Leisure Sciences*, No. 19, pp. 17–29; and Curran, J., Gurevitch, M. and Woollacott, J. (1987), 'The study of the media: theoretical approaches', in Boyd-Barrett, O. and Braham, P. (eds), *Media, Knowledge and Power*, London: Croom Helm, pp. 55–79.

45. Randall, S. (2000), 'How does the media influence public taste for food and beverage? The role of the media in forming customer attitudes towards food and beverage provision', in Wood, R.C. (ed.), *Strategic Questions in Food and Beverage Management*, Oxford: Butterworth-Heinnemann, pp. 81–96; Randall, S. (2000), 'Mediated meanings of hospitality: television food programmes', in Lashley, C. and Morrison, A. (eds), *In Search of Hospitality*, Oxford: Butterworth-Heinnemann, pp. 118–133.

46. A phrase used by Roy Wood in Wood, (2000), 'Why are there so many celebrity chefs and cooks (and do we need them)? Culinary cultism and crassness on television and beyond', in Wood, R.C. (ed.), *Strategic Questions in Food and Beverage Management* (note 45), pp. 129–152.

47. Shown in most areas of the UK on BBC2 on 26 September 1996, 8.30 p.m.

48. Randall, S. (1999), 'Television representations of food: a case study. A semiotic analysis of Rick Stein's Taste of the Sea television food programme', in the *International Journal of Toursim and Hospitality Research*, Vol. 1, No. 1., pp. 41–54, quoted from p. 45.

49. See, for further detail, Mennell, S. et al., *The Sociology of Food* (note 7).

50. Warde, A., *Consumption, Food and Taste* (note 4).

51. As Warde found in his comparison of women's magazines of the 1960s and 1990s. See Warde, A., *Consumption, Food and Taste* (note 4).

52. Goody, J. (1978), *The Domestication of the Savage Mind*, Cambridge: Cambridge University Press; and Mennell, S., *All Manners of Food* (note 4).

53. Bryman, A. (1998), *Quantity and Quality in Social Research*, London: Routledge; and Mason, J. (1996), *Qualitative Researching*, London: Sage Publications.

54. Bauer, M.W. and Aarts, B. (2000), 'Corpus construction: a principle for qualitative data collection', in Bauer, M.W. and Gaskell, G. (eds), *Qualitative Researching with Text, Image and Sound. A Practical Handbook*, London: Sage Publications, pp. 19–38.

55. Short, F. (2002), 'Cooking skills in late twentieth century England', thesis for Thames Valley University, Centre for Food Policy. See also Short, F. (2003), 'Domestic cooking skills – what are they?', in the *Journal of the Australian Institute of Home Economics*, Vol. 10, No. 3, pp. 13–22; and Short, F. (2003), 'Domestic cooking practices and cooking skills: findings from an English study', in *Food Service Technology*, Vol. 3, Parts 3/4, pp. 177–185.

Chapter 3 What do Cooks Think of Cooking?

1. Ripe, C. (1993), *Goodbye Culinary Cringe*, St Leonards: Allen and Unwin.

2. Stitt, S., Jepson, M., Paulson-Box, E. and Prisk, E. (1996), *Research on Food*

Education and the Diet and Health of Nations, Liverpool: John Moores University Consumer Research.

3. See Bell, A. (1998), 'Storm in an egg cup as Gary says Delia's cookery advice is "insulting"', the *Independent*, 27 October.

4. See www.dictionary.com, www.m-w.com, and www.encarta.msn.com

5. See, for example, www.dictionary.cambridge.org

6. Murcott, A. (1995), 'Raw, cooked and proper meals at home', in Marshall, D.W. (ed.), *Food Choice and the Consumer*, Glasgow: Blackie and Academic.

7. See Dickinson, R. and Leader, S. (1997), 'The role of television in the food choices of 11–18 year olds', in the *British Food Journal*, Vol. 99, No. 9; Anon. (1998), '1997 Food Survey', *Sainsbury's The Magazine*, 9 April; Health Education Authority UK (1998), *Health and Lifestyles: a Survey of the UK Population 1993*, London: Health Education Authority UK.

8. Lang, T., Caraher, M., Dixon, P. and Carr-Hill, R. (1999), *Cooking Skills and Health*, London: Health Education Authority UK.

9. Royal Society of Arts (1999), *Working Report of a Joint Survey by the RSA's Focus on Food Campaign and the Health Education Trust UK*, 3 June.

10. They were shared by the majority of the informants who took part in the main informing study.

11. See Kuehn, G. (2002), *Ignorance, Knowledge, Despair, Bliss ...How Much "Extensive" Eating Can We Handle?*, available www.americanphilosophy.org/archives/2002_Conference/2002_papers/respons

12. See, for example, Barer-Stein, T. (1999), 'You eat what you are', in *People, Culture and Food Traditions*, Buffalo: Firefly Books; Gabaccia, D.R. (2000), *We Are What We Eat. Ethnic Food and the Making of Americans*, Cambridge: Harvard University Press; and Birch, L.L. (2000), 'Acquisition of food preferences and eating patterns in children', paper for the Danone Institute's Symposium on Food Selection, Paris, available www.danoneinstitute.org/danone_institutes_intiatives/pdf/05_birch.pdf

13. Drake McFeely, M. (2001), *Can She Bake a Cherry Pie? American Women and the Kitchen in the Twentieth Century*, Amherst: University of Massachusetts Press, p. 6.

14. Douglas, M. (1998), 'Coded messages', in Griffiths, S. and Wallace, J. (eds), *Consuming Passions: Food in the Age of Anxiety*, Manchester: Manchester University Press, pp. 103–110.

15. Sutton, D. (2001), *Remembrance of Repasts. An Anthropology of Food and Memory*, Oxford: Berg Publishers, p. 104.

16. Murcott, A. (1985), 'Cooking and the cooked: a note on the domestic preparation of meals', in Murcott, A. (ed.), *The Sociology of Food and Eating*, London: Sage Publications, pp. 178–193.

17. Murcott, A. (2000), 'Is it still a pleasure to cook for him? Social changes in the household and the family', in the *Journal of Consumer Studies and Home Economics*, Vol. 24, No. 2, pp. 78–84.

18. Marshall, D.W. (1995), 'Eating at home: meals and food choice', in Marshall, D.W. (ed.), *Food Choice and the Consumer*, Glasgow: Blackie Academic and

Professional, pp. 264–287.

19. See Griffiths, S. and Wallace, J. (eds), *Consuming Passions* (note 14); and Fischler, C. (1988), 'Food, self and identity', in *Social Science Information*, Vol. 27, No. 2, pp. 275–292.

20. Poncet, E. (2000), 'From eaters to consumers. An interview with Claude Fischler', in *Dizajn*, No. 26, available www.designzine.com/2001_02_16/html/articleDizajn Frame.html

21. Wood, R. (1995), *The Sociology of the Meal*, Edinburgh: Edinburgh University Press; and de Certeau, M., Giard, L. and Mayol, P. (1998), *The Practice of Everyday Life. Volume 2: Living and Cooking*, Minneapolis: University of Minnesota Press.

22. de Certeau, M. et al., *The Practice of Everyday Life* (note 21), p. 190.

23. Beardsworth, A. and Keil, T. (1997), *Sociology on the Menu. An Invitation to the Study of Food and Society*, London: Routledge, pp. 168–172.

24. Marshall, D.W., 'Eating at home' (note 18).

25. Reichl, R. (2001), *Comfort Me with Apples: More Adventures at the Table*, New York: Random House; Uvezian, S. (2001), *Recipes and Remembrances from an Eastern Mediterranean Kitchen: A Culinary Journey Through Syria, Lebanon and Jordan*, Northbrook, USA: Siamanto Press; Bourdain, A. (2001), *Kitchen Confidential*, London: Bloomsbury; Ginsberg, D. (2000), *Waiting: The True Confessions of a Waitress*, London: Harper Collins; and Mayle, P. (2002), *French Lessons: Adventures with Knife, Fork and Corkscrew*, New York, USA: Vintage Books.

26. Shapiro, L. (1995), 'Do women like to cook?', in *Food. The Vital Stuff*, Granta 52, London: Granta Publications, pp. 155–162.

27. Shapiro, L. (2004), *Something from the Oven. Reinventing Dinner in 1950s America*, New York: Viking, p. xxi.

28. Endrijonas, E. (2001), 'Processed foods from scratch: cooking for a family in the 1950s', in Inness, S.A. (ed.), *Kitchen Culture in America. Popular Representations of Food, Gender and Race*, Philadelphia: University of Pennsylvania Press, pp. 157–174.

29. See Lang, T. et al., *Cooking Skills and Health* (note 8); Nicolaas, G. (1995), *Cooking, Attitudes and Behaviour*, a report on survey data for the Nutrition Task Force for the Department of Health, London: Crown Copyright; Health Education Authority UK, *Health and Lifestyles* (note 7); and Anon., 1997 'Food Survey', (note 7), pp. 36–41.

30. Leith, P. (1997), 'Food in Britain. Your chance to have a say', in *Sainsburys The Magazine*, November, pp. 58–65, quoted p. 58.

31. Lang, T. et al., *Cooking Skills and Health* (note 8).

32. See, for example, Mintz, S. (1996), *Tasting Food, Tasting Freedom: Excursions into Eating, Culture and the Past*, Boston: Beacon Press; Beardsworth, A. and Keil, T., *Sociology on the Menu* (note 23); and Warde, A. (1997), *Consumption, Food and Taste. Culinary Antinomies and Commodity Culture*, London: Sage Publications.

33. See Henly Centre (1994), *Leisure Futures*, London: Henly Centre; and Caraher, M. and Lang, T. (1998), 'The influence of celebrity chefs on public attitudes and behaviour among the English public', paper given to the Association for the Study of Food and Society Conference, San Francisco.

34. Goody, J. (1988), *The Domestication of the Savage Mind*, Cambridge: Cambridge University Press, p. 140.
35. Attar, D. (1990), *Wasting Girls' Time: The History and Politics of Home Economics*, London: Virago, p. 14.
36. Griffiths, S. and Wallace, J. (eds), *Consuming Passions* (note 14).
37. Demas, A. (1995), 'Food Education in the elementary classroom as a means of gaining acceptance of diverse, low fat foods in the school lunch program', PhD thesis, Ithaca: Cornell University, p. 225.
38. Sutton, D., *Remembrance of Repasts* (note 15).
39. All are mentioned by informants who took part in the main informing study.
40. From James Oliver's website, www.jamieoliver.com
41. From Gray, R. and Rogers, R. (1998), *River Café Cookbook Two*, London: Ebury Press.
42. Stead, M., Caraher, M., Wrieden, W., Longbottom, P., Valentine, K. and Anderson, A. (2004), 'Confident, fearful and hopeless cooks: findings from the development of a food skills initiative', in the *British Food Journal*, Vol. 6, No. 4, pp. 274–287, quoted p. 283.
43. Brown, M.A. and Cameron, A.G. (1977), *Experimental Cooking*, London: Edward Arnold.
44. McKie, L. and Wood, R. (1992), 'People's source of recipes: some implications for an understanding of food related behaviour', in the *British Food Journal*, Vol. 94, No. 2, pp. 12–17, quoted p. 17.
45. Lawson, N. (1998), 'Can't cook, don't want to', the *Guardian*, 13 October, pp. 6–7.
46. Mennell, S., Murcott, A. and Van Otterloo, A. H. (1994), *The Sociology of Food: Eating, Diet And Culture*, London: Sage Publications.
47. Goody, J., *The Domestication of the Savage Mind* (note 34), quoted p. 140.
48. Royal Society of Arts (n. d.), primary schools reference folder for teachers, for the Focus on Food Campaign.
49. See note 5.
50. Attar, D., *Wasting Girls' Time* (note 35), p. 14.
51. Murcott, A. (ed.), *The Sociology of Food and Eating* (note 16).
52. Swinbank, A.V. (2002), 'The sexual politics of cooking: a feminist analysis of culinary hierarchy in Western culture', in the *Journal of Historical Sociology*, Vol. 15, No. 4, pp. 464–494.
53. Goody, J., *The Domestication of the Savage Mind* (note 34), p. 140.
54. Oakley, A. (1985), *The Sociology of Housework*, Oxford: Basil Blackwell.
55. Oakley, A., *The Sociology of Housework* (note 54), pp. 58–59.
56. Lyon, P., Colquoun, A. and Alexander, E. (2003), 'Deskilling the domestic kitchen: national tragedy or the making of a modern myth?', in Edwards, J.S.A. and Gustafsson, I.-B (eds), *Culinary Arts and Sciences IV, Global and National Perspectives*, Bournemouth: Worshipful Company of Cooks Research Centre, pp. 402–412, quoted pp. 408–410.
57. An argument of Wood, R. (1996), 'Talking to themselves: food commentators, food snobbery and market reality', in the *British Food Journal*, Vol. 98, No.10, pp. 5–11.

58. Lawson, N., 'Can't cook, don't want to' (note 45).

59. See Stevenson, R.D. (1985), *Professional Cookery: the Process Approach*, London: Hutchinson; and Pepin, J. (1987), *La Technique. An Illustrated Guide to the Fundamental Techniques of Cooking*, New York: Papermac.

60. Lupton, D. (1996), *Food, the Body and Self*, London: Sage Publications, p. 194.

61. Mennell, S. (1985), *All Manners of Food. Eating and Taste in England and France from the Middle Ages to the Present*, Chicago: University of Illinois Press, p. 330.

62. Warde, A., *Consumption, Food and Taste* (note 32), pp. 160–161.

63. Consumers' Association (1998), 'Food, lessons for real life?' *Health Which?*, October, pp. 14–17, quoted p. 15.

64. See Finkelstein, J. (1989), *Dining Out: A Sociology of Modern Manners*, Cambridge: Polity Press; Fischler, C. (1980), 'Food habits, social change and the nature/culture dilemma', in *Social Science Information*, Vol. 19, No. 6, pp. 937–953; and Beardsworth, A. and Keil, T., *Sociology on the Menu* (note 23).

65. See Pinch, T., Collins, H.M. and Corbone, L. (1996), 'Inside knowledge: second order measures of skill', in *Sociological Review*, Vol. 44, No. 2, pp. 163–186; Singleton, W.T. (1978), *The Study of Real Skills. Volume 1 The Analysis of Practical Skills*, Lancaster: MTP Press; and Wellens, J. (1974), *Training in Physical Skills*, London: Business Books.

66. Charron, K.C. (2003), *Grandma's Apple Pie*, available www.stclairc.on.ca/programs/departments/journalism/journ2

67. *Ready Steady Cook* shown on BBC1 in most parts of the UK on Wednesday, 19 November 2003. See www.bbc.co.uk/food/readysteadycook

68. Randall, S. (1999), 'Television representations of food: a case study. A semiotic analysis of Rick Stein's Taste of the Sea television food programme', in *International Journal of Tourism and Hospitality Research*, Vol. 1, pp. 41–54.

69. Schlanger, N. (1990), 'The making of a soufflé: practical knowledge and social senses', in *Techniques of Culture*, Vol. 15, pp. 29–52, quoted p. 44.

70. See Pinch, T. et al., 'Inside knowledge'; Wellens, J., *Training in Physical Skills*; and Singleton, W.T., *The Study of Real Skills* (note 65).

Chapter 4 Who can Cook?

1. Fort, M. (2003), 'The death of cooking, in food, the way we eat now', the *Guardian*, 10 May.

2. See Leith, P. (2001), 'Choice for children', in *Resurgence*, No. 205, available http://resurgence.gn.apc.org/issues/leith205.htm and Bateman, M. (2000), 'Food for the future', in the *Independent on Sunday*, p. 25, 23 May.

3. Bell, A. (1998), 'Storm in an egg cup as Gary says Delia's cookery advice is "insulting"', the *Independent*, 27 October; www.geest.co.uk/html/profile/markets/2002; and www.healthyeatingclub.com/info/articles/food-proc/cooking-skills.htm

4. See Consumers' Association, (1998), 'Food, lessons for real life?', *Health Which?* October, pp. 14–17; Orr, D. (1999), 'Modern life on a plate', in the *Independent*, 22

January; and Demos (2003), *Hungry in a Consumer Society?*, available www.demos.co.uk.

5. See, for example, Bonzo, G., Kitson, N. and Wardrop, J. (2000), 'Talking food: a conversation about Zimbabwe, cooking, eating and social living', in *Mots Pluriels*, No. 15, available www.arts.uwa.au/MotsPluriels; Zubaida, S. and Tapper, R. (2001), *A Taste of Thyme. Culinary Cultures of the Middle East*, London: IB Tauris; *Foodshare* (2002), available www.foodshare.net; Perineau, L. (2002), 'France: dining with the doom generation', in *Gastronomica. The Journal of Food and Culture*, Autumn, Vol. 2, No. 4, pp. 80–82; and Tsering Bhalla, S. (n.d.), *Mum's Not Cooking Any More*, available www.singapore-window.org

6. von Rumohr, B. (1993), *The Essence of Cookery: Geist der Kochkunst*, translated by Yeomans, B., London: Prospect Books, pp. 52–54, quoted in Symons, M. (1998), *A History of Cooks and Cooking*, Chicago: University of Illinois Press, p. 328.

7. Mitchell, J. (2001), 'Cookbooks as a social and historical document: a Scottish case study', in *Food Service Technology*, Vol. 1, No. 1, pp. 13–23, quoted in Lyon, P. Colquoun, A. and Alexander, E. (2003), 'Deskilling the domestic kitchen national tragedy or the making of a modern myth?' in Edwards, J.S.A. and Gustafsson, I.-B. (eds), *Culinary Arts and Sciences IV*, Bournemouth: Worshipful Companmy of Cooks research Centre, p. 404.

8. See Chapter 1 and also, for a good summary, Gofton, L.R. (1992), 'Machines for the suppression of time: meanings and explanations of change', in the *British Food Journal*, Vol. 94, No. 7, pp. 30–37.

9. Bahr Bugge, A. (2003), 'Cooking – as identity work', paper presented at the 6th Conference of the European Sociological Association, Murcia, Spain, p. 1.

10. See Lang, T. and Baker, L. (1993), 'The rise and fall of domestic cooking: turning European children into passive consumers?', paper for the 13th International Home Economics and Consumer Studies Research Conference, Leeds, UK; Street, P.A. (1994), 'An investigation into the prevalence and degree of cooking skills in North Reddish', unpublished dissertation for the Department of Consumer Science, Manchester Metropolitan University, UK; Rodrigues, S.S.P. and Almeida, M.D.V. (1996), 'Food habits: concepts and practices of two different age groups', in Edwards, J.S.A. (ed.), *Culinary Arts and Sciences. Global and National Perspectives*, London: Computational Mechanics Publications; and Nestle Family Monitor (2001), Number 13, *Eating and Today's Lifestyle*, MORI.

11. Finlayson, A. (2002), 'Boiling an egg', in the *Guardian*, 7 February and Fort, M. (2003), 'The death of cooking', in the *Observer*, pp. 1–3, both available *www.guardian.co.uk*. See also Meikle, J. (1999), 'Poor to be offered cooking lessons to improve diet', in the *Guardian*, 12 May, referring to the UK's Food Standards Agency's policy.

12. Lyon, P. et al., 'Deskilling the domestic kitchen' (note 7), pp. 402–412.

13. Warde, A. and Hethrington, K. (1994), 'English households and routine food practices: a research note', in *Sociological Review*, Vol. 42, pp. 758–778, quoted p. 764.

14. See Chapter 3.

15. de Certeau, M., Giard, L. and Mayol, P. (1998), *The Practice of Everyday Life.*

Volume 2: Living and Cooking, Minneapolis: University of Minnesota Press.

16. Ekstrom, M.P. and d'Orange Furst, E. (2001), 'The gendered division of cooking', in Kjaernes, U. (ed.), *Eating Patterns. A Day in the Lives of Nordic Peoples*, pp. 213–234, quoted p. 217.

17. Symons, M. *A History of Cooks and Cooking* (note 6).

18. de Certeau, M. et al., *The Practice of Everyday Life* (note 15), p. 157.

19. See Pinch, T., Collins, H. M. Corbone, L. (1996), 'Inside knowledge: second order measures of skill', in *Sociological Review*, Vol. 44, No. 2, pp. 163–186; Wellens, J. (1974), *Training in Physical Skills*, London: Business Books Limited; and Singleton, W.T. (1978), *The Study of Real Skills. Volume 1 The Analysis of Practical Skills*, Lancaster, UK: MTP Press.

20. Scott, J. (1998), *Seeing Like a State: How Certain Schemes to Improve the Human Condition Have Failed*, New Haven: Yale University Press, p. 329, quoted in Sutton, D.E. (2001), *Remembrance of Repasts. An Anthropology of Food and Memory*, Oxford: Berg Publishers, p. 127.

21. Sutton, D. (2001), *Remembrance of Repasts* (note 20), p. 134.

22. de Leon, D. (2003), *Actions, Artefacts and Cognition: An Ethnography of Cooking*, Lund University Cognitive Studies, available www.lucs.lu.se/Abstracts/LUCS_Studies/LUCS104.html

23. de Leon, *Actions, Artefacts and Cognition* (note 22), p. 3.

24. de Certeau, M. et al., *The Practice of Everyday Life* (note 15), pp. 157–158.

25. Wellens, J., *Training in Physical Skills* (note 19); and Singleton, W.T., *The Study of Real Skills* (note 19).

26. See www.colstate.edu/pubs

27. Pinch, T. et al., 'Inside knowledge' (note 19); and Wellens, J., *Training in Physical Skills*, (note 19).

28. See Chapter 2 and Rappaport, L. (2003), *How We Eat. Appetite, Culture and the Psychology of Food*, Toronto, Canada: ECW Press.

29. Lang, T., Caraher, M., Dixon, P. and Carr-Hill, R. (1999), *Cooking Skills and Health*, London: the Health Education Authority UK, p. 1.

30. DeVault, M. (1991), *Feeding the Family: The Social Organization of Caring as Gendered Work*, Chicago: University of Chicago Press.

31. Anon. (2002), in *Cook School*, the magazine of the Royal Society of Arts Focus on Food Campaign, p. 55.

32. All are requests and preferences mentioned by those who took part in the main informing study.

33. See Lee, D. (1982), 'Beyond deskilling: skill, craft and class', in Wood, S. (ed.), *The Degradation of Work? Skill, Deskilling and the Labour Process*, London: The Anchor Press, pp. 146–162.

34. See, for example, Wellens, J., *Training in Physical Skills* (note 19); Singleton, W.T., *The Study of Real Skills* (note 19); and Lee, D., 'Beyond deskilling' (note 33).

35. Anon. (1993), 'Some coaching on poaching', in *Restaurants and Institutions*, pp. 190–191, quoted p. 191.

36. See for explanation, Bode, W.K.H. (1994), *European Gastronomy. The Story of*

Man's Food and Eating Customs, London: Hodder and Stoughton; and Gillespie, C. (2001), *European Gastronomy into the 21ˢᵗ Century*, Oxford: Butterworth-Heinemann. Saulnier, L. (1985 [first published in 1914]), *Le Répertoire de la cuisine*, London: Leon Jaeggi and Sons.

37. Fine, G.A. (1996), *Kitchens. The Culture of Restaurant Work*, Berkely, USA: University of California Press, pp. 19–37 and pp. 88–89.
38. Based on the practices of one of the informants for the main informing study.
39. See Fernandez-Armesto, P. (2002), 'Meals make us human, in the *Guardian*, 4 September, available www.guardian.co.uk/comment/story; and Symons, M., *A History of Cooks and Cooking* (note 6), p. 342.
40. de Certeau, M. et al., *The Practice of Everyday Life* (note 15), pp. 210–212.
41. A point made by Oakley, A. (1974), *Housewife*, London: Allen Lane.
42. Anon. (2002), 'The perfect pie crust', in *Cook School, The Food Education Magazine*, Launch Issue, pp. 18–19.
43. Silva, E.B. (2000), 'The cook, the cooker and the gendering of the kitchen', in *Sociological Review,* Vol. 48, No. 4, pp. 612–627.
44. Drake McFeely, M. (2001*), Can She Bake a Cherry Pie? American Women and the Kitchen in the Twentieth Century*, Amherst: University of Massachusetts Press, pp. 157–159.
45. Schwartz Cowan, R. (1983), *More Work for Mother. The Ironies of Household Technology from the Open Hearth to the Microwave*, New York: Basic Books.
46. See note 19.

Chapter 5 What is a Cook?

1. Symons, M. (1998), *A History of Cooks and Cooking*, Chicago: University of Illinois Press, p. 355.
2. de Certeau, M., Giard, L. and Mayol, P. (1998), *The Practice of Everyday Life. Volume 2: Living and Cooking*, Minneapolis: University of Minnesota Press, pp. 151–247 on cooking.
3. See, for example, Drake McFeely, M. (2001), *Can She Bake a Cherry Pie? American Women and the Kitchen in the Twentieth Century*, Amherst: University of Massachusetts Press; and Theophano, J. (2002), *Eat My Words. Reading Women's Lives through the Cookbooks They Wrote*, New York: Palgrave.
4. Shapiro, L. (2004), *Something from the Oven. Reinventing Dinner in 1950s America*, New York: Viking, p. xvii. See also Shapiro, L. (1995), 'Do women like to cook?', in *Food. The Vital Stuff*, Granta 52, London: Granta Publications, pp. 155–162.
5. See, for example, Charles, N. and Kerr, M. (1988), *Women, Food and Families*, Manchester: Manchester University Press; DeVault, M. (1991), *Feeding the Family: The Social Organization of Caring as Gendered Work*, Chicago: University of Chicago Press; Kjaernes, U. (ed.), *Eating Patterns. A Day in the Lives of Nordic Peoples*, Lysaker, Norway: National Institute for Consumer Research; and Martens,

L. and Warde, A. (2000), *Eating Out. Social Differentiation, Consumption and Pleasure*, Cambridge: Cambridge University Press.

6. See, for example, Coxon, T. (1983), 'Men in the kitchen', in Murcott, A. (ed.), *The Sociology of Food and Eating*, London: Gower; and Kyle, R. (1999), 'Middle class men's conceptualistions of food: a sociological investigation', unpublished PhD thesis for South Bank University, London.

7. Fine, G.A. (1996), *Kitchens. The Culture of Restaurant Work*, Berkeley: University of California Press.

8. Inness, S.A. (2001), *Dinner Roles. American Women and Culinary Culture*, Iowa City: University of Iowa Press, p. ix.

9. Humphreys, E. (1952), 'Whose kitchen is it anyway?', in *House Beautiful*, April, pp. 189–191, quoted by Inness, S.A., *Dinner Roles* (note 8).

10. Hollows, J. (2003), 'Oliver's twist: leisure, labour and domestic masculinity in The Naked Chef', in the *International Journal of Cultural Studies*, Vol. 6, pp. 229–248.

11. Nestle Family Monitor (2001), No. 13, *Eating and Today's Lifestyle*, research by Market and Opinion Research International (MORI), available www.mon.com/polls/2001/pdf/nfm13/html

12. Stead, M., Caraher, M., Wrieden, W., Longbottom, P.,Valentine, K. and Anderson, A. (2004), 'Confident, fearful and hopeless cooks: findings from the development of a food skills initiative', in the *British Food Journal*, Vol. 106, No. 4, pp. 274–287.

13. Wansink, B. (2003), 'Profiling nutritional gatekeepers: three methods for differentiating influential cooks', in *Food Quality and Preference*, Vol. 14, No. 4, pp. 289–297.

14. Shapiro, L., *Something from the Oven* (note 4).

15. Fisher, M.F.K. (1988), 'Loving cooks beware', in Davidson, A. (ed.), *On Fasting and Feasting: A Personal Collection of Favourite Writings on Food and Eating*, London: McDonald Orbis, pp. 12–15.

16. Thorne, J. (1996), *Fat Cook, Thin Cook*, available www.outlawcook.com

17. Barnes, J. (2003), *The Pedant in the Kitchen*, London: Atlantic Books.

18. I asked informants to describe making, either in the oven or on the stove, a stew, casserole, curry or something similar.

19. Duruz, J. (2004), 'Haunted kitchens: cooking and remembering', in *Gastronomica*, Vol. 4, No. 1, pp. 57–68.

20. Hollows, J. (2003), 'Feeling Like a Domestic Goddess: Postfeminism and Cooking', in the *European Journal of Cultural Studies*, Vol. 6, pp. 179–202.

21. Eyre, H. (2003), 'What do you mean, let's cook? Isn't that a seventies thing?', in the *Independent*, 24 August, p. 4.

22. See Gillon, E., McCorkindale, L. and McKie, L. (1993), 'Researching the dietary beliefs and practices of men', in the *British Food Journal*, Vol. 95, No. 6, pp. 8–12. See also Counihan, C.M (2004), *Around the Tuscan Table. Food, Family, and Gender in Twentieth-Century Florence*, London: Routledge; and Pink, S. (2004), *Home Truths. Gender, Domestic Objects and Everyday Life*, Oxford: Berg Publishers.

23. Warde, A. and Martens, L. (2000), *Eating Out: Social Differentiation, Consumption and Pleasure*, Cambridge: Cambridge University Press.

24. DeVault, M. (1991), *Feeding the Family* (note 5).

25. See, for example, Beardsworth, A. and Keil, T. (1997*), Sociology on the Menu. An Invitation to the Study of Food and Society*, London: Routledge.
26. Eyre, H., 'What do you mean, let's cook?' (note 21).
27. Valentine, G. (1999), 'Eating in: home consumption and identity,' in *Sociological Review*, Vol. 47, No. 3, pp. 491–524.
28. Mars, G. and Mars, V. (1993), 'Two contrasting dining styles: suburban conformity and urban individualism', in Mars, G. and Mars, V. (eds), *Food, Culture and History Vol. 1*, London: The London Food Seminar, pp. 49–60.

Chapter 6 What do Cooks Cook, and Why?

1. Fieldhouse, P. (1995), *Food and Nutrition, Customs and Culture*, London: Chapman and Hall, p. 70.
2. Child Poverty Action Group Briefings (1999), *School Meals in Scotland*, available www.cpag.org.uk
3. Lang, T., Caraher, P., Dixon, P. and Carr-Hill, R. (1996), 'Class, income and gender in cooking: results from an English survey', in Edwards, J.S.A. (ed), *Culinary Arts and Sciences: Global and National Perspectives*, Southampton: Computational Mechanics Publications, pp. 415–425; Burke, L. (2002), 'Healthy eating in the school environment – a holistic approach', in the *International Journal of Consumer Studies*, Vol. 26, No. 2, pp. 159–163; Hanes, F. (1986), 'Can I afford a healthy diet?, in *Modus*, November, pp. 321–323, quoted in Lyon, P., Colquoun, A. and Alexander, E. (2003), 'Deskilling the domestic kitchen: national tragedy or the making of a modern myth?', in Edwards, J.S.A. and Gustafsson, I.-B (eds), *Culinary Arts and Sciences IV, Global and National Perspectives*, Bournemouth: Worshipful Company of Cooks Research Centre, pp. 402–412.
4. Mulligan, M., Deputy Minister for Communities (Scotland) (2003), quoted in *Fare Choice, The Quarterly Newsletter of the Scottish Community Diet Project*, Autumn, Issue 25.
5. Lang, T., Caraher, M., Dixon, P. and Carr-Hill, R. (1999), *Cooking Skills and Health*, London: Health Education Authority.
6. Nestle Family Monitor (2001), No. 13, *Eating and Today's Lifestyle*, research by Market and Opinion Research International.
7. Laudan, R. (2001), 'A plea for culinary modernism: why we should love new, fast, processed food,' in *Gastronomica*, Vol. 1, No. 4, pp. 108–125.
8. See www.unclebens.com/products/our_products.asp
9. See Pinch, T., Collins, H.M. and Corbone, L. (1996), 'Inside knowledge: second order measures of skill', in *Sociological Review*, Vol. 44, No. 2, pp. 163–186; and Wellens, J. (1974), *Training in Physical Skills*, London: Business Books; and Singleton, W.T. (1978), *The Study of Real Skills. Volume 1 The Analysis of Practical Skills*, Lancaster, UK: MTP Press.
10. Lang, T. et al., *Cooking Skills and Health* (note 5); Nicolaas, G. (1995), *Cooking, Attitudes and Behaviour*, produced on behalf of the Nutrition Task Force for the

Department of Health UK, London: Crown Copyright; and Mulligan, M. in *Fare Choice* (note 4).

11. See Chapter 4 and Pinch, T. et al., 'Inside knowledge' (note 9); Wellens, J., *Training in Physical Skills* (note 9); and Singleton, W.T., *The Study of Real Skills* (note 9).

12. For a wider discussion, see, for example, DeVault, M. (1991), *Feeding the Family: The Social Organization of Caring as Gendered Work*, Chicago: University of Chicago Press; Dowler, E. (2002), 'Food and poverty in Britain: rights and responsibilities', in *Social Policy and Administration*, Vol. 36, No. 6, pp. 698–717; Millstone, E. and Lang, T. (2002), *The Atlas of Food: Who Eats What, Where and Why*, London: Earthscan Publications; Murcott, A. (1998), *The Nation's Diet. The Social Science of Food Choice*, Harlow: Addison Wesley Longman; and Sutton, S., Conner, M. and Armitage, C.J. (2002), *The Social Psychology of Food*, London: Open University Press.

13. Fieldhouse, P., *Food and Nutrition, Customs and Culture* (note 1), p. 70.

14. See Chapter 3.

Chapter 7 So How is Cooking?

1. Moskowitz, D. (2004), 'Heartland cooking with fish sauce', in *City Pages. The Online News and Arts Weekly of the Twin Cities*, Vol. 25, 25 August, available www.citypages.com.

2. Food Standards Agency UK (2003), *Evaluation of Food and Nutrition Competencies Amongst 14 to 16 year olds*, Final Report (Getting to Grips with Grub), p. 52, available www.food.gov.uk/multimedia/pdfs/competencyevaluation.pdf

3. Rhodes, G. (2002), 'Famous last words, Rhodes from school', in *Cook School: The Food Education Magazine*, January, Halifax, UK: Design Dimension Education Trust, p. 36.

4. Hardyment, C. (1995), *Slice of Life: The British Way of Eating Since 1945*, London: BBC Books, p. 56. And see Chapter 4.

5. See, for example, Cesarini, V. and Kinton, R. (1991), *Practical Cookery*, London: Hodder and Stoughton; and Leith, P. and Waldegrave, C. (1991), *Leith's Cookery Bible*, London: Bloomsbury Publishing.

6. See Christie, I., Harrison, M., Hitchman, C. and Lang, T. (2002), *Inconvenience Food. The Struggle to Eat Well on a Low Income*, London: Demos, available www.demos.co.uk/catalogue/inconveniencefood; Fieldhouse, P. (1995), *Food and Nutrition, Customs and Culture*, London: Chapman and Hall; Mintz, S. (1996), *Tasting Food, Tasting Freedom: Excursions into Eating, Culture and the Past*, Boston: Beacon Press; and Warde, A. (1997), *Consumption, Food and Taste. Culinary Antinomies and Commodity Culture*, London: Sage Publications.

7. Ritzer, G. (1996), *The McDonaldization of Society*, Thousand Oaks: Pine Forge Press, p. 102.

8. Warde, A., *Consumption, Food and Taste* (note 6).

9. Shapiro, L. (2004), *Something from the Oven. Reinventing Dinner in 1950s America*, New York: Viking.

10. See, for example, Fieldhouse, P., *Food and Nutrition, Customs and Culture* (note 6); Mintz, S., *Tasting Food, Tasting Freedom* (note 6); and Warde, A., *Consumption, Food and Taste* (note 6).

11. Gofton, L. (1995), 'Convenience and the moral status of consumer practices', in Marshall, D.W. (ed.), *Food Choice and the Consumer*, Glasgow: Blackie Academic and Professional, pp. 152–182.

12. Fine, G.A. (2003), 'Crafting authenticity: the validation of identity in self-taught art', in *Theory and Society*, Vol. 32, No. 2, pp. 153–180; and Stebbins, R.A. (1992), *Amateurs, Professionals, and Serious Leisure* Montreal and Kingston: McGill-Queen's University Press.

13. Wearing, B. and Wearing, S. (1991), 'Identity and the commodification of leisure,' in *Journal of the Leisure Studies Association*, Vol. 11, No. 1, pp. 3–18.

14. Drake McFeely, M. (2001), *Can She Bake a Cherry Pie? American Women and the Kitchen in the Twentieth Century*, Amherst: University of Massachusetts Press.

15. Rappaport, L. (2003), *How We Eat. Appetite, Culture, and the Psychology of Food*, Toronto: ECW Press, p. 149.

16. de Certeau, M., Giard, L. and Mayol, P. (1998), *The Practice of Everyday Life. Volume 2: Living and Cooking*, Minneapolis: University of Minnesota Press, p. 206.

17. Schwartz Cowan, R. (1983), *More Work for Mother. The Ironies of Household Technology from the Open Hearth to the Microwave*, New York: Basic Books, p. 23.

18. See (and for further references) Tannahill, R. (1988), *Food in History*, London: Penguin Books.

19. Schwartz Cowan, R., *More Work for Mother* (note 17), p. 7.

20. Laudan, R. (2001), 'A plea for culinary modernism: why we should love new, fast, processed food', in *Gastronomica*, Vol. 1, No. 1, Winter, pp. 36–44.

21. de Certeau, M. et al., *The Practice of Everyday Life* (note 16), p. 211

22. Drake McFeely, M., *Can She Bake a Cherry Pie?* (note 14), p. 2.

23. de Certeau, M. et al., *The Practice of Everyday Life* (note 16).

24. See Chapter 4 and Schwartz Cowan, R., *More Work for Mother* (note 17).

25. See Chapter 4 and Drake McFeely, M., *Can She Bake a Cherry Pie?* (note 14).

26. Mennell, S., Murcott, A. and Van Otterloo, A.H. (1994), *The Sociology of Food: Eating, Diet and Culture*, London: Sage Publications, p. 90.

27. Anon. (1998), 'Food, lessons for real life?', in *Health Which?*, October, Consumer's Association, pp. 14–17, quoted p. 15.

28. Warde, A. and Martens, L. (2000), *Eating Out: Social Differentiation, Consumption and Pleasure*, Cambridge: Cambridge University Press, p. 160.

29. Lang, T., Caraher, M., Dixon, P. and Carr-Hill, R. (1999), *Cooking Skills and Health*, London: The Health Education Authority, p. 31; and Lang, T. and Caraher, M. (2001), 'Is there a culinary skills transition? Data and debate from the UK about changes in cooking culture', in *Journal of the Home Economic Institute of Australia*, Vol. 8, No. 2, pp. 2–14.

30. Drake McFeely, M., *Can She Bake a Cherry Pie?* (note 14), p. 9.

31. See Dowler, E. (1996), 'Nutrition and poverty: the case of lone parent families in the UK', unpublished PhD thesis for the University of London; Dowler, E., Turner, S. and Dobson, B. (2001), *Poverty Bites: Food, Health And Poor Families*, London: Child Poverty Action Group; Christie, I. et al., *Inconvenience Food* (note 6); and Lang, T. et al., *Cooking Skills Health* (note 29),

32. de Certeau, M. et al., *The Practice of Everyday Life* (note 16).

33. Beechey, V. (1982), 'The sexual division of labour and the labour process: a critical assessment of Braverman', in Wood, S. (ed.), *The Degradation of Work? Skill, Deskilling and the Labour Process*, London: The Anchor Press, pp. 53–73, quoted p. 64.

34. de Certeau, M. et al., *The Practice of Everyday Life* (note 16), p. 217; and see Schwartz Cowan, R., *More Work for Mother* (note 17) for further discussion.

35. Nestle Family Monitor (2001), *No. 13, Eating and Today's Lifestyle*, research by Market and Opinion Research International (MORI), available www.mori.com/polls/2001/pdf/nfm13/html

36. See, for example, Street, P.A. (1994), 'An investigation into the prevalence and degree of cooking skills in North Reddish, with particular reference to mothers on a low income with young children', dissertation for the Department of Food and Consumer Science, Manchester Metropolitan University; and Lang, T. et al., *Cooking Skills and Health* (note 29).

37. Wrieden, W.L., Anderson, A.S., Longbottom, P.J., Valentine, K., Stead, M., Caraher, M., Lang, T. and Dowler, E. (2002), 'Assisting dietary change in low-income communities: assessing the impact of a community-based practical food skills intervention (CookWell)', report to the Food Standards Agency (UK). See also note 57.

38. See Symons, M. (1998), *A History of Cooks and Cooking*, Chicago: University of Illinois Press, p. 62, referring to American cookbooks on Chinese cookery.

39. de Zwart, M.L. (2003), 'From baking powder biscuits to Chinese chews', paper presented at Canadian Symposium VII: Issues and Directions in Home Economics/Family Studies Education, Richmond, Canada, 30 March.

40. As on the Cook Club pages of the British Nutrition Foundation at the time of writing (2004/5), available www.nutrition.org.uk

41. See Fort, M. (2003), 'The death of cooking, in food, the way we eat now', the *Guardian*, 10 May and Finlayson, A. (2002), 'Boiling an egg', in the *Guardian*, 7 February, report on a Guide Association survey that says 'four out of every 10 British schoolgirls are so ignorant about cooking that they can't even boil an egg'.

42. Lyon, P., Colquoun, A. and Alexander, E. (2003), 'Deskilling the domestic kitchen: national tragedy or the making of a modern myth?', in Edwards, J.S.A. and Gustafsson, I.-B (eds), *Culinary Arts and Sciences IV, Global and National Perspectives*, Bournemouth: Worshipful Company of Cooks, pp. 402–412, quoted p. 403, from Hanes, F. (1986), 'Can I afford a healthy diet?', in *Modus*, November, pp. 321- 323, quoted p. 323.

43. Roux, C., Le Couedic, P., Durand-Gasselin, S. and Luquet, F.-M. (2000), 'Consumption patterns and food attitudes of a sample of 657 low-income people in France', in *Food Policy*, Vol. 25, No 1, pp. 91–103, quoted p. 102.

44. Arnould, E.J. and Price, L.L. (2001), 'Bread of our mothers. Ruptures and continuities in families and homemade food traditions', paper presented at the 8th Interdisciplinary Conference on Consumption, 26–28 July, Paris, La Sorbonne.

45. Sutton, D. (2001), *Remembrance of Repasts, An Anthropology of Food and Memory*, Oxford: Berg Publishers, p. 148, referring to Leitch, A. (2000), 'The social life of lardon: slow food in fast times', in the *Asia Pacific Journal of Anthropology*, Vol. 1, pp. 103–118.

46. Shapiro, L., *Something from the Oven* (note 9), pp. 4–5.

47. Murcott, A. (1997), 'Family meals–a thing of the past?', in Caplan, P. (ed.), *Food, Health and Identity*, London: Routledge, pp. 32–49, quoted p. 46.

48. Sutton, D., *Remembrance of Repasts* (note 45) referring to Field, C. (1997), *In Nonnas's Kitchen: Recipes and Traditions from Italy's Grandmothers*, New York: Harper Collins.

49. Endrijonas, E. (2001), 'Processed foods from scratch: cooking for a family in the 1950s', in Inness, S.A. (ed.), *Kitchen Culture in America. Popular Representations of Food, Gender and Race*, Philadelphia: University of Pennsylvania Press, pp. 157–174, quoted p. 164.

50. Drake McFeely, M., *Can She Bake a Cherry Pie?*, (note 14), p. 12.

51. Bowers, D. E. (2000), 'Cooking trends echo changing roles of women', paper for the Economic Research Service, United States Department of Agriculture, available www.ers.usda.gov/publications/ foodreview/jan2000/frjan2000d.pdf

52. Drake McFeely, M., *Can She Bake a Cherry Pie?* (note 14), p. 1.

53. Drake McFeely, M., *Can She Bake a Cherry Pie?* (note 14), p. 13.

54. See Fernandez-Armesto, F. (2002), 'Meals make us human', in the *Guardian*, 14 September; Leith, P. (1998), 'Cooking with kids', in Griffiths, S. and Wallace, J. (eds), *Consuming Passions: Food in the Age of Anxiety*, Manchester: Manchester University Press; Mintz, S., *Tasting Food, Tasting Freedom* (note 6); and Ripe, C. (1993), *Goodbye Culinary Cringe*, St Leonards, Australia: Allen and Unwin.

55. Laudan, R., 'A plea for culinary modernism', (note 20).

56. See Chapter 1, also Fischler, C. (1980), 'Food habits, social change and the nature/culture dilemma', in *Social Science Information*, Vol. 19, No. 6, pp. 937–953; and Beardsworth, A. and Keil, T. (1997), *Sociology on the Menu. An Invitation to the Study of Food and Society*, London: Routledge.

57. Stead, M., Caraher, M., Wrieden, W., Longbottom, P., Valentine, K. and Anderson, A. (2004), 'Confident, fearful and hopeless cooks. Findings from the development of a food-skills initiative', in the *British Food Journal*, Vol. 106, No. 4, pp. 274–287, quoted p. 278.

58. Oakley, A. (1974), *Housewife*, London: Allen Lane, p. 119.

59. Lave, J. and Wenger, E. (1991), *Situated Learning. Legitimate Peripheral Participation*, Cambridge: Cambridge University Press. See also Ingold, T. (2001), *The Perception of the Environment: Essays in Livelihood, Dwelling and Skill*, London: Routledge; The Association of Experiential Education at www.aee.org; and The Edible Schoolyard, details about children's experiential cooking classes, available www.edibleschoolyard.org

60. Warde, A., *Consumption, Food and Taste* (note 6), p. 137.
61. Shapiro, L., *Something from the Oven* (note 9), pp. 224–225.
62. Altheide, D.L. (1997), 'Media participation in everyday life', in *Leisure Sciences*, No. 19, pp. 17–29, quoted p. 18; and Kitzinger, J. (1997), 'Media influence', in *Sociology Review*, Vol. 6, No. 4, pp. 6–9, quoted p. 7.
63. Randall, S. (2000), 'How does the media influence public taste for food and beverage? The role of the media in forming customer attitudes towards food and beverage provision', in Wood, R.C. (ed.), *Strategic Questions in Food and Beverage Management*, Oxford: Butterworth-Heinemann, pp. 81–96; and Randall, S. (2000), 'Mediated meanings of hospitality: television food programmes', in Lashley, C. and Morrison, A. (eds), *In Search of Hospitality*, Oxford: Butterworth-Heinemann, pp. 118–133.
64. Caraher, M., Baker, H. and Burns, M. (2004), 'Children's views of cooking and food preparation', in the *British Food Journal*, Vol. 106, No. 4, pp. 255–273, quoted p. 264.
65. Jill Dupleix quoted in Eyre, H. (2003), 'What do you mean, let's cook? Isn't that a seventies thing?', in the *Independent*, 24 August, p. 4.
66. Warde, A. and Martens, L., *Eating Out* (note 28), p. 132.
67. Warde, A. and Martens, L., *Eating Out* (note 28), p. 3.
68. Wrieden, W. et al., *Assisting Dietary Change* (note 37), p. 8; and Stead, M. et al., 'Confident, fearful and hopeless cooks', (note 57), p, 279.
69. See Goody, J. (1988), *The Domestication of the Savage Mind*, Cambridge: Cambridge University Press; and McKie, L. and Wood, R. (1992), 'People's source of recipes: some implications for an understanding of food related behaviour', in the *British Food Journal*, Vol. 94, No. 2, pp. 12–17.

Chapter 8 What to Do about Cooking

1. Laudan, R. (1999), 'A world of inauthentic cuisine', paper presented at symposium on Cultural and Historical Aspects of Food held at Oregon State University, April; and Laudan, R. (2001), 'A plea for culinary modernism: why we should love new, fast, processed food', in *Gastronomica*, Vol. 1, No. 1, Winter, pp. 36–44.
2. Warde, A. (1997), *Consumption, Food and Taste. Culinary Antinomies and Commodity Culture*, London: Sage Publications.
3. Symons, M. (1998), *A History of Cooks and Cooking*, Chicago: University of Illinois Press, p. x.
4. Foods described by informants to the main study.
5. Christie, I., Harrison, M., Hitchman, C. and Lang, T. (2002), *Inconvenience Food. The Struggle to Eat Well on a Low Income*, London: Demos, p. 24, available www.demos.co.uk/catalogue/inconveniencefood
6. Stead, M., Caraher, M. Wrieden, W., Longbottom, P., Valentine, K. and Anderson, A. (2004), 'Confident, fearful and hopeless cooks. Findings from the development of a food-skills initiative', in the *British Food Journal*, Vol. 106 No. 4, 274–287, quoted p. 274.

7. The Cookshop Program, see www.actionforhealthykids.org
8. See Meadows, M. (2003), 'Food choices and individual dynamics', in *Fare Choice, the Newsletter of the Scottish Colloquium on Food and Feeding*, Issue 25, available www.dietproject.org.uk; and Wrieden, W.L., Anderson, A.S., Longbottom, P.J., Valentine, K., Stead, M., Caraher, M., Lang, T. and Dowler, E. (2002), 'Assisting dietary change in low-income communities: assessing the impact of a community-based practical food skills intervention (CookWell)', unpublished report to the Food Standards Agency (UK). See also note 6.
9. Lave, J. and Wenger, E. (1991), *Situated Learning. Legitimate Peripheral Participation*, Cambridge: Cambridge University Press.
10. See, for example, Lang, T., Caraher, M., Dixon, P. and Carr-Hill, R. (1999), *Cooking Skills and Health*, London: The Health Education Authority; Ripe, C. (1993), *Goodbye Culinary Cringe*, St Leonards, Australia: Allen and Unwin; and Stitt, S., Jepson, M., Paulson-Box, E. and Prisk, E. (1996), *Research on Food Education and the Diet and Health of Nations*, Liverpool: John Moores University Consumer Research.
11. See, for example, Charles, N. and Kerr, M. (1988), *Women, Food and Families*, Manchester: Manchester University Press; and Oakley, A. (1974), *Housewife*, London: Allen Lane.
12. Ridgewell, J. (1996), *Working with Food in Primary Schools*, London: Ridgewell Press, p. 5.
13. Scarborough, J. (1996), personal communication, speaking on behalf of the (UK) National Association of Teachers of Home Economics and Technology.
14. Focus on Foods, (n. d.), a campaign from the Royal Society of Arts etc. and Waitrose, unpublished promotional material sent to teachers, 'Why focus on food?', p. 4.
15. Anon. (2002), in *Cook School: the Food Education Magazine*, Halifax, UK: Design Dimension Educational Trust, p. 3.
16. Bateman, M. (2003), 'The cooking class war', in the *Independent*, 4 June.
17. Farrell, A. (n. d.), 'Food in the National Curriculum: balanced diet or seriously mal-nourished?', article for the Food Forum, available www.foodforum.org.uk/hot/National_Curriculum-Tea-Fis.shtml
18. See, for further insight, Stevenson, D.R. (1985), *Professional Cookery: the Process Approach*, London: Hutchinson.
19. The Parents Jury, 'an independent watchdog which campaigns for healthier, safer food in the UK', gave celebrity television chef Jamie Oliver a 'food hero' award.
20. Dixey, R. (1996), 'Gender perspectives of food and cooking skills', in the *British Food Journal*, Vol. 98, No. 10, pp. 62–74; and Attar, D. (1990), *Wasting Girls' Time: The History and Politics of Home Economics*, London: Virago, p. 14.
21. Street, P.A. (1994), 'An investigation into the prevalence and degree of cooking skills in North Reddish', unpublished dissertation for the Department of Consumer Science, Manchester Metropolitan University.
22. Swinbank, V.A. (2002), 'The sexual politics of cooking: a feminist analysis of culinary hierarchy in western culture', in the *Journal of Historical Sociology*, Vol. 15, No. 4, pp. 464–494.

23. Stead, M. et al., 'Confident, fearful and hopeless cooks (note 6).

24. Fieldhouse, P. (1995), *Food and Nutrition, Customs and Culture*, London: Chapman and Hall, p. 70.

25. See, for examples, American Culinary Federation Chef and Child Foundation, *Cooking is for Kids. A Culinary Education Program for Children*, available www.acfchefs.org/ccf/ccfcook.html; and both the British Nutrition Foundation's and National Heart Forum's responses to the Food Standard Agency's *Getting to Grips with Grub. Food and Nutrition Competencies* of 14–16-year-olds, available www.nutrition.org.uk/medianews/pressinformation/gripsgrub/2003.htm and www. heartforum.org.uk/pdfs/NHF_grips_grub.pdf

26. See, for example, Caraher, M., Baker, H. and Burns, M. (2004), 'Children's views of cooking and food preparation', in the *British Food Journal*, Vol. 106, No. 4, pp. 255–273; and Gilbert, M. (2004), '"All aboard the food bus?" Report of the Food bus project', unpublished report for the Bristol North Primary Care Trust. See also unpublished for further explanation, Lupton, D. (1994), 'Food, memory and meaning: the symbolic and social nature of food events', in *Sociological Review*, Vol. 42, No. 4, pp. 664–685.

27. Gilbert, M., 'All Aboard the Food Bus? (note 26).

28. Stead, M. et al., 'Confident, fearful and hopeless cooks' (note 6), quoted p. 281.

29. Stead et al., 'Confident, fearful and hopeless cooks', (note 6), p. 275.

30. McGlone, P., Dobson, B., Dowler, E. and Nelson, M. (1999), *Food Projects and How they Work*, York: Joseph Rowntree Foundation. See www.jrf.org.uk/pressroom/r eleases/170399.asp

31. Lawton, L. and Stockley, L. (2003), *Evaluation of the Get Cooking! Pilot Courses Held in the Rhondda,* report prepared for the Food Standards Agency Wales, available www.food.gov.uk/wales

32. Steingarten, J. (1997), *The Man Who Ate Everything*, London: Review, p. 37, quoted in Fernandez-Armesto, F. (2001), *Food: A History*, London: Macmillan, p. 229.

Index